Madhouse

Also by Jeffrey H. Birnbaum
Showdown at Gucci Gulch (with Alan S. Murray)
The Lobbyists

Madhouse

The Private Turmoil of Working for the President

JEFFREY H. BIRNBAUM

TIMES BOOKS

RANDOM HOUSE

Grateful acknowledgment is made to *The Washington Post*
for permission to reprint an excerpt from an article by
Howard Kurtz from the October 14, 1993, issue of *The
Washington Post.* Copyright © 1993 by The Washington
Post. Reprinted with permission.

Library of Congress Cataloging-in-Publication data is
available.
ISBN 0-8129-2325-1

Printed in the United States of America on acid-free paper
2   4   6   8   9   7   5   3
First Edition
Book design by Mina Greenstein

For DEBORAH, MICHAEL, and JULIA

CONTENTS

Madhouse

Into the Madhouse

How often does someone get to sit on top of the world? And not just at the highest point either. On top of the world and also at the center of the universe. Not very often. But that is precisely where the people who work for the president of the United States think they are. And few would doubt them.

When a senior White House staffer wants to go somewhere, all he or she has to do is call the motor pool. Within minutes, a late-model, American-built, leather-appointed, chauffeured car with cellular telephone shows up at the nearest curbside. When a staffer wants to talk to someone—almost anyone—all he or she has to do is contact the White House switching center, called the signal operator, and, like magic, the other person is soon on the line. And when a staffer travels with the Big Man Himself, it is possible to be released from the bounds of mere mortals and lose all sense of time and space. Air travel is direct and on schedule. On the ground, police stop traffic at every intersection. There are no stoplights. There is no waiting. The best seats are always reserved.

That is enough to qualify as top of the world. Yet life as a staffer is even grander than that. Yes, there are the free boxes at the Kennedy Center with champagne bottles embossed with the presidential seal. But the greater glory is meeting the people who sit there too. To be a White House aide is to see and sometimes get to know the most important, most impressive people on earth: heads of state and titans of industry, virtuosos and scholars, heroes and heroines of every sort. The best the country—and the world—has to offer is waiting at the doorstep.

There is also history, past and in the making. Momentous events and fateful decisions suffuse every corridor and cubicle in the White House, and it is the rare aide who does not tingle at the thought of going to work for that reason alone. Franklin Roosevelt broadcast his fireside chats from the Diplomatic Reception Room. Military movements during World War II were charted in the Map Room. And here I am, staffers think, making my mark on history too. They never quite get over it. For many, it is the peak experience of their lives. It is the time they cast the longest shadow.

But most of all, staffers feel empowered because of their proximity to the Big Man Himself. The Boss. The Commander in Chief. In the slang of the Secret Service, the POTUS (President of the United States). For any White House aide, no honor is greater than to get "face time"—to be permitted to be with the president in a meeting. No commodity is more precious than the president's waking hours. And no infraction is more grievous than to waste that time. Reverence hardly approaches the emotion staffers have when they work closely with him. To aides like George Stephanopoulos, getting a desk near the Oval Office was the fulfillment of a childhood dream. He could not imagine wanting to be anyplace else. Other aides, such as Jeff Eller, will tell—and retell—until they die the story of picking up a phone, saying, "Get me the President," and actually making it happen.

Just being in the president's vicinity is intoxicating. When Paul Begala had his chance to go to Camp David, for instance, he tried to soak in as much presidential aura as he could. He checked out the chapel George Bush had built for his daughter's wedding. He found the officers' club and shot some pool. Then he snuck into Aspen Cottage, which houses the president's own office. With no one around, he sat on the president's desk, picked up the phone, and called his wife. "Hey, I'm in Camp David!" he told Diane Begala excitedly—just as President Clinton and Vice President Gore walked into the room. "Honey," Begala said, leaping to his feet, "I've got to go," and hung up as fast as he could. Clinton and Gore were not angry, though. They understood. People do not get to the center of the universe very often. They even allowed the young aide to keep a Camp David coffee mug as a souvenir of his visit to the top of the world.

There is, of course, a danger to attaining such high altitude: it is a very long way down. But of all places to work, surely the White House is one where a steep decline might be avoided. It is, after all, the center—as well as the summit— of all political power. Isn't it?

It is indisputable that the White House staff is important—more important in many ways than the members of the president's cabinet. The upper-level and midlevel staffers who are the subject of this book are, more than anyone else, responsible for translating the president's vision into action. They are smart, hardworking people who come to their jobs full of honest optimism, ecstatic at the prospect of reaching one of their greatest goals: working for a president they support.

But in the end, the reality of their day-to-day existence is surprisingly different from their anticipation, and it is harsh. The White House turns out to be far less potent and immensely less forgiving than any outsider can conceive. A staffer's best effort never seems good enough. And that is a crushing blow to the many good people who go to work for their president.

While exhilarating, life on the staff can also be exhausting. Aides' brush with greatness takes a heavy toll. Work in the White House is nonstop. It consumes almost every waking hour. Family life falls by the wayside; the First Family is the only family that a staffer really has time to serve. A twelve-hour day is a short one. Fourteen and even eighteen hours are more common. And nobody who works at the White House is ever free from its grip for long. The place is on permanent overload.

With little time to think, and barely enough time to act, mistakes are made often. Too often. Serious misjudgments become commonplace. Anywhere but the White House, those mistakes would be considered a problem, a problem destined to be solved. But in the center and at the top of things, foibles are portrayed as crises. The simplest injury is made to appear beyond repair. At every turn, there are "tragedies" and "disasters," not merely setbacks that need to be fixed. One result is a huge burnout factor among the staff, and a very rapid turnover. The Secret Service refers to the White House grounds as Eighteen Acres. The average life expectancy of a White House aide is only eighteen months.

It does not take long for aides to understand why their tenures are likely to be so short. Gene Sperling, one of President Clinton's more tenacious staffers, guided an impromptu tour through the West Wing late one night a year and a half into the administration. As he threaded his way through the empty, narrow passageways, he did not focus on the artwork or the secret meeting places of the mighty and the influential. Instead, he went door to door and called out the names of the staffers who had once worked there but no longer did. More than half of those doors had new people working behind them, and Sperling ended the tour with a shake of his head and a whispered wish that he would not be the next victim.

This book retells the experiences of a half-dozen aides in the Clinton White House. Its objective is to delve beneath the patina of celebrity to reveal a compelling and little-known story that applies to all recent White Houses: more often than not, people who reach the pinnacle of public service on the White House staff leave their posts weary, diminished, sometimes even broken. The sad fact is that life at the top, while exciting, can be too much to bear. Employment in the White House can be hazardous to your health.

Working for a president turns out to be a lot like looking directly into the sun: a great temptation but debilitating to anyone who tries. It is wrong, in fact, to think of the president and his staff as striving warriors or visionary leaders. Rather, they are better imagined in a defensive crouch, waiting for the next crisis to erupt and then scurrying to cope as best they can. The White House is a madhouse almost all the time.

Admittedly, a number of factors have made working in the Clinton White House more hazardous than in previous White Houses. Bill Clinton, a newcomer to Washington, had a radically impaired view of what he could actually accomplish. He severely underestimated the potency of the forces arrayed against him on several fronts.

In addition, the inexperience—and lack of decorum—of a few of his aides made Clinton's madhouse even madder than usual. Stories abound. During takeoff on Clinton's first trip as President, for example, Steve Rabinowitz, the White House director of production, known as Rabbi, could not resist an old campaign stunt. As *Air Force One* nosed into the sky from Andrews Air Force Base, he stood on a dinner tray and "surfed" down the aisle, allowing the motion of the plane to propel him along. In the eyes of the other aides who cheered him on, the maneuver was a paean to their hard-fought struggle to win the White House and was one of the spoils of victory. But in the eyes of the Air Force stewards in charge of the flight, it was a ridiculously childish display. On future flights they refused to give Rabinowitz a tray before takeoff. One steward explained that he was just trying to save the aide from himself.

Even when the Clinton White House tried to do things right, chaos always seemed to intervene. Preparation for presidential speeches began weeks in advance, but they inevitably became last-minute scrambles caused by the President's notorious lack of discipline. For instance, a few hours before Clinton's first State of the Union Address, in 1994, aides were tripping over one another to make changes the President had dictated to them in the midst of what was supposed to be a practice session. And even after those changes were made, he kept on refining. He secretly made his final edits in his kitchen over a snack of apple pie with the help of a nonstaffer, Diane Blair, the wife of the Tyson Foods executive who had helped Hillary Clinton with her controversial commodities trades. In the Clinton White House, it was sometimes hard to tell who was in charge of the asylum.

Still, the Clinton experience reveals some universal truths about the hardships that staffers will face in any White House. For one thing, the modern presidency is not the all-powerful institution many suppose. The Constitution never envisioned a truly strong president; checks and balances were designed to take care of that. Nowadays, in fact, a pres-ident does not *govern* anything. Almost any initiative is an uphill fight. The once mighty bully pulpit has been whacked down to size by a proliferation of media outlets and television channels, all of which churn out competing messages and criticism that drown out the president's voice. Real power is diffused among bigger, global forces, especially financial markets. The paternal president is a myth that derives more from the primordial desires of the populace than from any reality of governance. "There is always the exaggerated view that the next guy who is president will ride in on a white horse," says Charles Jones of the University of Wisconsin, "and as a result, presidents are bound to take a fall."

Along with the president, none fall harder than members of the White House staff. Like voters, top-level White House aides start off starry-eyed about a new presidency, then lose their spark as they see the many obstacles that stand in its path to success. But their loss is far more painful than the public's. Whereas the voters can simply turn away in disgust, a White House aide must live each day with the fact of gradual decline and still shoulder the unending self-sacrifice that is the daily staple of the job.

This situation is made worse by the staff's lack of preparedness. Their training is almost nonexistent. It is almost by happenstance that anyone at a senior level in the White House has actually held a similar job before. Unlike other countries, the United States does not have a government in waiting, or shadow government—at least officially. Rather, every four years or so, we have government by the seat of the pants, which has to be thrown together in a virtual frenzy in the few months that separate the election from the inauguration. And that is a prescription for calamity.

The inhospitable atmosphere of Washington also contributes to this problem. Starting with Watergate, during which much of the staff was involved in a criminal conspiracy, White House aides have been caught in scandal after scandal. The list of casualties is as long as it is familiar, ranging from Bert Lance to John Sununu and from Bud McFarlane to Bernie Nussbaum. The ultimate casualty, of course, was Vincent Foster.

Part of the reason for this trend is simply the sourness of the nation's capital. Press Secretary Dee Dee Myers frequently reflected on this. Her native Los Angeles is a self-absorbed place too. But there, at least, people poke fun at themselves—and make movies about their shortcomings. Washingtonians do not possess the same funny bone. People in official circles in Washington, Myers thought, actually believe that someday their admirers will build a monument to them on the Mall, no matter how transient or incremental their contributions really are.

The biggest causes of the staffers' woes, however, are the endemic difficulties of the jobs themselves. In many ways aides are asked to do the impossible. They have to master forces beyond their control. They are supposed to react to too many potential enemies and at too great a velocity. They cannot possibly meet the herculean expectations people place on them and their boss.

It is no wonder that so many staffers' reputations, and their personal lives, end in shambles. Instead of posting a uniformed sentry at the door of the West Wing, as is now done, the next president might consider erecting a sign that echoes Dante's admonition in the *Inferno:* ABANDON ALL HOPE, YE WHO ENTER HERE.

The White House staff is a relatively recent invention. It is usually traced back to 1933, when Franklin Roosevelt brought together a dozen or so aides to assist him with the fight to end the Great Depression. From there the staff grew and grew—in rough parallel to the federal government. When Roosevelt aide James Rowe returned from World War II, he noticed that the Truman White House had nine people doing what he alone used to do. Some twenty-five years later, he observed that there were three hundred.

Lately, the number of aides directly around the president has leveled off at about four hundred. There is a national security staff, a domestic policy staff, and a newly formed economic policy staff. The White House has its own law firm, called the Counsel's Office, and a variety of departments to help the president with scheduling, security, and personnel decisions. The rest of the organization deals with outreach: to Congress, the federal agencies, state and local governments, the political parties, special-interest groups, and the press.

This growth has been outpaced only by the ability of the chief executive to coordinate it. No president has yet found the right formula. When President Truman's friend Ed McKim tried to create a management system, Truman promoted him right out of the White House. President Eisenhower introduced the first chain of command, but he did not have organizational charts. Presidents Kennedy and Johnson had even more fluid arrangements. The only constant over the years has been a tendency to increase the system's complexity. President Reagan had four levels of management and twenty subunits. President Clinton had twenty-three subunits and, by one count, access to a total budget of nearly $1 billion. And still it was a madhouse.

Secretary of the Interior Bruce Babbitt predicted early that the outlook for the Clinton presidency was for "trench warfare" and a life of hand-to-hand combat for its soldiers—the members of the White House staff. And he was right. According to Dee Dee Myers, "It was very clear to me right away that we were making this up as we went along. There was no instruction manual."

The following is a portrait of what six White House aides learned as they went along.

• Chief White House lobbyist Howard Paster got the job he most wanted in life. But he found it infinitely tougher than he had foreseen; lawmakers were so independent minded that even the accepted method of trying to coax them into action—corraling the support of their legislative leaders—was not nearly sufficient anymore.

• Media Affairs chief Jeff Eller reached the top of his profession too. But when he got there he discovered that all the fanciest new gadgets and narrow-casting techniques of his public relations trade could not make voters listen to the President's message.

• Policy advisers Bruce Reed and Gene Sperling thought when they reached their exalted positions it would be a snap to help people in need. But they saw their best and most heartfelt ideas fail under the weight of highly organized, and politicized, opposition.

• White House Press Secretary Dee Dee Myers was overjoyed to be the first woman to hold the title. But she came to understand, despite lip service about diversity, that the White House was still very much a man's world.

• And the political consultant Paul Begala thought the nimble rhetoric of a campaign would be enough to keep his President afloat. But he learned that governing is entirely different, and incredibly more arduous, than running for election.

President Clinton also made a fundamental error that had a profound effect on his staff. At one of his first, informal dinner parties in the White House residence, the President rose from his seat and derided the many naysayers who had greeted his arrival in the capital. They were wrong, he said confidently. As President, he really was in charge of things. It was possible—indeed only right—that he should make good on his campaign promises. He would be able to accomplish astounding new things because he worked in the hallowed White House. He declared that he and his wife would flatly refuse to move slowly from one limited goal to the next, as the fainthearted advised. Instead, he would work on the "hard things" all at once and right from the start. He would not be denied. After all, he was on top of the world, at the center of the universe. And the many friends around him applauded heartily.

In fact, both he and his staff would soon learn how perilous an ambition that was.

HOWARD PASTER

1

Too Much Stimulus

ON THE MORNING OF INAUGURATION DAY, HOWARD PASTER bundled his wife and two children into their maroon Ford Explorer for the first part of their trek from their high-priced neighborhood in Northwest Washington to the Capitol. When they arrived, they were feted at a comfortable Senate reception, then walked to choice seats not far from the podium. Paster was exuberant, but he also felt a little guilty. Unlike many of the other new White House staffers, he had not labored for months to get Clinton elected. He was an interloper, a late arrival, and he knew it. Then again, he was among friends when he walked onto the inaugural platform. From all sides, members of Congress, many of whom he had raised money for over the years and helped as a foot soldier in legislative battles, teased and heckled him as he made his way, proudly, to a seat near the front.

The forty-eight-year-old Paster had finally arrived at the place he most coveted in his professional life. He was chief congressional lobbyist to the President of the United States. It was the job that some of his best friends and former partners had held many years before, when they were young and ambitious. They had used the post to catapult themselves into the prominent position in the private sector that Paster had already attained. He was one of Washington's most experienced and best paid corporate lobbyists. One of his old partners had been a White House lobbyist for Jimmy Carter; another had dealt with Congress for Ronald Reagan. Now, belatedly, it was Paster's chance to show that he too could hold the premier lobbying job in town, assistant to the President for legislative affairs. And he was thrilled to get the chance.

Before he took the assignment, Paster's friends in the lobbying fraternity tried to warn him about what he was getting into. "You will have the hardest job in the administration," they told him. They said he would be compelled to deal with unwieldy forces from above—the inbred backbiting among the President's courtiers—and from below—the maelstrom of interests that clash in the U.S. Congress. He would be the man in the middle. But Paster laughed, said, "I doubt that," and went on with full confidence that he knew how to do his job.

There was something comical about the way Paster looked, and that was just as well, given his odd profession. As a lobbyist, he needed to convince people to trust him, and his peculiar appearance and personality helped him most of the time. He had thinning hair that sometimes stood straight up on his round pate, giving him the look of a friendly porcupine—with glasses. He was short and keenly intelligent, and had a tendency to turn conversations into little conspiracies. "Yes," he seemed to say by the end of a talk, "now we are leveling with each other"—even when he was not.

The people he most often tried to level with were Democrats, a connection he came by honestly. He was born into a politically active, politically left-wing family in Flatbush, New York, and grew up in suburban Nassau County. Even his first profession was liberal leaning. He went to Columbia University's Graduate School of Journalism and worked for a short time as a reporter for the *Suffolk Sun* newspaper on Long Island. There he was nicknamed Faster Paster because of the pace of his speech. Many people, including some members of Congress and fellow White House staffers, saw rudeness in that mannerism. But his sister, Ann Brody, explained it this way: "Howard is not a man of a lot of unnecessary words. You don't need to have very long conversations with him to know what he's thinking. He has his opinions, and he states them clearly."

Paster certainly succeeded at whatever he tried. He was a standout Democratic staffer in Congress, first for Congressman Lester Wolff of his home state, New York, and then for liberal senator Birch Bayh of Indiana. He left Capitol Hill in the late 1970s to become the chief lobbyist for the United Auto Workers union and did well there too. He helped navigate the historic Chrysler bailout bill through the balky Congress. At first few believed the $1.5 billion loan guarantee program could pass. But Paster worked hand in glove with corporate lobbyists in the prototype for what would later become a standard lobbying technique: forming a coalition that included both labor and management.

His reputation made, Paster decided to try a different challenge—and go for the big bucks. In typical fashion, as they say, he came to Washington to do good and ended up doing well. He was at the vanguard of a trend that grew huge through the 1980s of Democratic staffers leaving Capitol Hill to join lobbying firms representing mostly corporations of the kind that were not traditionally Democratic. Paster became a key link to the Democrats for Timmons & Company, which represented such usually non-Democratic enterprises as banks, defense contractors, oil companies, and even the National Rifle Association. He was their entree to the power brokers on the Hill.

It was Paster's job to make and maintain close ties to the

barons in Congress. Knowing them well was what his clients paid him to do. And he did so with aplomb. In return, Paster and his clients were often favored with vital information about pending legislation. He also was able to get written into law the small amendments and marginal changes that are lobbyists' bread and butter. A little fix by Paster could mean millions of dollars in taxes avoided or regulations deferred for his big-business clients. And that was why they kept him on annual, multi-hundred-thousand-dollar retainers.

Over the years, Paster grew especially close to House Commerce Committee chairman John Dingell of the autoworkers' state of Michigan and to Senate Majority Leader George Mitchell of Maine, which also has a sizable labor electorate. But Paster developed into far more than a former union guy; that identity provided just his initial introduction. His real clout was as a fund-raiser. Thanks to the substantial resources of the corporations he represented, he was able to direct thousands of dollars into the always needy coffers of top-level Democrats. And that money was all the more needed when Paster was at the height of his fund-raising prowess, in the 1980s. Republicans held the White House, and Democrats were perennially in danger of losing control of the Senate. Along the way, Paster also became expert in congressional politics, though he focused on the doings of the liberal elite who held most of the power.

He came late but well recommended to the Clinton campaign effort. The Democratic congressional leaders he had cozied up to for so long all said he was the person they wanted to head the President's lobbying of Capitol Hill. And Paster did not want anything more in this life. Timmons was sold to the parent company of Hill & Knowlton thanks in part to Paster's business skills, and, in the fall of 1992, he became the chairman of Hill & Knowlton's main operation in Washington. His ambition was to take charge of the entire public relations and lobbying company worldwide, but he insisted that his half-million-dollar-a-year contract contain a clause allowing him to leave the company if he were offered the top lobbying job in the White House. That post, he decided, was the ultimate honor for any lobbyist. "Given the chance to do public service," he said, "where better to do it than the White House?"

In the White House, Paster was paid a fraction of his former salary—$125,000 a year—but he did not mind. He managed eleven professionals, the White House lobbyists to the House and the Senate, and guided sixteen other lobbyists in cabinet agencies. His responsibilities kept him working seven days a week until all hours, though he sometimes snuck home for dinner with his family—only to return afterward. He did not mind that either. At first.

After the inaugural address, Paster made his way triumphantly back into the Capitol and through the marble-floored hallways to, appropriately enough, the President's Room. Located just outside the Senate on the building's second floor, the ornate chamber is where presidents traditionally rest before speaking to Congress and where they wait to sign late-passing legislation. The paintings on the walls feature members of George Washington's first cabinet. And, as Howard Paster entered the room, he found President Clinton standing at a felt-topped table in the center, signing papers that designated the nominees for his own cabinet, the very group that had been Paster's preoccupation since he had joined the transition staff. For weeks Paster had methodically paraded all twenty of Clinton's cabinet designees before the leaders of the Senate, whose blessings they needed to secure their jobs.

The whole of Paster's attention—and the attention of the two dozen other people who ringed the room—was on the President. And the world was watching through the lenses of television cameras located nearby. Clinton, using a black-and-gold pen inscribed "Bill Clinton, The White House," signed a series of documents with his more presidential-sounding name: William J. Clinton. He signed a proclamation declaring January 22 a National Day of Fellowship and Hope—in keeping with his inaugural themes. He also signed an executive order that would make it harder for Paster, and every other Clinton appointee, to lobby in the private sector after leaving government. But Paster had no qualms. He saw himself as a long-term employee of William J. Clinton.

"Congratulations, Mr. President," he said as he reached to shake Clinton's hand. It was the first time Paster had called him Mr. President. Until then he had called him Governor. But the change seemed natural—and exciting.

The next moment also was important to the President's top lobbyist. Democratic senator Howell Heflin approached Clinton. "We met before," Clinton said as he greeted the portly Alabaman. "When I was teaching law at Fayetteville [in Arkansas], I went to Stanford to hear you speak." Both Heflin and Paster were impressed. The speech Clinton remembered had taken place nearly two decades earlier. If the President really had that kind of memory, and the presence of mind to use it at the right times, as he just had, Paster thought congressional relations were going to go smoothly.

He did not have to wait long for evidence of just how smoothly. Abby Saffold, a senior aide to Senate Majority Leader Mitchell, walked over to Paster and whispered that confirmation was in the offing, that very day, for the Big Three of Clinton's cabinet: Secretary of State Warren Christopher, Secretary of the Treasury Lloyd Bentsen, and Secretary of Defense Les Aspin. All of Paster's pleading was about to pay off.

Everything was looking up. In a national poll for NBC News and *The Wall Street Journal,* 61 percent of those interviewed said they were optimistic about the next four years. Roughly the same percentage expected things to change for the better during that period and anticipated that the President and Congress would work together to make that happen.

But Washington is not that easy—or predictable—a place. The very next day, the White House's phones were jammed because of a roiling controversy over, of all things, a nanny. Zoe Baird, the forty-year-old general counsel for Aetna Life & Casualty Company, was the first woman ever nominated to become the attorney general. But she also admitted she had broken the law. In 1990, she and her husband, Yale Law School professor Paul Gewirtz, had hired an undocumented Peruvian woman to serve as baby-sitter for their young son and the woman's husband to work as their part-time driver. Not only did they hire these people in violation of immigration laws but they also failed to pay Social Security taxes on their paltry wages.

Radio talk-show hosts across the nation had a field day, and the public responded with outrage. Why does a person who earns $500,000 a year need to hire help on the cheap? And how could the nation's chief law enforcer be a scofflaw herself? The calls came by the thousands, not just to the White House but to the offices of senators who were considering the Baird nomination. And that's where they made the real difference.

As the White House's primary liaison with Congress, Paster began to get calls from angry lawmakers almost the moment the issue became public. He marveled at how quickly the good feeling of the inauguration seemed to have disappeared. But he saw his job as keeping abreast of the problem. And there was a lot to track. First thing in the morning, respected Republican senator Nancy Kassebaum of Kansas circulated a statement opposing Baird's confirmation. At a lunchtime caucus of Democrats, Senators Barbara Mikulski of Maryland and Dianne Feinstein of California expressed their own reservations. Later, other Democrats did the same.

The speed of Baird's decline was breathtaking, but Paster dutifully passed along to the President each shred of bad news, often through George Stephanopoulos and White House Chief of Staff Mack McLarty. Finally, at day's end, he was summoned to the Oval Office. Paster had wanted that moment to be special. It was, after all, his first visit to the President's office, and he wanted to savor the feeling. He had seen this scene in his imagination for years. But the White House is not what people expect it to be. And this day was a perfect example.

When the time came to talk to the President in the Oval Office, neither Paster nor anyone else had much to say. Like so much else they had to deal with, the Baird situation had simply gotten out of control. As a longtime Washingtonian, Paster had seen similar waves crash down on one appointee after another: John Tower, Robert Bork, many others. But he had never witnessed it from the White House. It was eerie to stand at the right hand of power, in the Oval Office itself with the President of the United States, and be all but completely helpless.

He also discovered how hard it was even to do a simple thing like end a single nomination. Part of the problem was the inexperience of people around him. Both the President and his politically tone-deaf counsel, Bernie Nussbaum, wanted the decision to come from Baird herself. Clinton, it turned out, had a weak spot when it came to personnel and a saying when faced with a hard choice involving his appointees: "OK, do it," he would tell his staff, "but don't rub it in their eye." Such was the case with Zoe Baird. So Paster and Nussbaum went to the Hill to muddle through.

The two men were chauffeured in one of the American-built sedans, driven by Army officers, that are on call at all times for top appointees of the President. After they arrived at the Dirksen Senate Office Building, where Baird was testifying, Paster and Nussbaum went to a room borrowed from Senator Donald Riegle of Michigan and spoke in private to Baird and her husband, Paul Gewirtz. The White House aides laid out the difficulties ahead and the fact that support was waning. But Baird and Gewirtz, especially Gewirtz, wanted to tough it out.

So Paster walked down the hall to gather more intelligence to bolster his case. He talked to Senators Paul Simon of Illinois, Howard Metzenbaum of Ohio, and Howell Heflin of Alabama. Their concerns differed in degree, but all made the same point without saying so outright: the nomination was in deep trouble, and the White House should pull the plug. Paster returned to the White House to convey this news and helped arrange for Senator Mitchell and Judiciary Committee chairman Joseph Biden of Delaware to convey to the President what dire straits Baird was in.

Still, Clinton did not act. He wanted Baird to choose. He ordained that the hearing would be allowed to run its course. She would have her chance to defend herself before any announcement was made. In the meantime, the White House tried to keep up appearances. Poor Dee Dee Myers was sent out to reporters, in essence, to mislead. "At this point, the President is standing behind her," she said that evening, even as the nomination was crumbling. But for the sake of honesty she added, "It is a situation that we are paying close attention to, obviously."

Paster kicked himself for not forestalling the firestorm that was consuming Baird. True, he had warned Baird and others that her breach of the law would cause problems. So had Biden. During their first meeting on Capitol Hill, Biden had contradicted some transition officials who had dismissed the infraction as "a traffic ticket." Biden told Baird, "It was more like a freeway crash." But Baird and her backers had believed she still had a chance, and no one had contradicted them. Now Paster was suffering from that error.

In the meantime, Clinton and his staff had no system to deal with such turmoil—and no place to deal with it either. So at about 11:30 Clinton walked into, of all places, George Stephanopoulos's office down the hall from the Oval. He was wearing a running suit and sneakers. By telephone, the final arrangements were made. Baird insisted on knowing a few things before she accepted the inevitable. Could she get some sort of job in the Clinton administration down the road? Yes, the President said. Could she get her old job back at Aetna? Yes, the company said. So letters of withdrawal and acceptance were faxed back and forth until the wording was agreed upon—at 12:42 A.M.

Paster was in a whirl. On his first full day on the job, the Clinton White House already had suffered a major defeat. The lobbyist chafed at the unfairness of it. Earlier the same day, the Senate had confirmed, without opposition, the entire rest of the cabinet. But nobody would notice. Instead, it was all bad news, a troubled presidency, a misplayed hand with Congress. And it had started with such high expectations just the day before.

Paster's assignment was unique—and uniquely difficult—in the White House. As his friends had warned him, he not only had to satisfy his boss, the President, which was hard enough, but also had to keep happy one of the world's largest groups of egotists and chronic malcontents, the 535 members of Congress. When a lawmaker wanted a photo with the President for an important constituent, or a meeting with a senior White House staffer, or the President's imprimatur for a tiny amendment, or even an invitation to a social gathering, Paster had to take the call. And no matter how much he did for the lawmakers, it was never enough. "I would get calls from people complaining they hadn't seen the President for months who had just seen him two weeks before," Paster said, shaking his head at the memory.

The pressures from the White House side were sometimes

even more intense. In exchange for all his so-called constituent service to members of Congress (for the lawmakers
were, in effect, his constituents), Paster was expected to deliver votes for the President's programs. And, despite what
the public thinks about such matters, it is only on rare and
special occasions that those kinds of favors translate directly
into votes. Paster tried his best to keep track of the favors.
There was no centralized data bank for members of Congress.
Instead, he spent hours reading the mountains of paper that
the White House's budget office produced about the legislative goodies given out to members' pet projects. But all the
record keeping and benefit bestowing he could muster often
was just not enough.

Paster also had an extra problem. To the close-knit Clinton
crew, he was an outsider. He was everything the Clintonites
were not. He was eastern, liberal, and a veteran Washington
deal maker. He could be as brusque and sharp-tongued as
they were southern and genteel. Worst of all, he had not even
been a Clinton loyalist until the very end of the campaign. In
a prescient remark to *The Washington Post,* Tom Korologos,
a former lobbying partner of Paster, said, "Howard's problem
may be that he wasn't there at the creation. He didn't know
Clinton from kindergarten." In short, Paster was not a member of the extended Clinton family, and so much of the administration was run in a clannish way that missing that link
became a serious flaw.

Paster was also, in many ways, precisely the kind of person
Clinton and his people had vowed to banish from Washington. In his acceptance speech at the Democratic National
Convention in 1992, Candidate Clinton said of President
Bush, he "won't break the stranglehold the special interests
have on our elections and the lobbyists have on our government. But I will." Yet Clinton, like all presidential candidates
who ran as non-Washingtonians, needed people like Paster if
he was to have any chance to succeed with his legislative
agenda. So the chief lobbyist was a necessary evil and, there-

fore, in a second way, the man uncomfortably caught in the middle.

Still, Paster forged ahead, concentrating on the things he thought would do the President the most good. During the budget process, he believed his job was to keep his White House colleagues mindful of the odd, almost medieval ways of Capitol Hill. Committee chairmen there were like feudal lords. They had their own perks and privileges, and did not relinquish them easily. Paster lobbied inside the White House against proposals that would disrupt their way of life.

One tradition in Congress was for appropriations chairmen to control a slush fund system of sorts that allowed them, at their discretion, to dispense a bridge or a roadway to a specific member as a way to buy a vote. At Paster's insistence, the President agreed to keep this "highway demonstration project" system alive and under the control of the congressional chairmen. Paster also harped on the notion of regional equity, insisting the President remember the need to balance the budget's benefits and sacrifices among the various parts of the country. Clinton had to be particularly careful of the big bloc of farm state lawmakers, he counseled, because they could doom the budget, especially in the Senate. As a result, the President kept cutbacks in farm subsidies to a minimum.

Surely, Paster thought, keeping the big boys happy was a good way to get the President's budget passed.

If only Paster's job had been that straightforward! No sooner had Zoe Baird withdrawn than the President was back in the trenches again, this time defending that ill-fated campaign promise to end the ban on gays in the military. It was clear by then that Clinton could not change the prohibition with the stroke of a pen. He had once believed he could end it by signing an executive order. But few things in the White House work by fiat.

A single alteration in policy or law requires more work than anyone who has not seen the system close up could ever imagine. Clinton's proposal on gays ran headlong into opposition on many fronts: at the Pentagon; among the Pentagon's many supporters in the Senate, especially Democratic senator Sam Nunn of Georgia, chairman of the Senate Armed Services Committee; and among the conservative activists who wanted to do Clinton in anyway.

But the President still thought compromise was possible. So he asked Secretary of Defense Aspin, a former member of the House, to devise one. On the Sunday before the inauguration, the two men agreed on its outlines: they would lift the ban within six months and end dismissals and other legal actions against homosexual military personnel immediately.

There was only one problem: Clinton and Aspin did not bother to clear the proposal with the many powers that be in Congress and elsewhere. Paster was circumvented and was thus unable to spread the word among his "constituents." Try as he might, he could not keep track of everything that was happening at the White House. No single person can, especially in a new White House in which the system was still in an uproar. The result was another embarrassment. On the same day he promised a health-care reform proposal within one hundred days (something else that never happened), the President held a long meeting on gays with the Joint Chiefs of Staff. And, in private, both Nunn and Joint Chiefs chairman General Colin Powell opposed him. "If there's a strategy there, it hasn't been explained to me," Nunn said. "I just am not part of the strategy."

Such lack of consultation was a fundamental mistake, and Paster, trapped as he was between the White House and Congress, caught hell from both sides, even though the lack of communication was not his fault. On the Hill, lawmakers prepared amendments that would retain the gay ban and threatened to attach them to almost any piece of legislation that moved. So Clinton, through Paster, tried to bring Nunn into the fold. One evening in late January, the Democratic members of Nunn's committee were invited to a meeting in the Roosevelt Room. And the President sat, and listened. Some senators, including Charles Robb of Virginia, a gung-ho Vietnam veteran, supported lifting the ban. But others continued to resist. Long-winded Senator Robert Byrd of West Virginia even reminded the President that a Roman army had once been defeated when homosexuality was permitted in the ranks. Paster listened to the remarks and felt his stomach churn.

Most of the senators in the room agreed with Byrd, and Nunn appeared unmoved. Worse yet, no matter what the President did or said, the only issue reporters asked about was this one. "It was too good an issue," George Stephanopoulos moaned. "It had military, it had sex, it had controversy, it had homosexuality, it was a made-for-TV crisis."

Clinton tried to put the best face on the situation, but he clearly had lost. Asked if the gay issue was taking attention away from his economic program, the President could not contain his anger. "No, it's distracting you," he charged. "It's not distracting me." But Paster saw that something more than the press was to blame. After the Roosevelt Room meeting, he told Mack McLarty the controversy was not about what was right or wrong on the issue. "This is about Nunn beating the President," he said. It was nothing more or less than the old power game of Washington. The wily veteran senator wanted to teach the newcomer a lesson, and he did. The President was forced to capitulate. After negotiations with Nunn, Clinton directed the Pentagon to study an end of the ban and report back in six months. And Paster began, even in those early days, to doubt the wisdom of his ambition to work in the White House.

February brought another stab at filling the job of attorney general. Clinton chose Janet Reno, and Paster was hopeful that this time the nomination would go well. Clinton was confident too, enough so that, in Paster's presence, he teased

Bernie Nussbaum just before the Rose Garden ceremony announcing the appointment.

"OK, Bernie, don't blow it," the President said in the Oval Office. "If you do blow it, you know what happens."

"No," Nussbaum replied. "What happens?"

"You'll have to have a sex change operation so I can appoint you as attorney general."

Some time later, Clinton presented Nussbaum with a photograph of himself talking to Reno and pointing at Nussbaum. Clinton inscribed it, "Bernie, You [were] spared the operation."

By that time, nominations had become a sideshow for Paster and his fellow aides. The real action dealt with the President's budget proposal. The total program was simultaneously one of the largest deficit-reducing proposals ever offered and one of the largest government expansions. Hundreds of billions of dollars were at stake, and aides had to remind themselves at times just how much that was. Once, after Gene Sperling got his colleagues to agree to move $200 million from one account to another, Paster had to admonish him to slow down. "You know, Gene," he said, "it isn't Monopoly money." And Sperling could only grin in reply.

The economic program had three distinct parts: deficit reduction and two parts that actually increased the deficit. One of those was called the stimulus package; the second, for longer-term spending, was called the investment package. The President insisted that all three were needed. Republicans—and the general public—would soon doubt that conviction, and Paster would be one of the early victims of the conflict.

The budget's first major test in Congress was its smallest part in dollar terms, the stimulus package. On Tuesday, March 2, Paster went into full swing to lobby on its behalf. But the day turned out to be an example of just how multidimensional a president's relations with Congress must be, and how tough a spot his chief lobbyist is in.

Clinton was scheduled for separate meetings that day with Republican House members and GOP senators. In the Oval Office that morning, the President joked that he was about to enter "the lions' den." As the White House's top lobbyist, Paster had to make sure he was not eaten.

He borrowed a trick from his days as a corporate lobbyist. Back then he had represented the baseball commissioner, and he knew nothing soothes a politician more than an athletic souvenir. He also knew that that day was the seventieth birthday of House Minority Leader Robert Michel. So before the meeting with the senior members of the House Republican Conference, Paster gave the President a replica 1914 Chicago Cubs baseball cap for presentation to Michel. The Illinois Republican, a big Cubs fan, could not have been more pleasantly surprised. He also loved the two other Paster touches: a large sheet cake with candles that was wheeled into the meeting room and the fact that the President himself led the singing of "Happy Birthday."

But the gesture did not deflect every concern; the flattery part of lobbying can only go so far. Congressman Henry Hyde, also from Illinois, complained that the Republicans had not been briefed about the food shipments to Bosnia the President had just agreed to begin. Afterward, as they walked down the hallway together, Clinton told Paster, "The guy has a point," and he instructed Paster to keep the Republicans better informed. Satisfying members of Congress was a never-ending chore.

At the Senate meeting, Republican leader Bob Dole tried a few lobbying tricks himself. He served Clinton Big Macs in deference to the President's predilection for fast food. And the panderama continued when Clinton teased New Mexico's Pete Domenici, the top GOP member of the Senate Budget Committee, that he had followed his career on C-SPAN and was unsettled at the very notion that they might not agree on an economic plan. At the same time, Clinton showed he could play hardball. In a studied act, the President refused to return the telephone call of Republican congressman Dick Armey of Texas, later the House majority leader, who had made some uncomplimentary remarks during an earlier White House meeting.

At the end of the day, back at the White House, Clinton told Paul Begala the meetings had gone well. "You know, I love this stuff," he said. But no matter how hard he tried, Paster came away wondering if he would ever be able to control it all.

Later that month, Paster was given hope. Robert Byrd, the imperious chairman of the Senate Appropriations Committee, asked to visit Clinton in the Oval Office specifically to tell him how the stimulus package was going to succeed. Paster was more than happy to arrange the meeting.

To help spur his committee to pass the stimulus package quickly, Byrd asked Paster to get a letter from the President that made clear how important the legislation was to his overall strategy. And, dutifully, Paster drafted the missive before the meeting. As Byrd arrived, Paster handed Clinton the letter in a large manila envelope.

"I'm going to get this bill done," Byrd told the President confidently.

"I appreciate it," Clinton replied and began to fiddle with the envelope.

But before the President could take the letter out, Byrd reached for the envelope and began to scribble on the outside. The senator explained he was diagramming the series of amendments he intended to attach to the measure in order to pass it smoothly. Both Paster and the President were impressed. The last thing on their minds had been to ask for more details. "Who else were we going to rely on to pass an appropriations bill," Paster said, besides the appropriations chairman?

Paster thought his faith in the barons of Congress was being proven sound. Congressman William Natcher, chairman of the Appropriations Committee in the House, had also trekked to the White House to tell Clinton he was going to pass the stimulus package. And late on Thursday, March 18, he did just that. On the same day, the outline of the President's entire $1.5 trillion budget plan also was approved by the House.

Shortly thereafter, Byrd telephoned to tell Paster that his committee was about to approve the stimulus package. The committee chairman also proudly reported that the two senior Republicans on the panel, Mark Hatfield of Oregon and Ted Stevens of Alaska, were voting to send the bill to the floor. And with that Paster relaxed. But he soon learned there was never time to rest in the madhouse.

As quickly as the stimulus package's prospects rose, they fell. Just because a bill passes the committee does not guarantee it will become law. Far from it. And complaints about the package came first from the Republicans. They disparaged the $16.3 billion legislation as larded with swimming pools and golf courses for the constituents of favored lawmakers. How could the President be for reducing the deficit, they asked, if he also favored such giveaways?

Then the Democrats started to ask the same questions. The leading alternative, in fact, was authored by two Democrats, Senators John Breaux of Louisiana and David Boren of Oklahoma. Their bill would have allowed the full amount in the stimulus package to be spent, but not until after spending cuts and tax increases were enacted to pay the new costs. To prove they were not kidding about that kind of strict adherence to fiscal conservatism, Breaux and Boren filibustered the stimulus package for four and a half hours on Thursday, March 25.

Paster began to shuttle back and forth to the Senate to find a compromise. Senate Democrats were eager for a way out of the problem, but there was no obvious answer. The White House staff was riven. Some argued the President should embrace Breaux-Boren. But Paster said no. The President had pledged to other Democrats that he would not make alterations. Besides, if a deal had to be cut, Paster said, it had to be cut with Republicans. They held the balance of power.

Making matters worse, Clinton was not in town to give clear guidance. He was more than 3,000 miles away at a summit meeting in Vancouver with Russian president Boris Yeltsin. And the distance hurt. Taking their cue from Breaux and Boren, Senate Republicans began their own filibuster, and there was nothing Paster could do. "We're losing them," Paster shouted, pounding a table. "We have to do something!" But everything he tried went nowhere.

How could he have blundered so badly? If only he had questioned Senator Byrd more closely. If only he had listened to his own advice: a January 15 memo to McLarty in which Paster warned that the President needed to work closely with Republicans. "Failure to consult in an appropriate fashion will haunt us," he wrote. "Republicans need to know we are interested in doing business; we need to convey a willingness to work with those who will work with us. Not only will we need Republican votes to break Senate filibusters, access to Republican votes may be necessary on legislation when Democratic support is soft."

But it was too late now. Paster had relied on the word of the leaders of Congress—his old friends and comrades—to predict the outcome of legislation. Perhaps when he had started in Washington, some two decades before, that had been good enough. And when he had worked on tiny parts of legislation as a lobbyist, that rule also had probably applied. But in the contemporary world of the White House, no votes could be taken for granted on the big bills that made or broke a presidency. Now he had to win vote by vote.

Paster could have kicked himself. The Congress had been growing more balky and independent minded for years. He knew the background well. It had all started with the post-Watergate congressional reforms in 1974. The once impregnable seniority system had been demolished, and committee chairmanships were no longer automatically given to the lawmakers with the longest tenure. That gave rank-and-file members more clout. In addition, the number of subcommittees had greatly expanded, which granted a vastly larger number of relative newcomers to Congress their own staffs, their own power bases, and their own chances to be "Mr. Chairman."

Around the same time, campaign finance laws had been changed to expand the ways individual candidates were able to raise funds separate from their party. Paster often wished Bill Clinton had the authority Lyndon Johnson had exercised to promise campaign money to lawmakers who voted with him and deny funds to lawmakers who refused. But now any member of Congress, given an enhanced power base in the expanded committee system, could raise campaign contributions almost at will and tell the President to buzz off.

Paster also longed for the days when Dwight Eisenhower could sit with Speaker Sam Rayburn and decide what would or would not become the law of the land. And he envied Larry O'Brien, a senior staffer to both Kennedy and Johnson, who would regularly meet with key Democratic party constituencies and predict with precision which bill would pass and when. OK now, he might say, Medicare wins in the Senate next week. And it would. Such guidance from above was unheard of anymore. Even the GOP filibuster that was dragging down the stimulus package was a product not of the Republican leadership (Senate Republican Leader Bob Dole seemed willing to deal) but of the younger Republican upstarts, especially senators Trent Lott of Mississippi and Don

Nickles of Oklahoma. They saw a chance to wound the Democratic President and decided to press their advantage.

Paster knew there were not a lot of people who commanded blocs of votes, but he did not realize how completely atomized the process had become. He tortured himself for not having called more senators himself early on. He had been lulled by his success at getting the bill out of committee. But in the new, fragmented world of Congress, he said, "You can't presume."

The lesson was not academic to Paster. The long hours of work and the fruitless negotiations over the stimulus package were beginning to take their toll. Paster was barely seeing his family. And still his efforts were not producing the right result. The pressure, the fatigue, the frustration were beginning to get to him.

On the night of Wednesday, April 7, with the stimulus bill still languishing in the Senate, Paster worked in his study at home until 11:30. He could endure no more that day. So he walked down the hall to bed and set the alarm, as usual, for 4:30 A.M. But his sleep was restless that night. At the sound of the alarm, he woke up and had what he could only describe as an epiphany. All of a sudden his situation became clear. "I said to myself, 'You are an asshole, this can't go on.' "

He drove in to the office and met with Mack McLarty as soon as he found a chance. "I'll be either divorced or dead if this goes on," Paster told him. And he came to realize he and his staff had to slow down. But that is never possible in the perpetual motion machine known as the White House.

At the end of the month, the stimulus package finally died, killed by a solid phalanx of Republican senators and their unstoppable filibuster. The action was the President's first significant loss of legislation in Congress and raised doubts about his ability to enact his entire, ambitious agenda, which included the much larger and more complicated measures to overhaul the health-care system and reduce the budget deficit. The President's approval rating fell five points in the *Wall Street Journal*/NBC News poll.

Paster was devastated. He regretted the Oval Office meeting at which he and the President had mutely nodded their assent to Senator Byrd. He also wished he had spoken up when Byrd had told him the bill had been approved by his committee. Had he to do it over again, he would have asked committee Republicans, such as senators Hatfield and Stevens, if they would also back the measure on the floor. As it turned out, they did not, and that had been the beginning of the end of the stimulus package.

Paster took responsibility for the screwup, and his colleagues at the White House were more than happy for him to have it. In the final days of the stimulus fight, he had met with his equals around McLarty's conference table and debated the merits of one compromise or another. Stephanopoulos and McLarty had argued in favor of the Breaux-Boren compromise. But Paster, failing to anticipate that Republicans would be unwilling to deal at all in the end, had said that would be a mistake. The Republicans saw a chance to portray Clinton as a big-spending liberal, and that sweet opportunity was what led to defeat.

Paster was caught in the vise endemic to his job. Not only had he failed to bring along the members of Congress who were his responsibility but he had also hurt himself with the people he reported to at the White House. He was being squeezed in just the way his old friends had warned him he would be. And his pinch was tighter than usual because of the way he had failed. Clinton's first chief of staff did not function as the boss of the White House the way some of his predecessors had. Mack McLarty was more of an ambassador for the President to the groups that he already was close to. One of those groups was oil state lawmakers such as Boren and Breaux, especially Breaux. A large part of McLarty's job was to make sure Breaux, a leader of the moderate wing of the

Democratic party, voted for Clinton's initiatives. So if Paster was going to throw Breaux out of the Clinton tent, as he had during this debate, he had better make sure the tent was full enough otherwise. In this case, he had not, and the damage was irreparable. McLarty, and many others in the White House, never looked at Paster the same way again.

As the difficulties of his job became clearer to him, Paster began to wonder why he had ever aspired to the post. Gail Paster, his wife and a Shakespearean scholar, gave him a quotation from Thomas Floyd's "Pictures of a Perfect Commonwealth" that conveyed what he felt. It read: "Governours . . . are always to be emploied in matters of great consequence, whereof the charge is such, that if they discharge their duty, they shall hardly have so much leisure, as to treat their meat, and take their rest, unlesse they omit some of that time which should be emploied in publicke affaires."

What was left of Paster's reputation was on the line for his next assignment, to navigate the broad deficit-reduction bill through the House Ways and Means Committee. One of the knottiest parts of the measure concerned the President's plan to impose a new broad-based energy tax. A freshman Democrat on the panel, Bill Brewster of Oklahoma, had gathered enough votes to kill the tax unless it was watered down. Paster's job was to save the bill as a whole by persuading the committee's chairman, Dan Rostenkowski of Illinois, to give Brewster what he wanted. So Paster telephoned Rostenkowski and begged.

"I have to get this one," he said. "If I don't get it done, I'm dead meat. I'll be worth shit at the White House."

In case pleading did not work, Paster also tried a threat. He said if Rostenkowski did not accommodate Brewster then he, Paster, would be demoted and, in effect, leave all tax negotiations from the Clinton administration in the hands of Rostenkowski's nemesis, Lloyd Bentsen. Before he was secretary of the Treasury, Bentsen had been chairman of the Senate's tax-writing panel, the Finance Committee, and an adversary of Rostenkowski for years.

So Rostenkowski relented and permitted Brewster to modify the proposal. But the energy tax was still in trouble, and so was Paster. Bentsen was out for his hide, and Paster's promise to keep the secretary out of the talks proved empty.

Before a meeting of Ways and Means Democrats some time later, Bentsen made his wishes plain to Clinton. Paster watched silently as the secretary looked straight at the President and said, "It needs to be clear that only one person can represent you on tax matters." And that person, he said, was Lloyd Bentsen.

Clinton said little about the comment then, but with the congressmen in the Roosevelt Room moments later he said, "Lloyd Bentsen is clearly my chief agent on tax matters." And that was the end of that. Paster was caught in the middle again.

The next attack on Paster came from Congress, in the person of Senator Boren. There were rumors that Boren was talking to other senators about getting rid of Paster in revenge for having opposed the lawmaker's compromise on the stimulus package. After another White House meeting, Boren walked up to Paster and said, "I'm not after your job." To Paster, that was all the confirmation he needed that the senator wanted him fired.

The combination of setbacks made Paster even more paranoid than usual. It seemed that everyone was on his case. In mid-May, *Newsweek* magazine ran a picture of Paster with the caption "Former Gucci Gulch lobbyist under fire for blowing the stimulus-package fight." And for weeks afterward, as hard as he tried, Paster could not get over it.

The pressure was palpable. Despite his long hours, the chief lobbyist lay awake on many nights. He had stopped exercising, was eating more junk food, and was gaining weight.

His ingestion of Diet Coke, always impressive, grew to be prodigious; he bought the stuff by the case. And a stress-related rash forced him to visit a dermatologist—twice.

Worse, the job was beginning to hurt his family. Early on, he had been tempted to feel like a big man: getting paged at his son's baseball game and calling the White House on his cellular phone from the stands. But that got old fast. "That makes you important," Paster realized. "It doesn't make you good." Another time he got a page that read, "Call Secdef ASAP," which meant he should call the secretary of defense right away. When he did so from Hamburger Hamlet, he returned to find that his son had already finished his meal. Paster apologized but, as with the *Newsweek* slap, could not make himself forget the injury he had caused.

Paster could understand making mistakes. What he could not get over was that the same mistakes kept recurring. The White House seemed to be incapable of learning. Or, more to the point, the sitting-duck situation the White House was in during so many of its self-generated controversies made the chance of correction remote. That certainly was the case during the horrific episode of Lani Guinier.

Pressure was building in Congress for Guinier, a University of Pennsylvania law professor and old Clinton friend, to withdraw her nomination to head the Civil Rights Division of the Justice Department. Republicans opposed her almost by rote. But Democrats also were worried that she was too much an advocate of racial quotas. It was an echo of Zoe Baird, and, once again, it was up to Paster to make sure his colleagues at the White House knew. He tried to tell them every chance he got—on the telephone, in the hallways, at the senior staff meeting each morning. But somehow, the message was not getting through. At last, on Wednesday, June 2, Paster and other top aides met in the Oval Office for a long talk with the President.

This time, it seemed, Clinton understood. Paster's impression was that he wanted Guinier to withdraw for her own sake and for the good of the administration. But personnel decisions were still the most vexing in the Clinton White House. Guinier insisted that her opponents' view of her as a "Quota Queen" was simply untrue, and she refused to withdraw. Once again McLarty asked Paster to talk to the ill-fated nominee.

"Do you want me to tell her whether the President is going to withdraw the nomination?" Paster asked.

"No," McLarty replied.

"Why not?" Paster said plaintively, although he already knew the answer too well. He was getting used to being the man in the middle.

The White House was not organized for decisiveness. It was more like a debating society than an executive office. And that led to unending tension among the staffers. Their constant battle against the chaos would have been hard even if they had had a system to organize their responses. But they did not have such a system, and that made life inside the madhouse even harder. For example, the politically inept Bernie Nussbaum was adamant that Lani Guinier be allowed to defend herself. Almost everyone else thought she should withdraw. But in the Clinton White House, a single voice was enough to silence all the others. And Nussbaum's was a little louder than most. He almost always reflected the view of his champion, Hillary Clinton, and she played a large role in choosing the Justice Department's staff. She was so close a friend of Guinier that she had attended her wedding in 1986.

So Paster faced another impossible challenge. He knew Guinier was not confirmable. Both Senate Majority Leader Mitchell and Senate Judiciary Committee chairman Biden had conveyed that to the President directly. Yet Paster was not given the authority to demand she withdraw. He was being forced, instead, to speak obliquely—to deliver harsh news without saying it aloud. At about 7:30 that evening, he went to the attorney general's conference room at the Justice Department to deliver the bad but not decisive message. His sense of déjà vu was agonizing.

Guinier was waiting defiantly, surrounded by supporters. Indeed, the room was packed with people, from both inside and outside the administration. All eyes were on Paster as he sat next to Guinier and turned his chair so he was looking at her. He wanted to make himself as clear as he could given the circumstances. He began this way: the Democratic leaders of the Senate believed she would not be confirmed.

She did not get the hint. She and her backers argued that she wanted—and deserved—her day in court and that he was wrong about her support in the Senate. Paster tried not to show his outrage. He could not believe a lawyer from Philadelphia was questioning his vote count. He *knew* where the votes were, and where they were not. He had learned the secrets of vote counting from some of the great ones, Phil Burton of California, and John Dingell and David Bonior of Michigan. From them and from personal experience, Paster knew that to get a credible count he had to ask specific questions and then pay close attention to the answers. A less than direct response, or even a flickering doubt shown in the eye, was enough to know the vote was not a certainty. He often returned to ask his questions as many as three times before he was sure he had a solid reply. Guinier naively believed that just because a member of Congress said something complimentary, she should expect a vote in her favor.

Paster also tried to explain to Guinier that the courtroom analogy did not apply. There are no standards of evidence, and certainly no standards of fairness in a political inquiry of the kind she was facing. She could not prevail. Even some of the senators who seemed to support her were running away, he said.

In the end, he faced the same stalemate he had faced when he entered. "Well, look, you sleep on it," he concluded, dejectedly. "But I can't tell you the view of the White House will be different in the morning." He then faced another indignity. Guinier wanted to appear on ABC's *Nightline* that night to make her case. Oh, my God, was all Paster could think. From an office down the hall, he telephoned McLarty at the White House, who brought Stephanopoulos into the conversation.

"OK, it's you and Koppel," Paster told her before he left the Justice Department after nine o'clock, trying to make light of what he knew was another impending disaster.

The next day, at last, Vice President Gore intervened. He urged the President to read some of Guinier's law review articles and make up his mind. During a helicopter flight that day, Clinton finally did. Afterward Gore, McLarty, and Paster, among others, attended another meeting in the Oval Office. To Paster's relief, Clinton said, "Had I read what she wrote earlier, I wouldn't have nominated her." But even that was not the end of it. There was still a spirited debate. Paster and others urged the President to withdraw the nomination and argued that fighting a losing battle over Guinier would hurt his chances to win passage of other, bigger priorities. Nussbaum said Guinier deserved a chance to explain her views before the Judiciary Committee. To abandon her without a fight, he and others argued, would offend blacks, liberals, and women.

At one point Nussbaum suggested, "We'll call it a failure of the confirmation process." And Paster could not believe his ears. "How about some accountability around here?" he challenged. This was the worst example of Clinton's "jump ball" management style, Paster thought. As in basketball, whoever made the greatest effort to take over an issue or event often got the go-ahead but was never fully held accountable for the result.

Finally, Vernon Jordan put an end to the squabbling. "Mr. President," he said at the Oval Office meeting, "it's two minutes to midnight. We can't delay." Even then, however, Clinton did delay. Guinier was summoned to the White House and allowed to take an hour and a half of the President's precious time. Afterward, Clinton went before the White House press corps to announce he was withdrawing the nomination. He did so with tears in his eyes.

During the most stressful times of his life as a private lobbyist, Paster had gone to work filled with optimism. Even during the most turbulent times back then, such as when everyone else doubted the future of the Chrysler bailout, he did not give up. He never felt defeated. He looked forward to his work each day and was confident that, somehow, he would win. But the unrelenting turmoil of the White House, the way it spun out of control so often and at such velocity, was debilitating even to Paster. Sure, he could be more than a little high-strung, and at times peevish. But this was different. His deep sense of gloom and exhaustion was new— and frightening. On the morning of Friday, June 4, the day after the dispiriting interlude of Lani Guinier, Paster left his house not long after dawn with a sharp pain in his stomach. The thought of another day was almost more than he could bear.

On the one hand, he had gotten rid of the burden of dealing with Guinier. On the other hand, another daunting personnel challenge loomed. The search team was working to find a confirmable replacement for Supreme Court justice Byron White. The lead candidate at the moment was Secretary of the Interior Bruce Babbitt, but who knew for sure?

"They're killing me," he told a friend later, and, after a mere five months, vowed to himself to leave the job he had most wanted in life by the end of the first year.

.　.　.

Paster reported at 8:15 on the morning of Sunday, June 6, for a meeting in the Oval Office with the President. The subject: choosing a new Supreme Court justice. With Mario Cuomo out of the running, the President had all but decided Babbitt would be the nominee. The secretary was a veteran politician of the kind Clinton wanted. He had served as both governor and attorney general of Arizona and had once run for president, though not against Clinton. He was a graduate of Harvard Law School and was well respected by both Democrats and Republicans. One such Republican was a sitting justice, Sandra Day O'Connor. Babbitt had appointed her to the Arizona bench when he was governor.

At the Oval Office meeting, the President directed that Babbitt be given a more vigorous background check, or vetting. And over pizza in the secretary's spacious office that evening, Paster saw nothing in the documents he reviewed that made him think Babbitt would not take the next step toward actual nomination.

As far as Paster was concerned, Babbitt was all but a done deal. He and other top staffers even had agreed that if Babbitt were nominated he would have to give up control of the Department of the Interior right away to avoid any appearance of conflict. Paster already was having informal conversations about the secretary's confirmability with senators influential in judicial appointments. He had learned the hard way he had to consult with *everyone.*

But the vise of his position began to close in again. At the annual White House–Congress barbecue two days later, one western-state lawmaker after another pulled Paster aside to protest that the public-lands issues that were the heart of Interior's mission would suffer if Babbitt left. The complaints came from Congressmen Bill Richardson of New Mexico and Norm Dicks of Washington. "Don't let Bruce leave the department," implored Congresswoman Jolene Unsoeld, also from the state of Washington. Paster watched warily as these and other lawmakers whispered to the President as well. He could almost feel the momentum slow.

The next day Babbitt was no longer the front-runner. And Paster was disappointed again. As he had seen so terribly often before, the next candidate on the White House counsel's list rose to the top: appeals court judge Stephen Breyer of Massachusetts. Paster felt dizzied by the change.

That morning, Gail Paster saw her husband's torment over the Supreme Court nominee and anticipated there would be more to come. Hearing that Babbitt was out and Breyer on the rise for the job, she shook her head. A white male would be a disappointment to liberal groups, she said. Paster thought the President would not succumb to such pressures, especially since he and other staffers were going to such great lengths to check Breyer's background. Even though the judge was in a Boston hospital at the time, a slew of Clinton aides undertook an eight-hour interview of him anyway.

One reason it took so long—much to Paster's distress—was that Breyer had a Zoe Baird problem of sorts. Zoe Baird! It all seemed to come round, and round again. Some aides tried to dismiss it. But Paster knew better. He warned that the President could not afford to nominate someone with such a flaw so soon after Baird had been forced to withdraw.

So the Counsel's Office went back to the list again. And this time, as Gail Paster had predicted, they plucked a woman: appeals court judge Ruth Bader Ginsburg. By Sunday, June 12, Bernie Nussbaum was going through tax documents in Ginsburg's duplex in the Watergate. Much to his delight, the records were impeccably ordered, including all Social Security tax payments. The only problem was caused by Nussbaum, who stupidly answered the telephone when it rang. On the other end was Ruth Marcus, a reporter for *The Washington Post,* who had suspected, but then knew for sure, that Ginsburg was the new front-runner for the job.

At about noon, Ginsburg went to the White House to

lunch with Clinton in the residence—just the two of them. Afterward, the President went to the golf course with lobbyist James Free, Vernon Jordan, and Alan Wheat, a Democratic congressman from Missouri. Typical of the tightly held way Clinton preferred to keep such consultations, he did not tell any of his companions with whom he had just met. They all had their suspicions, though. Their game was supposed to begin after noon but did not get under way until about 1:30.

The group played only nine holes, even though they had expected to play all eighteen. The President said he had to get back to the White House, and who would argue with him? Ginsburg, in the meantime, finished with Nussbaum and was told she might know the result by about 5:00 P.M.

That, of course, did not happen. But it did look to Paster like the President was getting close. Still wearing his golf clothes, Clinton told his staff what he thought of the latest candidate. "She's a solid person," he said, "a workhorse, not a show horse." But, still unwilling to commit, the President changed into a clean shirt and went to a previously scheduled barbecue he was hosting for the White House press corps. After the dinner, which was held under a huge white tent on the South Lawn, Clinton slipped off to the residence to make the Supreme Court choice. And while the President made his last calculations, Paster watched basketball on television in his office.

At about eleven o'clock the decision was made—it would be Ginsburg—and Paster walked over to the residence to help the President telephone congressional leaders. The actual calling was postponed, however, until the Chicago Bulls won the basketball game at the close of an exciting triple overtime—a fitting metaphor for the Supreme Court selection.

Sitting in the kitchen—his favorite spot in the residence— Clinton called senators Mitchell, Biden, Hatch, Kennedy, and

Moynihan. Paster reached Senator Dole's top aide when efforts to raise the senator himself proved unavailing. Nussbaum had called Ginsburg earlier to tell her not to go to sleep. After all the necessary calls were made, the White House operator tried to get Ginsburg, but there was a bad connection. Clinton dialed back himself, and when he got her on the line around midnight, he told her that she had an outstanding record, a mainstream record, and that she had made signal achievements for women. He now thought she would become a leader on the court as well.

Clinton also called the losers. He told Babbitt he "had never seen an outpouring of support for a secretary of the interior" like the one he had just witnessed. "I have people calling, saying, 'If he quits, I want the job, but if you let him, you're crazy as hell.' " He told Breyer how impressed he was with him and assured him he would be a major contender for the job in the future, which proved prescient indeed.

As he drove home in the wee hours, Paster thought how privileged he was to have been so close to the making of history, and how glad he was that that particular part of history was over. He did not know how much more history he could take.

Back at the White House, the deficit-reduction bill loomed as the next crisis. And Paster began to feel even more like an outsider. He felt closed out by McLarty, with whom he feuded more and more.

Paster had plenty of reasons to dislike the chief of staff. The basic one was that McLarty did not give him the leeway he needed to come even close to getting his job done. McLarty left the most simple things unaccomplished. For months Paster had tried to find patronage posts for a couple of associates of Congressman Steny Hoyer, a Maryland member of the House Democratic leadership and a loyal Clinton follower. But repeated entreaties and memos to McLarty went unanswered. "I'm so pissed, I can't see straight," Paster said after one such attempt. "I fight and I fight and I fight and I wear myself out." The disorganization of the place, overall, he concluded, made it hard for anyone to work.

In self-defense, he tried to insulate himself and his staff from the turmoil, but he could not. He tried to give his staff more private time, assuring them the office would close at 7:30 P.M. when Congress was not in session. But that never happened. He vowed that everyone would get one weekend off a month. But that did not happen either.

Paster suffered in the meantime. In the entire year, he did not once visit his daughter at college. And, in general, he did not like the person he was becoming. He had lost touch with friends and family. There were guards and Secret Service agents in the West Wing whom he saw almost daily but never bothered to meet. "I had begun to lose just a little bit of my humanity," he confessed.

The job "sucks," he said in one of his more dejected moments. "You're constantly being yelled at by members of Congress for other people's mistakes."

The President and McLarty scheduled one of their by then typically overlarge, endless meetings in the White House residence for Wednesday, August 11. The issue of the day: how to make enough time for the President to deal with his huge agenda, which included anticrime legislation, health-care reform, reinventing government, and the North American Free Trade Agreement, known as NAFTA. The convergence of so many major issues was referred to among the White House staff as "the train wreck." And, to avoid it, the Clintons and their senior staff convened in the White House residence at 9:00 P.M.

Hillary Clinton arrived uncharacteristically late. And political consultant James Carville greeted her in a way that only he could: "The game isn't over until the fat lady sings," he said, "and the meeting doesn't begin until the First Lady arrives." Hillary Clinton listened patiently and then replied with a straight face, "That's a pretty good suck up, James, but you have got to do better."

The First Lady said she wanted to discuss the crowded schedule for the fall, suggesting that to make it work required an extra measure of discipline—something the White House had woefully lacked. Paul Begala dropped the pretense of brownnosing that his partner had started and took the hardest line of the meeting. He argued forcefully that health care was the penultimate issue for the President and that the other priorities should be trimmed back.

If anyone in the room should have agreed, it was Paster. As a former labor lobbyist, he had no great attachment to free trade. He also knew how hard it would be to find the votes to pass NAFTA. But by now he knew meetings like this one were ridiculous. He had been to enough to know that nothing was going to be set aside. The President knew what he wanted, and no one could tell him otherwise.

"So we have a full schedule?" Paster asserted. "So what?"

That choice became inevitable when Carville switched positions, disagreed with Begala, and took Paster's side. It would be unwise for the President to be seen backing away from any of his main priorities, Carville reasoned. He was already being forced to backtrack enough, and his tendency to accommodate was hurting his image.

And so it was. Roy Neel, who was acting as the scheduler, set up a chart that showed blocks of the President's time devoted to each major issue: health care, NAFTA, and reinventing government. Crime was "put off" until the next year. Only in Washington . . .

At the end of the three-hour session, Clinton was so exercised he wondered aloud if he had time to take his upcoming vacation. "But, Mr. President," Begala said, "people will think you're weird if you don't take a vacation." The President paused, then replied, "I *am* weird."

.   .   .

After the meeting, Paster was deeply disturbed. He felt he had to tell the President how frustrated he was. "Every meeting in this place has fifteen people," he grumbled. And that last gathering in particular had just been "nonsense." Paster believed the President would never do anything less than his full agenda; the meeting was just another extraordinary waste of time.

So, Paster thought, it was time to speak up. Before he left the White House that night, he asked to talk to the President privately. When the two were sitting alone, he told Clinton it was possible he would quit at year's end. And, according to friends of Paster, the President asked him not to act so hastily. He said he hoped Paster would decide not to go. Big challenges lay ahead. Clinton suggested Paster take some time to rest, and reassess things when he returned. Paster said he would and vowed to talk to the President more about his concerns.

Paster was enormously tired, and he planned a ten-day vacation in the mountains of Northern California and in San Francisco. But he did think he knew what was wrong. The problem, he believed, rested largely with Mack McLarty. "One of Mack's greatest faults," he said, "is that he's too inclusive; he ought to be more autocratic." But he did not have the time or the inclination to mention that to Clinton, who was, after all, McLarty's lifelong friend.

Before Paster had a chance to discuss White House management more with the President, the next crisis erupted, and in an unlikely place, Somalia. Few Americans knew where the country was or why the United States still stationed troops there. But starting Sunday, October 3, Somalia was all the networks and newspapers cared about. Out of nowhere, one of the country's warring factions, provoked by an American ambush, had cornered a contingent of U.S. soldiers and killed eighteen of them in a wild firefight. To bring the tragedy

home, pictures were published and broadcast of the sparsely
clad corpse of a downed helicopter crewman being dragged
by a rope through the streets and a bloodied and terrified pilot named Michael Durant being questioned by his Somali
captors.

For the White House, it was a policy and public relations
disaster, and it brought the usual response: top aides were
summoned to talk about it in meeting after meeting. Clinton
cut short a trip to California to join the conversation, and, to
Paster's now familiar horror, the jump-ball principle of management went quickly into play.

After two long days, Paster had sat through enough skull sessions. He thought it was time to act. But he faced resistance,
this time from Les Aspin. The secretary of defense did not
want to brief his former colleagues on Capitol Hill about
Clinton policy in the region, even after Paster had gone to the
trouble of arranging the meeting.

To Paster, this was simply not acceptable. "If we cancel it,
we have *real* problems," he warned, and it was hard to argue.
Paster's office was fielding a steady stream of irate phone calls
from members of Congress who demanded to know what was
going on. Paster told Aspin he could not back out, and in the
end the secretary was persuaded.

The meeting room in the New West Front of the Capitol
was jammed with 250 lawmakers, all eager to hear what the
President's policy would be. This was the big chance, Paster
knew, for the White House to make sense of things and clear
its name. The stakes were high. Instead, the lawmakers got
a rambling discourse by an obviously ill-prepared defense
secretary who did not even bother to tell them the facts as
he knew them about the firefight. Aspin ended up asking
for *their* opinions rather than telling them what Clinton
was thinking. He also allowed himself to be pummeled
with angry questions, to which he gave jumbled and con-

tradictory answers. Paster squirmed in the rear of the room.

Later, Aspin complained to the President that Paster should not have scheduled the briefing at all, and, when Paster found out about the complaint, he raged. The ill will hurt Paster deeply and erased any good feelings he might have retained from his vacation. "I don't give a rat's ass anymore," he swore. "Fuck 'em."

The next week Paster formally notified McLarty and the White House counsel that he was preparing to look for other work. The notification was required by the rules of the White House to avoid conflicts of interest. And, by now, Paster was more than ready to move on. His first inclination was to return to Hill & Knowlton, but this time as chairman of the entire company. That was the job he had had his eye on before he joined the White House, and now, less than a year later, he still had a chance to claim it.

It seemed the right time for him to go. If he stayed beyond the first of the year, he would have to stay through the next election cycle—one more full year—and he was too tired and disgruntled for that. The setbacks of 1993 had mounted up and had never been allayed. He still felt McLarty was not allowing him to do his job.

He asked the chief of staff to allow him to speak to the President. But McLarty said, No, not yet. Wait until after the NAFTA fight was over. And so, yet another insult was added to Paster's litany of complaints.

Like everything else, NAFTA was a bear to pass. Its opponents had largely defined the issue in their favor, making the White House's task harder. But this time the staff tried something new: bipartisanship, an idea taken from that long-ago Paster memo—and sad experience. On Friday, November 12, Paster took part in an extraordinary meeting in the

Roosevelt Room that included such former Republican White House aides as Kenneth Duberstein, Rich Bond, Craig Fuller, and Alan Kranowitz—then all lobbyists for corporations that favored free trade. Also in attendance was the top staffer to House Republican Leader Bob Michel, William Pitts. This time, Paster vowed, Republicans would be part of the team, the biggest part. That way there would be at least a chance to win.

Still, Paster continued to clash with McLarty. Dick Gephardt had long declared his opposition to NAFTA, and Paster was doing his best to work around that fact. He knew he had no choice but to divide the Democratic caucus and keep a solid Republican majority if NAFTA were to pass in the House. McLarty was not so attuned to the congressional mathematics. He continued to try to woo Gephardt back. But the more McLarty and Gephardt met, the more nervous the necessary Republican lawmakers became.

"If you cut a bad deal with Gephardt, we'll start cutting out," House Republican whip Newt Gingrich warned Paster.

"Newt," Paster replied, "we're not going to do that."

But McLarty kept talking to Gephardt until George Stephanopoulos took Paster's side, a fact that only added fuel to the Paster-McLarty fight.

The White House strategy on winning NAFTA was blanket coverage. In the final weeks before the vote, Clinton met with every undecided Democrat in the House. He met them in small groups and large groups, and talked to many of them individually on the telephone. He was aided in this by William Daley, the brother of Chicago mayor Richard Daley and son of the former mayor of the same name, who was brought in to coordinate the effort. Daley, in turn, was helped by two high-strung White House staffers, Rahm Emanuel and Tom Nides. Many mornings, the two aides would sit on either side of Daley at a long conference table in the Old Executive Office Building and moan about the fix they had gotten themselves into. "My career is ruined!" Emanuel exclaimed one day, and vowed not to name any of his children using an initial from the acronym NAFTA.

The White House also looked outside for help. Clinton aides played a role in coordinating a multimillion-dollar lobbying campaign by a group of well-heeled corporations that favored the pact, called USA NAFTA. In addition, they traded votes for special favors whenever they could. With Paster keeping track of the votes that were promised, the White House granted concessions to special interests ranging from glass blowers to citrus growers in order to gain specific lawmakers' support.

The battle cry became "NAFTA 'cause we hafta," and, having learned from his stimulus package mistakes, Paster was not leaving any vote unsought. The result was an easy victory. On Wednesday, November 17, by a vote of 234–200, NAFTA sailed through the House and on to the Senate, where no one feared defeat. After the House vote, Paster returned to the White House and asked McLarty if he could meet with Clinton. But McLarty again said no. Wait until after the Asian leaders' summit meeting that weekend in Seattle, he said. That would be a better time.

Paster finally learned about his departure from the White House staff by watching CNN. On Monday, November 22, Wolf Blitzer reported that Paster had resigned. The lobbyist immediately suspected McLarty of engineering the leak. As he returned from a visit to the Hill, he telephoned the chief of staff from the car and said, "I must see him tonight."

This time, McLarty did not stall. Paster finally got his chance to tell the President his plans. But, much to his irritation, McLarty sat through what Paster had wanted to be a private meeting, in effect not giving the President any chance to ask Paster to stay and preventing Paster from making his full complaint about McLarty.

"I'm going to submit my resignation on Wednesday," Paster told Clinton. "I don't want to leave, but I should leave. This is the job I always wanted, but the consequences to my family have been intolerable to me."

"That is the only reason I could accept your resignation," the President responded.

"I will help from the outside any way I can," Paster said, barely able to keep his emotions under control. And it was done.

The next morning, Paster got a standing ovation at the senior staff meeting and some ribbing from House Ways and Means chairman Dan Rostenkowski, whom he escorted to visit the President a little later. With affection, the burly lawmaker called Paster a "goddamned quitter." Oddly enough, Paster also got a phone call from Zoe Baird, who told him she was sorry to hear he was leaving.

At 9:30, the President met the joint leadership of Congress in the Cabinet Room. It was meant as a year-end session to commemorate for the cameras what a productive year it had been. After all, the budget and NAFTA were great successes. But the President also took a moment to thank Paster, without whom those victories would not have occurred.

At the White House, however, there is always bitter with the sweet. Press reports lumped Paster's departure with that of Roy Neel, then the deputy chief of staff, who resigned to head a telephone-company lobby group in town. Both men, reports said, were leaving the White House after just a year to become highly paid influencers of the government they had just been part of. In fact, antilobbying laws strictly prohibited either man from lobbying his former colleagues in the White House, and Paster was going to be chairman of a large public relations company, only part of which was involved in lobbying. He would not lobby himself. Still, such criticism, Paster knew by then—along with so many other things—was a price to be paid for working in the White House. Before he left, Paster got a call from Stan Lundine, the lieutenant governor of New York and a former congressman. "Be careful what you wish for," Lundine chided, "it may come true."

"What I didn't understand about the White House was the number and intensity of pressures that come to bear all the time," Paster said later. "You have to pay attention to everything." And, of course, that is not possible.

"I'm grateful to Bill Clinton. He gave me my life's ambition. And outside of my family, my time at the White House was the high point of my life," Paster said. But he added, speaking as if the tragedy of his service had happened to somebody else, "People leave, however gratified, somewhat frustrated they couldn't do more."

His position smack in the middle—between his own colleagues in the White House and the cacophony of the Congress—was the largest reason for his frustration. "I did it as well as I could," he said, but that probably could never have been well enough.

In his new suite of offices at Hill & Knowlton, with its view of the Potomac River in tony Georgetown, Paster kept several mementos of his days inside the White House: a signed photograph of himself with the President, a small slab of Virginia sandstone from the facade of the Capitol, commemorating the inauguration, and a crystal ashtray imprinted with a view of the White House. But although he returned to give advice to Leon Panetta, the new chief of staff, every once in a while, and tried to raise as much money for the Clinton reelection as he could, Paster could not imagine ever becoming a president's top lobbyist again.

His assistant both at the White House and at Hill & Knowlton, Unice Lieberman, age twenty-six, was still starry-eyed, however. To Paster's regret, she was thinking of leaving him to return to government service, maybe even in the White House. "I have missed the idea of working for something greater than myself," she said, and Paster understood. But the White House? Paster could only shake his head. "She's young," he said. It was the only explanation.

JEFF ELLER

2

Sisyphus on the Potomac

IN THE EARLY DAYS OF THE CLINTON ADMINISTRATION, WORK in the White House sometimes seemed quietly under control. In mid-February 1993, press aide Jeff Eller orchestrated so much good publicity in support of Clinton's economic plan that the President was pleased. And that meant Eller was happy too. So when the presidential motorcade pulled into a Comfort Inn in Chillicothe, Ohio, after a rousing speechmaking swing, neither Eller nor Clinton was ready to go to sleep. Not by a long shot.

Air Force One had arrived relatively early, about 9:00 P.M., and the traveling band had time to relax. Just like the old days on the campaign trail, they kicked back with Clinton at their side. In his hotel room, the President wore jeans and a casual shirt and played hearts with Dee Dee Myers and Bruce Lindsey. But as always, he could never do just one thing. He also listened to Paul Begala read the wires and talk politics, watched the movie *American Me* out of the corner of his eye, and made telephone calls to a dozen people in New Hampshire who had helped his campaign there. February 18 was the anniversary of his near-death experience in the presidential primary, and he did not forget the people who had helped him survive.

Eller cherished the scene. Sure, Clinton was playing hearts again as he had done so often on the campaign plane. But he also seemed comfortable in his new role. He was settled. The dark-suited valet who hovered in the background did not appear to be out of place. It just seemed right to have White House–installed telephones scattered around the room. On that bitterly cold, star-studded night, Clinton looked to be at home chatting on a phone with the presidential seal. And Eller was getting used to the scene himself.

If only he knew how temporary that feeling would be.

Few people would have taken Eller for the Indiana farm boy he was. For one thing, he was the White House's designated high-tech whiz, and his office in the Old Executive Office Building was always stacked high with computer magazines. His desk boasted two and sometimes three PCs, which he manipulated simultaneously while talking on the telephone through a headset. When he fantasized about the potential for his job, he had visions of wiring the whole Old EOB with fiber-optic cable and of starting a satellite network devoted exclusively to covering Clinton, called BCTV. In real life, he spent a lot of time placing the President's words into databases and corresponding via E-mail and fax with anyone who had the wherewithal to interface.

By any modern measure, then, Eller should have been a model White House staffer. He was thoroughly schooled in politics and expert in the latest methods of his particular part of the communications department. Few knew better than he, as they say, how to get the message out. He was also an accomplished supervisor, having run television news operations, sizable election campaigns, and, most recently, the Clinton public relations department that targeted local media markets. He also was no kid. He had weathered one divorce and was managing to keep a live-in relationship on track while working almost nonstop for Bill Clinton. He had suffered long yet proved his mettle on many fronts.

But Eller had a wild streak. True, at work he was, literally, buttoned down and usually wore blue oxford shirts. But he was a man of appetites—in the words of a friend, "all hormones and sweat glands." He rarely wore a tie, except at big meetings. He also smoked big cigars (in blatant violation of the Old EOB's no-smoking edict) and was a constant consumer of food and drink. He kept a pitcher of iced tea within reach at all times. For late-night bull sessions on his second-floor balcony, which overlooked the West Wing, he kept beer in the office refrigerator.

He was, at age thirty-seven, the man-child of the Clinton camp. He was the father-protector of the staff when they first arrived at the White House. And he was admired for his management skills at other times too: at parties he was always in charge—of the punch bowl.

This combination was evident from Eller's earliest days in Arcadia, Indiana. Before he went to school each morning, his chore was to feed the chickens—all 7,500 of them. After school, he had to find time to tend the draft horses and help with the corn and soybeans. As a result, he was well used to the kinds of hours he kept at the White House: 7:30 A.M. until 9:00 or 10:00 at night.

But he was also a bit uncontrollable. Eller wound up at the White House rather than in rural Indiana because he lacked the knack for agriculture his father and brother possessed and did not see it as a sacred calling. Rather, he reveled in the freedom of the open fields. He loved frozen ponds and parking lots for the chance they provided to spin his truck in "donuts" on the freshly fallen snow. He left Purdue University after just two and a half years and went straight to work in backwoods broadcast news, first at a radio station in Crawfordsville, Indiana, and later, in television, in a succession of small towns; Terre Haute, Indiana; Chattanooga, Tennessee;

and, ultimately, Nashville, where he became an assignment editor.

Eller, ever restless, left TV news as well. And probably that was wise. He liked to joke he had a face that was perfect for radio, dominated as it was by square glasses and a droopy mustache. So in 1985 he decided to try something new: politics. He became press secretary to Democratic congressman Bill Boner of Tennessee and learned a skill he would need for the rest of his career: crisis management. Three weeks after he signed on, the Justice Department began to investigate Boner for bribery.

As part of the probe, Eller was subpoenaed by a federal grand jury and, as he liked to say, came to learn what the words *bad day* really mean. But Eller was unscathed by the probe, and his boss was cleared. Boner later ran successfully for mayor of Nashville. Eller, who was by then known as a political operative, stayed in Washington to work as a troubleshooter for the House Democrats' reelection committee and roved from one difficult campaign to another.

Other political work, including a stint in Panama, occupied him until 1991. At that point he knew if he did not work in a presidential campaign, he probably never would. Although Eller was not old by the standards of most professions, his graying hairs were oddities in the young person's game of national politics. So he shopped around for the best candidate. He talked to several Democratic campaigns but settled on Clinton's, not because he agreed with the Arkansan on every issue—he did not—but because he thought Clinton had the best chance to win. And, for Eller, that was what mattered. He wanted a chance to win the White House before he was too old to reach that far.

And reaching that far, he thought, could get him even further. The route to the top of the political communications field, and the riches that could bring, runs straight through 1600 Pennsylvania Avenue. The White House was the ticket to a better place.

But Eller's ambition was not blind. He insisted on meeting the candidate before he started working for his campaign. And he did so, briefly, in a hotel in Charlotte, North Carolina. Eller's main impression was that Clinton was taller than he had expected, and not much more. Eller was a Democrat, and Clinton was the Democrat who could win. So Eller became a Clinton loyalist through and through.

He skillfully directed Clinton's victory in the Florida primary, then moved to Little Rock to run what became known as a state-of-the-art media operation. Eller is credited with bringing to the Democrats the "message of the day" disci pline for which only Republicans had been famous previously, then taking it to a new, more sophisticated level. He faxed "talking points" each day to Clinton backers all over the country so they could simultaneously spout the same message. He also monitored network satellite feeds so the campaign was always aware of how its message was being played. So when the Clinton White House needed a director of media affairs, Eller was the first choice for the job—deputy assistant to the President, for which he was paid $100,000 a year.

What Eller did for that money was on full display on Thursday, April 15, 1993, a gray, chilly day that made the ill-lighted hallways of the Old EOB seem darker than usual. And at a time in the evening when most Washingtonians were comfortably on their way home, Eller gathered his staff into a conference room for another hour or two of work. At first he tried to brighten his troops with banter. Then, abruptly, he got down to business. He placed several boxes of Julio's pizza in the center of the long, rectangular table and sat himself at the far end of it.

"OK," he declared, and the room quieted. Studying the schedule in front of him, he began, "What's the message?"

Years before, a president could command the attention of the nation almost any time he wanted. What he said was "the top of the news" on the networks and in the morning papers. But that started changing with the declines of presidents Johnson and Nixon. The proliferation of media outlets and television channels, as well as an increasingly skeptical press, meant the bully pulpit was in constant need of reinforcement. So the White House became, in many ways, a state-of-the-art public relations office.

Eller's job was to find ways to expose the President and his agenda to local and specialty media outlets. The results were almost always positive. The less sophisticated local press would broadcast and publish more of the White House message, and tamper with it less, than would the jaded national press corps. So every chance the President got, especially when he left town for a speech, he was linked by satellite and computer screen to local markets around the country—thanks to Eller and his staff.

During the planning meeting that Thursday evening, Eller ran through the schedule for a visit to Pittsburgh. In addition to the speech at the airport, Eller planned for the President to give an interview to the local newspaper. Surely that would be played big on Sunday, the day after the speech. But there was more. He directed Dave Anderson, the White House's satellite uplink expert, to arrange television interviews for Clinton with top stations in Buffalo, New York, and Burlington, Vermont. "Vermont's going to get a heavy dose of him [the President]," Eller said. Vermont senator Jim Jeffords, a moderate Republican, was a potential vote for the President's economic package.

"That's good," Eller concluded, and he went on with the rest of the schedule. On April 27 or 28, he said, the White House planned to introduce its campaign-finance reform bill. "The goal of campaign finance," he said candidly, "is to drop it in and get out of it"—meaning the President wanted the publicity of advocating the cause but would not press for its passage right away. Pushing for passage would cause too much friction with the Democratic leaders in the House, who were more interested in protecting their own reelections than in advocating any sort of reform. On Friday, April 30, the national service legislation would be introduced. And on Saturday night, May 1, Eller said, the President would attend the White House Correspondents Association dinner, which Eller mocked gently as "another press pander."

When he first came to the White House, the scrappy Eller brought with him the rough-and-tumble attitude of the Clinton campaign. "We're all products of campaigns," he said. "We've learned to scavenge and scam." Early on, for instance, he sent his employees all over the Old EOB to get as much good furniture and equipment as they could. When his staff was accused of theft, Eller said, in mock horror, "I'm shocked. Shocked!"

Such entrepreneurship was often necessary. A new White House does not work well even in the best of times. By Eller's count, for instance, it took visits by thirteen technicians before his primary computer could be connected to the in-house network. To get a decent system, he had to circumvent the White House bureaucracy entirely, enlisting experts from the National Science Foundation.

But Eller was more than a technician and a bureaucrat. He was a Clinton partisan, and he was well liked by the First Family for his willingness to take a punch on their behalf. When Dee Dee Myers insisted the press go along to the memorial service for Hillary Clinton's father in April, Eller was sent to keep them in line. In particular, the First Lady did not want photographs taken of family members as they emerged from the funeral, so it was up to Eller to inform the photographers they had to move away. Predictably, they resisted. Larry Downing of *Newsweek* started to tell Eller that it was his job to take the shot, and Eller exploded. "Don't lecture me," he said. "If you don't move I'll block the shot," which he did by placing vans between the photographers and the church.

. . .

Such devotion paid off. That same month, Larry Smith, Secretary of Defense Les Aspin's chief of staff, called George Stephanopoulos to ask if Eller was interested in becoming the Pentagon's press secretary. Eller had told Smith sometime earlier that the prestigious job at Defense, second only to his position at the White House, was his "dream." And it was no secret. Ever since the election, when, to campaign workers' amazement, all the best jobs in government became available to them like a candy store in front of children, Eller's wish list had included the Pentagon. An inveterate hobbyist, he was a student of military weaponry, and he often told people, "I like things that fly through the air and kill people." His taste for the armed forces had been even more keenly whetted by his stint as a political consultant abroad. He had even asked Stephanopoulos about going to the Pentagon after the White House. He figured the highest press job at the Defense Department was as much a ticket to the top as being media affairs chief in the White House. But Stephanopoulos said he was needed where he was.

Maggie Williams, Hillary Clinton's chief of staff, agreed with Stephanopoulos. She contacted Eller soon after the Smith overture to say the First Lady did not want him to leave either. Besides, she had a special assignment for him. At 4:00 P.M. on Thursday, May 6, Eller marched over to Hillary Clinton's office on the second floor in the West Wing and got an offer he could not refuse. She asked him to be the point person, her man in charge, for marketing the Clinton health-care plan. She said she wanted the health reform effort to be run like a campaign and wanted him to be, in effect, the campaign manager.

"So this counts out DOD?" Eller asked.

"No, you can't do that," she replied. At least, that was, for now.

At the end of the thirty-minute meeting, Eller was thrilled but also a little taken aback. He wanted to be sure the inter-

nal politics of his job change would go smoothly. He asked if
his elevation would offend fellow communications aide Bob
Boorstin, who had long had the thankless task of fielding
press inquiries. The First Lady checked with Boorstin, who
said Eller would be fine with him. Eller also worried that he
had no great store of knowledge about health as an issue. And
she reassured him about that. There were plenty of health experts around. His assignment was to sell the plan. Maybe not
knowing every fact and figure would actually help.

"Thank you for asking me," Eller concluded. "This is a
very daunting task."

"You're right," she replied.

That night, Eller wrote a note to the First Lady. "I'm in.
Let's win," it read. He gave it to Lisa Caputo, Hillary Clinton's press secretary, the next morning at 7:30 A.M.

Later that morning, Stephanopoulos told Eller, "We've got
to talk about this DOD thing."

"George," Eller replied, "I don't think I can do it."

"What do you mean you can't do it?"

"Well, the First Lady asked me to do some stuff on health
care, and I can't say no." So with understatement he dis-
guised the real excitement he felt. This was one mountain he
was eager to scale. Health care was the President's number
one priority. In Eller's mind, nothing was more important in
the entire White House operation.

But just as he reached the apex, Eller fell hard. The long days
and longer nights at the White House compelled him to wish
even more than usual for affection and relief, and a woman on
staff named Catherine Cornelius, blond and twenty-five years
old, provided both. In return, Eller was more than willing to
help her if he could, despite what to a clearer-thinking person
would have seemed an obvious risk to himself. The risk was
Cornelius's ambition to take over the White House travel office, which arranged official trips for the White House staff
and press corps. At her request, she was sent to work at the

office, essentially as a spy for fellow Arkansans David Watkins, the White House administrator, and Harry Thomason, the television-producer friend of Bill and Hillary Clinton. Thomason was part owner of an air-charter company that stood to benefit if Cornelius opened the White House travel operation to new bidders.

Gradually, Cornelius accumulated evidence of possible financial wrongdoing at the office and spurred Watkins to order a review of its books by KPMG Peat Marwick, the big accounting firm. But the travel office staff had many good friends in the press corps, having pampered them for years on presidential trips around the world, and Eller was brought in as a communications expert to discuss how to handle the press's reaction. The fateful meeting, which he attended at Cornelius's request, began at 10:00 A.M. on Thursday, May 13.

"Because of the relationship between these guys and the White House press corps," Eller said, "we need to get out ahead of the story." He agreed with Thomason that the seven-person travel-office staff should be fired at once. Prolonging the decision would only lead to leaks sympathetic to the travel staffers. Cornelius already had been the target of one such leak, Eller thought, when *Time* magazine had inquired if she was a relative of the President. (She was, in fact, a distant cousin.)

"Let 'em go," urged Thomason, who, despite his nonstaff status, had a special-access pass to every part of the White House and a temporary office in the East Wing.

"Give them their notices," Eller agreed. He suggested Watkins give them a letter saying, "Your services are no longer needed; we're restructuring the office."

But Watkins was not as sure. So the next day, Eller met in Mack McLarty's office with the chief of staff and Deputy White House Counsel Vincent Foster. Eller repeated his proposal, saying the staff should be dismissed by 5:00 P.M. that day. But the ever-cautious and understated Foster advised that the White House wait at least until the Peat Marwick review was completed before taking action. McLarty agreed. The Peat Marwick team began its review that day.

By Monday the evidence was in. Watkins drafted a memo that said Peat Marwick had found "abysmal management" at the office. As a result, he had decided to dismiss the seven employees and McLarty approved. Hillary Clinton was kept informed as well. But the announcement had to wait until Wednesday, May 19, when the staffers were all back in town.

In the meantime, on Tuesday, Eller had to go with Clinton on a trip to Los Angeles. While there, he had another run-in with the press, only this one was literal. During a presidential speech in Van Nuys, the ever-aggressive Eller was standing too close when a local cameraman came running by and whacked Eller in the head with his shoulder-held camera. The pain was so intense, Eller was unable to function. He limped back to *Air Force One* to lie down and drink some tea. While he was there, some sixty dignitaries, including the Hollywood superagent Michael Ovitz, came by as they toured the massive plane.

It was not until he woke up in his own bed the next morning that Eller realized Clinton had taken a very costly haircut around the time of the tour. "Oh fuck," he said aloud as he watched the story on television, still woozy from his injury. "Clinton doesn't even like the big plane. He thinks it's too much." But the coiffure, by a Beverly Hills hairdresser named Cristophe, was taking on a life of its own. The incident was initially (and incorrectly) reported to have caused major delays in air traffic at Los Angeles International Airport. But, more important, it gave the public another reason to think the White House was out of touch.

Eller had his own reason to worry as well. He knew that morning was when the travel office staff was going to be fired.

At 8:30 A.M., Watkins delivered "talking points" to Dee Dee Myers, explaining the dismissals in largely sanitized form. But there was one major exception on the list: a notation that the White House had asked the FBI to investigate. Thirty minutes later, Foster and William Kennedy, another member of the White House Counsel's Office, read the talking points and immediately called Watkins. They told him to delete any reference to the FBI and said there should not be any public discussion of the contact. White House meddling at the Justice Department was seriously frowned upon; those contacts were supposed to be handled by the Counsel's Office alone. Watkins then called Eller and asked him to tell Myers about the change. Watkins too kept trying. But Myers had gone with the President to Capitol Hill that morning, and she could not be reached right away.

By the time she was, it was too late. She had told one reporter about the FBI, and the entire episode began to spin out of control. The inexperienced White House had fallen into yet another scandal.

In the ensuing week, almost every aspect of the story was replayed on the front pages of major newspapers. The White House compounded its problem by releasing an FBI statement about the incident without the bureau's consent. Eller had been right about the likelihood of leaks from the travel staffers to their friends in the press corps. But he had been wrong that acting quickly would have headed it off. The problem was not with the reporters but with the way the situation was handled by the White House staff.

To stop the stories, McLarty finally announced on Tuesday, May 25, that he would conduct an internal review of "Travelgate" with the help of Leon Panetta. Meanwhile, Eller's personal life changed permanently. His long-term, live-in girlfriend, Heather Conover, a public relations executive, had not known of his relationship with Cornelius until she read about it in the newspaper. And when she did, she and Eller split. He moved out of the house in Washington they shared.

Eller was bitter and still less than 100 percent healthy after his run-in with the cameraman. For a while he blamed everyone but himself for the disaster. "I have never seen a more self-serving, disingenuous group than the White House press corps," he raged. "They care more about being kings than about saving money. We're going to save everybody a hundred dollars a head. Nobody cares. They care more about their gin and tonic."

But it was not the press that did Eller in. It was his misfortune to have made a mistake in a place where any error is a catastrophe.

While all this was happening, Eller was expected to keep promoting health care. For that purpose, he and other White House staffers met regularly among themselves and with selected leaders from Congress, such as Senators Jay Rockefeller of West Virginia and Tom Daschle of South Dakota. They were well on the way to deciding how to coordinate their message and respond rapidly to attacks from the plan's enemies. The only impediment: the plan itself was not complete.

Eller tried to sit in on the meetings to decide the substance of the plan. But he soon abandoned the practice. These were multihour affairs held in the Roosevelt Room with everyone from the President and the Vice President to Hillary Clinton and Ira Magaziner, senior adviser on policy development. They discussed such grindingly dull arcana as whether insurance cooperatives should be mandatory or voluntary and how far to go with managed competition and managed care, which, incredibly, were two completely different things. One meeting went on for so long that Eller, who was taking pain pills for his head injury, could not listen any longer. "I simply couldn't stay awake," he confessed. "It's stupid to sit in a meeting when you're falling asleep, especially when the President's there. I was sitting where he could see me."

Anyway, Eller wanted to focus on his main responsibility: setting up the War Room—his central campaign headquarters. His target date for getting the room running was June 1.

He even contemplated changing the room's name. What about calling it the Intensive Communications Unit? From then on he occasionally referred to the place as the ICU.

But it was not to be. At 6:30 P.M. on Thursday, May 27, Eller left yet another meeting with the First Lady in the Old EOB and walked across to the West Wing to talk to Dee Dee Myers. Over there, everyone was busy with the latest crisis: passing the budget through the House. Eller nervously watched the vote on television and felt immeasurable relief when it passed. A loss in the House would have been a set-back for health care. After the vote, Eller sent an E-mail message to a colleague's office that read, "Congratulations on Round One."

But he also knew tough times lay ahead. "This place doesn't work," he said, and predicted, "The long knives will be out for me eventually. It's going to be hard to make an omelet out of this without breaking any eggs." He needed the White House to concentrate on his project—health care—but most other aides were worried about the budget instead. And, judging solely by what he saw that evening around the television set, he reasoned that they were not so good at work-ing on more than one big project at a time.

The concern became common gossip in the Old EOB. And conspiracy theories abounded. It was no secret that many members of the President's economic team, especially Bob Rubin and Lloyd Bentsen, opposed the sweeping kind of health legislation advocated by the health team. As a result, Eller's friends saw dark motives behind every action of the economists. The health team talked among themselves about what they suspected were plans by Bo Cutter, a Rubin deputy, and Alice Rivlin, Panetta's number two, to sabotage the entire health-care effort, an accusation the two denied. So antago-nistic to any issue other than trade did Cutter seem that Howard Paster once allowed, "If Cutter comes to a White

House dinner, he better bring a taster." Eller would not have brought the poison, but he understood why someone might.

Meanwhile, on Friday, July 2, Eller had to take his medicine on Travelgate. The White House report on the firing of its travel staff was released by McLarty in the White House briefing room. In front of the press corps, the chief of staff apologized to the travel office employees who had been fired for the insensitive way they were treated and said five of the seven, who had had no financial or management role, would be reinstated in other government jobs.

Then he dropped a bomb on Eller. McLarty said Eller was one of four White House aides who would be reprimanded for poor judgment in their handling of the situation. The report mentioned Eller's personal relationship with Cornelius and criticized him for arguing that the travel office staff should be fired even before accountants reviewed their work.

When Eller heard those words, he flushed with anger, stood up from his seat in the Old EOB, and marched over to the briefing room in the West Wing. No one had told him he was going to be reprimanded, and he thought that was wrong. Very wrong. Eller waited until after the briefing and confronted McLarty face to face. "I'll take any punishment you'll give me, and I'll discuss it," he said. "But I did not know you were going to stand in the briefing room and publicly reprimand me. I deserved better than that." But McLarty had nothing more to say, and he gave Eller a cold stare.

Afterward Eller tried to remember why he was working so long and so hard at the White House at all. "I'm run down, tired," he said. "On any given day, I don't feel very good. I want to take four or five days off. I just don't see where I can do it. Three or four days, maybe, of uninterrupted sleep." With a sigh, he added, "After health care, I'm seriously thinking of moving on.

"They say the life expectancy of an appointee is eighteen months," he said, then predicted, "We're going to cross that line much closer to the one-year mark." The exit started to look pretty inviting, whether his ticket was punched or not.

Eller continued to attend health-care meetings starting at 8 o'clock each morning, but gradually their importance waned. His big fear came true. The budget issue was eating into health care's time. There was not room for both. One day, Bill Burton, a McLarty assistant, came by to say the budget effort was going to take over half of Eller's health-care War Room. Soon thereafter, Maggie Williams made clear that the War Room was being taken over completely by the budget-marketing staff.

Initially, Eller was distraught. He shouted epithets into the hallway to make his point known. But he came to accept the change—grudgingly. "We don't want to screw with the budget, because if we don't do the budget we don't do health care," he said. At the same time, he was still concerned about his reprimand over Travelgate and its effect on his relationship with his colleagues and the President. Maybe the wound would heal with a little more time.

But the impulsive Eller could not hold back. He still felt wronged by the way the reprimand had been handled. And, against the advice of friends, he complained to McLarty. He also expressed "overall frustration" at working in the White House. "It's hard to get a decision, and decisions don't stick," he said. "I'm not sure I want to stay. This isn't the easiest place to work."

Afterward, Mark Gearan, then the communications director, tried to settle Eller down. They got pasta salads from the White House mess and ate them in Gearan's office. Gearan suggested Eller take a couple of days off. But Eller would not cool down.

"I don't think I can right now," he replied. Besides, he said, there was so much to do. At least until the budget bill passed, Eller would have to play along.

. . .

On Friday, August 13, Eller was summoned to a five-o'clock meeting in McLarty's office. Several other health-care aides and David Gergen were there as well. Eller had hoped the meeting would be about the request by the television networks for time with the First Couple to talk about health care. But he was unpleasantly surprised. Not only would health care have to wait for the budget to pass but it would also have to wait for two other major initiatives to kick in: the North American Free Trade Agreement and the Vice President's effort to pare back the federal bureaucracy, called reinventing government.

The War Room was going to be turned back over to the health-care crew in September, they learned. But McLarty and Gergen said the meeting mostly was to inform the health-care team they had to work with the NAFTA and "re-go" parts of the White House operation as well. In his usual gentlemanly fashion, McLarty said health care would still be the centerpiece issue, but reinventing government and NAFTA were also going to be done in the fall. The President was insistent.

The message stung the health-care staff. Eller took deep offense, and he said so: "Look, we've been good soldiers and played by the rules, but people in this administration have overtly tried to undermine health care." He directed his meanest look at McLarty and continued. "At some point the word has to go forth that we're going to do health and we're going to do it as a team and everyone has to get on the team. As soon as the President makes the decision, we have to move, and that includes the secretary of the Treasury. Reporters have told us that Bentsen says he's for health care but then gives a wink and a nod."

McLarty just stared back. "Well, Jeff," Eller recalled him saying. "That's a very good point."

Eller pressed the point one step further. "Have you had the same meeting with the NAFTA people?" he asked. McLarty said he had.

But Eller did not really care what the chief of staff had to say. "I've been reprimanded and still have a job," he said later. "Hell, what are they going to do, fire me?"

The next day Eller traveled to Tulsa, Oklahoma, to prepare for a meeting of the National Governors' Association at which Clinton was scheduled to give a major health-care address. He already had planted a sizable article about the health-care plan in the *Tulsa World* newspaper. The paper's editor was a friend of Eller's from their Nashville days. He had called Eller out of the blue earlier in the week to say, "We want to give you a full page," and Eller had readily agreed. Bob Boorstin and his assistant Jason Solomon wrote the text, and Eller arranged to slip a copy of it under the door of every governor at the conference, just in case they missed it in the morning newspaper.

At the check-in counter, Eller was approached by Dan Balz, a reporter from *The Washington Post*. Balz asked if Eller would give him a copy of the article, and Eller said sure. But he must have still been rattled from his confrontation with McLarty. Instead of giving Balz a copy of the Boorstin-Solomon piece, he handed over a draft of the President's address, to be delivered on Monday, two days hence.

Balz was considerate enough to inform Eller about his error. But that hardly made the mistake less serious. "I screwed up in a really big way, a White House–size mistake," Eller said. "I felt stupid."

On Wednesday, August 18, the President went on vacation—sort of—and Eller went with him. The President rested—sort of—but Eller could not. Even as Clinton lounged on a private beach at a scenic lake near Fayetteville, Arkansas, his dog-tired aides, including Eller, scurried to find a photocopier to reproduce press releases that detailed his latest decisions: an invitation to five Caribbean leaders, the appointment of a new Public Printer of the United States, and the issuance of an executive order to establish the Domestic Policy Council formally.

Bill Clinton was allergic to sitting still, and that caused problems for his presidency and his staff. His insatiable interest in policy making was crowding out health care. His personal restlessness also hurt his ability to cope with the demands of the job. Clinton was the type of public official who needed to have constant activity and found it hard to recreate in ways that were not related to work. For those kinds of people the trouble comes when they do too much and everything gets clogged.

That was surely what was happening, and Clinton's staff was feeling the tension. Over the weekend, the President publicly upbraided one young aide on the tarmac in Vail, Colorado, for forgetting the telephone numbers and cellular phone he had requested. Earlier, and within earshot of others, he shouted at another staffer for misplacing his briefcase. The policy apparatus was getting pretty cranky as well. Eller was not alone living in dread of simultaneously taking on all three legs of the Clinton policy stool: NAFTA, re-go, *and* health care.

Previous presidents, even ones as energetic and ambitious as Clinton, had modulated their efforts more carefully. Franklin Roosevelt, for example, was known as a big vacationer and was forever leaving Washington on fishing trips. He also once remarked on the need for a president to pace himself. The public cannot always be attuned "to this highest pitch on the scale," he said. Not so Clinton. He made comments to the public almost every day and kept in close touch with his official duties. Optimistic aides had once planned for a three-week vacation. In the end, he agreed to only about half of that.

His refusal to put distance between himself and his work was exhausting and demoralizing the staff. Eller functioned as press secretary on the Arkansas trip, and the Clintons kept him on the go constantly, running back and forth from the hotel to their residence. Eller got away briefly for a barbecue lunch and a night of beer drinking at a local pool hall. But that was about it.

In early September, Eller formally moved into the War Room and set himself up more or less in the front. On a wall nearby was a sign he had inspired that read: "HONOR EVERY THREAT." But down deep the usually unflappable Eller was frightened by the prospect of taking on so huge a responsibility. "I seriously question whether I'm up to it," he confessed. "I've never done anything this big. Nobody can tell you the final outcome. It's like walking into this tunnel and not knowing when you're going to come out of it."

He knew that interest groups would spend a gargantuan amount of money to defeat the health-care plan, and that there were forces inside the White House almost as unfriendly. Later that day he met with Roy Neel, the scheduler, to try to find some more health-care time. But after forty-five minutes, he came away without even an extra second.

Each day became a blur of events and planning for future events. There were endorsement announcements by the American Medical Association and the Laborers' International Union. There were briefings for the networks by the First Lady and others. There were events to show that some small businesses *did* support the Clinton plan. And events to spotlight the positive comments about the plan by letter writers to the President. Words of praise were orchestrated by the War Room from C. Everett Koop, the former surgeon general.

So much was going on, in fact, that it was hard for people inside the White House to have any sense of what it meant or how it was playing. As soon as one event ended, preparations began for four more. No matter how much effort was put into anything, it never seemed enough. Eller and his staff became Sisyphus on the Potomac, pushing the stone each day but getting nowhere. Running down the hall of the Old EOB one afternoon, Bob Boorstin had time only to look over his shoulder and tell Eller, "Remind me never to do this again."

At one point, Eller lost perspective. He had worked from early morning until late each night and did not think he was getting enough support. So consumed with health care was he that on Thursday, September 9, three days before Israel and the Palestine Liberation Organization were scheduled to sign their historic agreement on the South Lawn, he was unable to see why the White House should spend more time on that issue than on his.

At the 7:30 meeting in Mark Gearan's office that morning, Eller made an impassioned speech about the need to focus on health care alone. He complained that the White House was incapable of doing more than one thing at a time. And when Stephanopoulos poked his head in, Eller erupted. "We're treating health care like just another White House project," he yelled. "It was always bigger than that, but we can't engage the West Wing. I'm scared to death that everything we've done will be undone." Stephanopoulos did not stick around to hear any more.

And later, to Maggie Williams, Eller confided, "I have doubts whether I can do this job." Some of the people who had seen his outburst began to think he might be right. Eller allowed himself to fantasize once again about the relief of leaving, long-term ambitions be damned.

Clinton had promised a health-care plan within one hundred days as one of his first acts as President. Now, eight months, and more than two hundred days later, there still was no plan, and only more delays were in sight. The antireform forces were massing rapidly, and effectively, but a full-scale response by the President was still not in place. The best Eller could accomplish was to direct a holding action, and that was less than satisfying.

So Eller's mind drifted back to his alternative ambitions

with the Defense Department—that could be the path to the top too!—and he decided to get that stone turning if he could. He got his chance on Tuesday, October 5, when reports drifted back to Washington about the murder and humiliation of American soldiers in Somalia. Eller immediately went to visit Roy Neel, then deputy chief of staff, and volunteered to help. When American-based reporters went to Somalia to check out the atrocities, what they found there would have a profound effect on the President. "The pictures coming in from Somalia over the next five to six days will be really important," Eller said. "If there's a role for the White House, there might be something for me." He reminded Neel of his political work in Panama and knowledge about the military.

Neel seemed agreeable, and later Eller made the same pitch to Kathleen deLaski, the top spokesperson at the Pentagon, and to Mack McLarty. "My concern," Eller told them, "is you'll have all these people show up in Mogadishu and there wouldn't be anyone doing care and feeding"—his term for providing reporters information favorable to the President.

On the morning of Friday, October 8, Eller was called to a meeting in the West Wing with David Gergen, Mark Gearan, deLaski, and others. They decided to send an "advance team" to Mogadishu that would include two Pentagon public affairs experts and, for the first time anyone could remember, a White House representative—Jeff Eller. In typical Eller fashion, he was happy but also wary. He knew the Pentagon believed it could handle the mission on its own and resented the interference.

Still, the prospect of going to a faraway land intrigued and excited Eller. He certainly needed a pick-me-up. The unrelenting intensity of the health-care War Room was beginning to suffocate him. So he made arrangements to detach himself for a few days. He got the blessing of Maggie Williams and assigned Bob Boorstin and a policy aide, Christine Heenan, to run the War Room while he was gone.

That afternoon, though, he got a call from deLaski, and

Eller's heart fell. "Thanks," she said in a hard voice, "but I don't think we're going to do it."

But Eller was not one to give up easily, and he did not this time. By nine o'clock that evening he got Gergen on the phone and was complaining about the reversal. Gergen also was displeased; he liked the idea of the White House exerting more influence and worried about how well the Pentagon would shape the story. So he promised to try again.

At 10:30 Eller got another phone call, this time at home, from a more soft-voiced deLaski. "If you guys really want to do this," she said, "we'll find a way to accommodate you."

The next day, Saturday, was a scramble to put the logistics together. At 9:30 A.M. Eller met Gergen outside Gergen's office in the West Wing and assured him the War Room would run smoothly in his absence. At ten o'clock, Eller contacted John Gaughan, the head of the White House military unit, to make his travel arrangements. "John, there's a chance I might need to get to Mogadishu fairly quickly. How do I do that?" he asked.

"I'll start making some phone calls," Gaughan replied. "How will you be traveling?"

"At the President's request," Eller said proudly, and he did not need to say any more.

"Then you need a letter from the NSC [National Security Council] asking for transport," Gaughan said. "And you're probably going to need to take some shots."

Eller sat at his computer and drafted a letter, which he had Sandy Berger of the NSC sign in the West Wing. He also visited the White House medical unit in the bowels of the Old EOB and got a necessary vaccination and some malaria pills. In the midst of all this, he got a page to check in with the White House switchboard; a call was holding from *Air Force One*. He called immediately and got Gergen, who was on the presidential trip that day to Yale University. "The First Lady and the President have given their approval," Gergen said. "Go ahead and go."

Eller's next call was to Gaughan. "This is a go," he said in mock military jargon, and the two began to arrange flights on military aircraft. Eller went home, ate dinner, packed, and tried to sleep. He left the next day, on a 4:45 A.M. flight from Andrews Air Force Base to another base in New York. There he caught a six o'clock flight on a huge C-5 transport jet direct, nonstop to Mogadishu—sixteen hours in the air. To help pass the time, the pilot allowed Eller to watch the in-flight refueling from the cockpit.

When the plane set down Monday morning, soldiers formed a security perimeter around it on the tarmac. Eller, who was listed on the manifest as a distinguished visitor from the White House, was given a flak jacket and a helmet. Wearing both, he helicoptered to the American compound in downtown Mogadishu. There he ate a breakfast of biscuits, gravy and eggs, canned fruit, coffee, and much-appreciated water. The place was dusty, ablaze with heat and sunlight, and more primitive and uninviting than anywhere Eller had ever traveled, even in Central America.

"Well, now what do you do?" asked the colonel in charge of press at the site, which was a cinder-block building that had once housed a school.

"I'm not here to tell you what to do," Eller answered, ingenuously, "I'm here to provide what advice I can."

Wednesday began with an astonishingly cold shower from spigots on the side of a trailer set up for the purpose. After Eller regained the ability to exhale, he looked forward to earning his keep by treating the pool of Pentagon reporters who had just arrived from the states to a briefing by Robert Oakley, the Clinton envoy. "If you pull this off," a military press aide told Eller, "it will be worth your coming over here."

Eller thought so too. He had worked out the details by telephone with Gearan the night before. "Mark, we have an opportunity here to have Oakley come and update the pool," he said. "There ought to be a benefit." Gearan agreed, and so did Tom Donilon, a senior State Department aide. The event was set.

But when the time approached, Eller saw that everything was not perfect. He realized that, rather than have Oakley exclusively for the Pentagon pool, the local staff had arranged for the event to be seen by every journalist in town. It was scheduled right after the daily United Nations briefing.

"Hey, what's going on here?" Eller asked of the chargé d'affaires. "Are you bringing Oakley over here?"

"Yeah, at ten-thirty," the man replied.

"I don't think that's the deal here," Eller protested.

"It got changed," the staffer said.

After a pointed, ten-minute discussion, Eller simply refused to accept the new plans. He pulled rank and insisted the envoy be presented to the pool exclusively at a press conference in the American compound. Overhearing this, CNN's on-the-scene camera crew began to shriek in protest. What kind of idiocy was Eller trying to perpetrate? What kind of exclusive? This was a war zone!

Eventually, they reached an accommodation: the pool would get the press briefing, but CNN would transmit the video back home via satellite.

Everyone was happy, including Eller, even though the point of the exercise seemed to have been lost. Luckily for Eller, when Oakley sat down with the pool, he provided the first good news for Clinton since the firefight. "If you're optimistic," he told the reporters, "there'll be two or three things happening in the next couple of days." He went on to imply that the good things might include the release of a hostage named Michael Durant.

To all but the handful of people who cared about such trivia as press relations, the entire event was thin gruel, and certainly something that could have been handled through regular channels. Still, Eller felt triumphant when he called Washington, which is seven hours behind Mogadishu time. He connected with the early-morning communications meeting, and Dee Dee Myers congratulated him and asked for some details about what it was like. Later, Gergen and Gearan also told Eller they thought the interview had gone well and asserted, without much apparent basis, that the President was aware of it and was grateful.

But Eller did not win praise outside that call. In fact, Myers was forced to defend him, and to little effect. At her regular press briefing later that day, she was asked, "With all the media minders that the Pentagon has over in Somalia, why do you find it necessary to dispatch Jeff Eller over there?" And, the questioner added, was he there just to spin?

"Absolutely not," she replied. "It's to make sure that the press has access to events in Somalia. [The Department of Defense] actually requested that somebody from the State Department go. The State Department couldn't send anybody there quickly enough, and so it was decided that Jeff would go."

That rendition of events, of course, was questionable, but none of the reporters at the briefing knew otherwise. So Myers had license to continue to support her colleague. "Jeff is very capable," she said. "He has a great deal of technical expertise, among other things. We wanted to try to facilitate the pool's trip over there to make sure that they got access that they needed and the kind of technical assistance they need."

Then, to change the subject, she tried a little humor. "I can't confirm or deny," she said, "that Jeff Eller will be traded for Michael Durant."

The tactic did not work. The next day, unflattering stories appeared about Eller's intervention in Somalia. Typical was the one by *The Washington Post*'s media writer, Howard Kurtz. It began:

> The White House has dispatched its media affairs director, Jeff Eller, to Somalia to help supervise an official pool of 18 American reporters, prompting criticism that the ad-

ministration is politicizing a function normally performed by career military officers.

While previous administrations were accused of trying to manipulate media coverage of military conflicts, this is the first time in recent history that a senior White House official has gone to a combat zone to deal with reporters. Eller, a former Nashville anchorman who coordinates local media interviews for President Clinton, has been in charge of galvanizing support for the President's health care plan.

Marlin Fitzwater, press spokesman for Presidents Ronald Reagan and George Bush, said Eller's presence "would tend to undermine the military and also to politicize the conflict. It sends a signal that you're sending political people over there to handle the press and the message and the image. He doesn't understand the military and may not be sensitive to all their concerns."

Still, on Thursday, Eller began the long trip back to Washington, this time via Cairo and Dover, Delaware. Despite the controversy over his own role, he was secure in the knowledge that his co-workers at the White House were satisfied with his performance. He returned to the other war—for health reform—with new eyes. And, he thought, having succeeded in Somalia might give him a leg up for the job at the Pentagon.

But after his stint in a real war zone, the War Room seemed quiet—too quiet. It troubled Eller a little. There was still more than he and his team were able to do, but none of it was very exciting, and, worse, nothing seemed to be making much of a difference. Clinton was even planning to launch health care—again—so turgid had progress been so far. All of that made the White House more oppressive than ever.

To break the chilling quiet in the health-care War Room on the afternoon of Tuesday, October 26, Jason Solomon heaved a green-and-purple football at Eller and Marla Romash, the health-care press secretary. Eller took his unlighted cigar out of his mouth, picked up the ball, and flung it back, catching the young man squarely between the shoulder blades. "If you knock out my computer," Romash growled at both of them, "you're dead." Then she, and everyone else, went back to the slow and steady business of marketing President Clinton's health-care plan.

In the face of declining popularity for the health-care program, Eller struggled to keep up public—and personal—enthusiasm. The flurry of activity surrounding the unveiling of the formal Clinton legislation on Wednesday, October 27, was an example of how he and his team hoped to accomplish that. Traditionally, the delivery of legislation to Congress is done without fanfare. But this event was a spectacle. Both Bill and Hillary Clinton made the trip and gave a speech. The War Room planned other such extravaganzas as well, including a presidential bus trip. Eller also arranged for television reporters from Pittsburgh and Buffalo to interview the First Lady, and for others from Dallas and Miami to interview the President.

But most of the health-care battle was a daily slog and, Eller increasingly believed, a treadmill. Keeping it all fresh and interesting was not easy. Maybe it was not even possible. "That's a never-ending battle," he conceded, sucking another unlighted cigar.

To Eller's distress, no amount of trying to force-feed the American public the President's view of things seemed to make them accept it. Even the bully pulpit of the presidency, with all that constant press attention, did not make his job as a communications specialist easier when the public was not willing to receive the message he was sending. In part this was Clinton's failing: he rarely embraced a clear point of view. But, more to the point, the public was not open to listening. And that was the new fact of work in the White House that proved the most remarkable to Eller.

The world of communication had become even more fragmented, diversified, and, most important, discerning than even he, a supposed expert on such matters, was able to master. People were watching and listening to all sorts of new carriers: the Internet, satellite transmissions, and ever-narrower cable telecasts. But the new and maddening twist for Eller was that this explosion of choices did not necessarily encourage people to learn more about their world, did not give him a real shot at opening their minds to Clinton. Rather, people tended to concentrate their limited time on the communications choices that validated their existing worldview.

Once, decades ago, Americans shared a vision of themselves. We were drawn together, rather than pulled apart, by television. We had Walter Cronkite on weeknights, *Bonanza* on Sundays, and, for many, the president almost whenever he spoke. No longer. As author Robert Wright pointed out in *Time* magazine, conservatives focus on National Empowerment Television and go to alt.fan.danquayle on the Internet. Nature buffs spend their time watching the Discovery Channel and browsing alt.politics.greens. As a result, Wright said, the President stands on only a "midsize soapbox" that people tune in if they choose to. And, to Eller's constant regret, usually they did not.

So while Eller was able to saturate a local media market with images of Clinton whenever he wanted, he was not able to monopolize the attention of the people who lived there. In fact, the residents could pay amazingly little heed to the visit. They could—and often did—see the event that was happening just down their street through the eyes of their favorite outsiders, such as Rush Limbaugh, Pat Robertson, or the National Rifle Association. To Eller's sorrow, the once vast political potency of the bully pulpit had been whittled down to size.

About the time Eller was getting good and sick of the health-care struggle, he got another chance at the Pentagon. And he jumped at it. On Monday, December 13, he and Dee Dee Myers could sense something big was in the works just by watching the comings and goings during the White House press corps Christmas party on the second floor of the White House mansion. Eller noticed David Gergen take the elevator to the private quarters. He sidled up to a Secret Service agent nearby and asked who else had gone up. The answer was Tony Lake, the national security adviser, and George Stephanopoulos. Myers also was watching, but from a different angle. When they saw each other as they were leaving the party, Eller put a name to his suspicion: Les Aspin. "Yeah," Myers said. "I know."

Two days later, Aspin ended his tumultuous tenure at the Pentagon by announcing he would leave after just twelve months. Inside the White House, word quickly circulated that Aspin's replacement, Admiral Bobby Inman (ret.), already was in tow, and changes were in the offing at the Defense Department. After the morning communications meeting, Eller spoke up about wanting to be part of those changes. Referring to Aspin's press secretary, he told Gearan and Stephanopoulos, "I'm not too good at killing people, but if Kathleen would leave, I'd like to take her place."

Later, Gearan called over to the War Room with what Eller thought was encouraging news. "Inman's going to be here," Gearan said. "Come over and meet him before the press conference." Eller felt lucky on more than one count. Not only was there a chance for him to get his job at the Pentagon but he also happened to be wearing a suit—a rare event—just as he was about to meet the man who could become his new boss. He was dressed for a gala that night being thrown by the Democratic party of Florida.

Eller rushed up to Room 450 of the Old EOB, where a pre-briefing meeting was taking place. There he saw Gergen, who told him, knowingly, "Your name has come up this morning." Eller nodded and repeated his mantra of the day, "I'm not good at killing people . . ."

"It's much too early," Gergen interrupted, "but it's in your interest to get in on the ground floor." So Eller stayed close to the action for the rest of the day, including watching Inman's announcement ceremony in the Rose Garden. Afterward, he went with Gearan to the West Wing office of Tony Lake, where they and several other top staffers met the gracious secretary designate. Eller gave him the telephone numbers of the many reporters who had called to speak to him. And at that moment, in effect, he became the press secretary for Inman's confirmation team.

It was not a position that required much work. The most he had to do that day was tell the Associated Press that Inman would return to his home in Texas and take time off over the holidays. The next morning, Inman telephoned Eller to say that, without his assistance, he had returned thirty of the press calls himself. Inman even weathered his first controversy with ease, and largely without Eller's intervention. On Monday, December 20, Dee Dee Myers put out a two-paragraph statement disclosing that Inman had a "Zoe Baird" problem but, like successful nominees for other posts since the Baird incident, was now in full compliance with the law.

The early reaction on Capitol Hill was that Inman's Social Security lapse would not impede the nomination unless the housekeeper was an illegal immigrant—which she was not. Eller made that plain to any newspaper that called, and many did. "We don't think this in any way will affect his confirmation," he said over and over again.

And he believed it. It looked like Eller was on the way to getting what he wanted—at last.

But on Tuesday, January 18, 1994, Eller's hopes took a tumble. That morning he was paged by Gearan while attending a health-care meeting in Ira Magaziner's office. Eller thought, Oh God, I screwed up. But when he arrived in the West Wing, he discovered he had done nothing wrong. Bobby Inman had.

"Inman is going to withdraw," Gearan told him, gravely.

"You're kidding," Eller said.

"No, I'm not."

Eller had to sit down. Well, he thought, no good deed goes unpunished.

A little later, the communications staff, including Eller and Myers, stared in wonderment at the televised press conference Inman gave in Texas. And after a while, everyone in the room arrived at the same question: had Inman lost his mind? He had been a senior official in several previous administrations, yet he complained about public criticism of him as if that were not the daily diet of almost any top aide. Surely the fellow was not living in the real world, the White House staffers thought, at least not the world they lived in. Bob Boorstin, who took medication to control his manic depression, commented, "At least I take my pills." And back in the War Room that evening, Eller received a page from a friend that read, "Please call Inman ASAP. Wants Planter's Peanut endorsement. Use booby hatch code word."

Eller laughed at the sarcasm, but his heart sank. Did this mean the end of his Pentagon ambitions?

Before long, Clinton went to the Rose Garden to name yet another secretary of defense, William Perry, who was Les Aspin's deputy. Inman had recommended the sixty-six-year-old Perry before he withdrew, and Clinton had agreed. But in an oblique reference to Inman's odd departure, the President said, "Bill Perry is a real pro—you can depend on him."

Eller did not know if *he* could depend on Perry. He still wanted the top spokesman's job at the Pentagon—it was the ticket he needed—but he knew Perry had worked closely with Kathleen deLaski. Just in case he was still a candidate, though, he secured permission from Hillary Clinton to pursue the position. And David Gergen was still on his side. Over the phone, Gergen made sure Eller understood how substantive the position of Pentagon spokesman was, and

Eller said he already knew a lot about policy and weaponry.
"I like talking about the Osprey," he said, referring to the
small transport plane that can take off vertically. There was
still a chance, Eller thought.

On the day after the State of the Union Address, Wednesday,
January 26, Dee Dee Myers took time to tour the Pentagon's
press operation at deLaski's request. Because of her background, Myers knew a lot more about the place than most of
the officers she met there thought she would. She was, after
all, a military brat; her dad had been a Navy pilot. And that
impressed them.

It also impressed Eller, who came by her office to find out
what it had been like. Myers teased him mercilessly. "Oh
man, it's really nice," she said. "It's got its own conference
table, a big closet, and a full-bird colonel outside the door.
You even have one-star generals working for you." Eller's
mouth was almost watering.

But news from the Pentagon was not encouraging. A few
days later, Gergen told Eller that the status of the spokesperson's job remained up in the air, and there was talk of
keeping deLaski while adding some aides above her. Also, the
list of contenders for jobs appeared to have grown to include
at least two people besides Eller. That was troublesome since
Perry had said he wanted to move quickly to fill out his top
team. "It doesn't feel a hundred percent good," Eller confessed with a pained expression on his face.

Health care was not making Eller feel any better. Despite
all the hoopla surrounding the State of the Union, the Clinton health plan faced increasing opposition. And on Wednesday, February 2, the ceiling fell in. The Business Roundtable,
a group of chief executive officers from two hundred of the
nation's largest corporations, voted, despite furious White
House lobbying, to support a much weaker health reform
plan advanced by Democratic congressman Jim Cooper of

Tennessee. To the public, Eller showed an optimistic face. "We think it was a mistake, and we regret their decision," he said. But he was furious. "The word *cocksucker* is being used a lot more around the War Room today," he said.

Eller actually suffered a double disappointment. Not only had the new year brought new trouble for health care but it had also brought new management to the issue. Hillary Clinton was determined to get more organized. So she put her longtime ally Harold Ickes, the new deputy chief of staff, in overall charge of the health-care effort, and it looked like he might bring in his own chief operations officer, who would, in effect, bump Eller aside.

Eller kept a brave face at the prospect. But, once again, he could only blame himself. He made no secret that he was on the verge of burning out and was looking for another job. Bringing in a pair of fresh legs, he thought, would not hurt the health-care campaign—or himself. He doubted he would be around the White House much longer anyway.

It had surely been a long road. He remembered his first day. While his colleagues hopped from inaugural gala to inaugural gala, Eller went to his office at 8:00 P.M., looked out the window at the West Wing, and penned a note to his parents. On simple white letterhead stationery, with the blue letters "THE WHITE HOUSE, WASHINGTON," printed at the top, he wrote:

> 1-20-93
> Dear Mom and Dad,
>   I made it! It does seem like the top of the mountain! I'm so tired and there's so much to do—but it's very exciting.
>   Much love,
>   Jeff

Now he was trying to convince himself to go on. But mid-February 1994 proved to be his limit. During a morning meeting as he was running down a list of upcoming media interviews, something in him snapped. He did not think the other staffers were listening to him as they should. He could hear them talking among themselves while he made his report, and it bothered him. Deeply. He did not want to be ignored anymore. He was tired of not getting things done. He was just tired in general. So he shouted, "Fuck it," threw his papers on the floor, and charged out of the room. For a long while he paced the first-floor hallways of the Old EOB, trying not to meet anyone's eyes. He was about to turn thirty-eight years old, and he knew it would not be a happy birthday.

When the day came, Wednesday, February 16, Eller awoke recovered enough to accompany the President on *Air Force One* to a health-care event in New Jersey. He tried to forget his troubles by burying himself in the routine of arranging local interviews and keeping track of logistics on the ground. He also apologized for his outburst to Harold Ickes and Maggie Williams, who said they understood. And, apparently, they did. On the plane ride back to Washington, the President and First Lady presented him with a birthday cake in the conference room. The President also gave him a cigar, and Hillary Clinton offered a kiss on the cheek. And they told him—ordered him—to take time off. News of his distress had reached the highest levels.

But where to go? In Eller's state of mind, he was likely to do anything, and he had given almost no thought to a vacation. Then an opportunity came from an unexpected source. One of his top assistants, Kim Hopper, was leaving the staff to take a job in California and planned to drive cross-country, with a stop to visit her mother in northern Florida. They decided to travel together. Seeing Eller's frazzled condition, she asked, "So, you want to drive with me for a while?" And he replied, "I might do that."

Eller and Hopper, who was twenty-eight years old, had not been personal friends. They worked together closely in the

media affairs department, and she was one of his most trusted
deputies. Her departure gave Eller a chance to ask—and get
approval—for raises for other members of his staff, since he
planned some restructuring. But travel together? Eller was
not so sure. Hopper insisted it would be fun, and at her
going-away party at the Dixie Grill on Saturday night, Eller
told her he would do it. They agreed to meet at the White
House the next morning.

The first leg of the trip did not go well. Hopper's Volkswa-
gen's radio and tape player were broken. So they stopped at a
Circuit City in Richmond, Virginia, to buy a boom box. Then
it turned out Hopper's taste in music was too contemporary
for the finicky Eller. She liked groups like Smashing Pump-
kins and Blind Melon; he preferred listening to the radio.
They stayed overnight in Charleston and kept their distance
from each other.

The next day they tried to content themselves by watching
the world go by as they made their way through rural Georgia by the back roads. They took pleasure in seeing the hanging moss, a barbecue joint called The Hog on the Log, and a
taxidermist whose motto was "You kill it, I'll fill it." Eller felt
himself begin to cool down and relax, but he remained com-
pulsive about work. He kept in touch with the White House
by telephone and computer and made sure to talk to Myers
every day. Hopper teased Eller about how often he spoke to
his friend.

By the time they reached Monticello, Florida, where Hopper's mother lived, Eller was not much to look at. He had
stopped shaving and was pretty scruffy. Hopper's mother did
not know what to make of him. Eller's family also was pretty
confused. On Tuesday he had a voice mail message from his
father that said, "Mom's really upset. She's afraid you've gone
off the deep end. You've run away with a strange woman."
Eller spent twenty minutes Tuesday night trying to convince
his mother he had not gone nuts. As proof, he thought, he
went out that night with Hopper to shoot a little pool.

On Wednesday, they left for Gulfport, Mississippi, where they played blackjack and slots on a barge and watched the Olympics from their hotel room. They were obviously enjoying themselves. On Thursday, Eller and Hopper visited a friend of Eller in nearby Bay St. Louis and feasted on gumbo and oysters. Afterward, Eller had planned to go his own way and maybe later take in some baseball spring training games. But he chose to stay with Hopper instead.

First they drove to Dallas and came to terms on music; Hopper allowed Eller to listen to tapes of Steely Dan and The Who—but only once each. They stayed Friday night in an inexpensive hotel in Santa Rosa, New Mexico, and by Saturday noon reached Santa Fe. There they splurged, staying at a hotel where they could sit in a hot tub and drink margaritas, which they did. That night they ate a fabulous meal, drank champagne, and fought about their relationship. "You never tell me about yourself," Hopper accused Eller. Later, they finally told each other about their lives.

The rest of the trip went well. They stopped at the Grand Canyon before pushing on to Los Angeles and the inevitable end of their journey. Eller stayed with Hopper for a few more days before he made his way back to Washington. But he returned with a beard and a new outlook. Even his still unsettled prospects of a job at the Pentagon did not bother him as much. He would give the White House another try.

Still, his constant setbacks took their toll. Eller was having a hard time figuring out what really mattered to him. He wanted a new job, preferably at the Pentagon, but that was not happening the way he had hoped. On Friday, March 11, the number two official there, John Deutch, asked him to be deputy press secretary. Eller, who was seeking the top job, had to think about that one.

Over the weekend, he stoked up more than his usual quota of cigars and drank extra glassfuls of iced tea. He counseled widely: Maggie Williams, Mark Gearan, Harold Ickes, Tony

Lake, Mack McLarty, and, of course, Dee Dee Myers. Her advice: do what makes you happiest. Eller also spent a long night playing pool and drinking beer at a joint called the Big Hunt on DuPont Circle with Doug Sosnik, a fellow White House staffer and a friend from the Clinton campaign.

At the pool table, the conversation kept returning to the lateral nature of the move. He already served, in effect, as a deputy press secretary—to the President. Why should he take the same job at the Defense Department? And closer to his heart was another point he and Myers had in common, and had discussed at length. They both had emotional attachments to the President that were hard to express but were always there. They had been through the wars together and come out on top. Now, when Clinton faced perhaps his biggest challenge, on health care, was not the right time to abandon him. "I wouldn't commit a felony, but there aren't too many things I wouldn't do for the President," Eller said.

There was also, of course, the mercenary consideration. The White House was the Big Time. A long-enough stint there would be the conduit to the best jobs in anyone's profession. One of Eller's overzealous friends from Tennessee advised him not to leave the White House too soon or for much less than a promise of $300,000 a year. And, to Eller's satisfaction, the job offers were already pouring in. He had a standing invitation to join the Washington public relations firm of Robinson, Lake. Burson-Marsteller also expressed interest. In addition, he had feelers from places as diverse as The Body Shop, a natural-ingredient toiletries firm, and a company that was negotiating to buy the Philadelphia Eagles football team.

So Eller decided to stay where he was. A few more months at the White House would give him the credentials he needed. He told McLarty the next week, and the chief of staff seemed relieved. Eller too was comfortable with his choice. He would still have a voice in health care and concentrate on what he did best: promoting the President to local media markets. He did not want to move up or move out—at least for the time being. "This is not my time," he said. That time would come soon enough. Just a few more months . . . his decision was made.

So Eller went back to what he knew. One of his specialties had always been to arrange town hall meetings. The freewheeling format suited the chatty President, and he did them regularly for a long while. They were among his main vehicles to bolster the plodding health-care plan, which suited Eller just fine. There were few things Eller liked better than to play the White House big shot and cut deals with local television stations. In mid-April he telephoned Channel 10 in Providence, Rhode Island, and asked to speak to the news director.

"I want to have a preliminary, off-the-record conversation," he said, about the possibility of the station hosting a presidential town hall meeting.

"We are *totally* interested," replied Ted Canova. "We commit right now. This is totally 'can do'—one hundred percent."

Eller had chosen WJAR by pure demographics: the White House usually used the most-watched news channel in the area, and Channel 10 was it. So the next week he visited the station, laid his eyeglasses on a conference table, and reeled off the particulars to a handful of deferential news executives.

First he gave them the bad news. "He tends to run a little late," Eller said about his boss. "He hasn't missed one yet, but we came close." The President once had arrived with just seven minutes to airtime in Detroit, he recalled.

"I think it would be fun television if he's late," Canova enthused.

"Don't say that," Eller replied, cringing at the thought.

The President was a stickler about the way he was stage-managed, Eller explained, as the others took notes. He insisted on a hand-held, wireless microphone, à la Phil Donahue, and refused to wear an earplug into which questions could be piped. Also, Eller said, the station need not worry about providing the President food or even the water he kept near his stool. A White House steward took care of that—for security reasons.

"Do you have any advice about picking the audience?" asked Linda Weir Sullivan, the station's general manager.

"Everybody has done it differently," Eller began carefully, but he noted, "Almost everybody prescreens questions. It gives you a better sense of the show." Realizing he did not want to sound as if he sought only favorable questions— reporters always suspected he tried to stack the audience—he added, "I don't want to know the questions." But he did allow that before the show he would like "a sense of what the audience is," so he could tell the President.

The President's one request, he insisted, was that "the questions not be disrespectful," which all but ruled out hostile confrontations of the kind that would most damage the cause.

"This does make your life a living hell for three days," Eller warned.

"That's fine," Canova replied with a wide smile.

For Providence, the town hall meeting was a very big deal, and Canova could hardly wait. "This industrial park," he said, "will be hopping."

The jaded citizens of the nation's capital often scoff at the prospect of yet another public appearance by the President. To them it mostly means traffic jams. But outside the Beltway, a town hall meeting was a major happening. Its sheer novelty was guaranteed to produce days of news stories about the preparations for the visit, then more reporting afterward about what the President actually did and said. The hourlong question-and-answer session would be aired in prime time not just in Providence but also in three other cities sprinkled throughout New England.

To Eller, that kind of blanket coverage was ideal, and a big reason televised town hall meetings had become one of Clinton's trademarks. Begun as a purely electoral tool, the town hall meeting had become fundamental to the way the Presi-

dent publicized his legislative initiatives, especially health
care. The War Room tried to target the meetings in districts
of important lawmakers in the debate. The selection of Providence was a play for the sympathy of Senator John Chafee, a
Republican on the Senate Finance Committee and the author
of a GOP alternative to the Clinton plan.

Eller said there was never any hope of a simple quid pro
quo—a vote in favor of the Clinton health bill in exchange for
the President's visit. Instead, he hoped to create a general
sense of goodwill that would help Senator Chafee and others
cast a yes vote in the end. Anyway, Chafee, a veteran of the issue, said his vote was not up for grabs. "We're always proud
to have any President come to our state—pleased and
proud," he said. But he added, "As far as influencing my position on health care, that wouldn't affect it."

In the end, Providence did hop, but Chafee did not vote for
health-care reform, and the citizens of Rhode Island did not
object. Eller got all the press coverage he planned on, but that
did not result in any change of public opinion about the President's initiative. Why? "It's pretty simple," Eller said. "There
was no clear and cutting message." Did the President want
the government to ensure health coverage for everyone or did
he not? Would it really work and make my life better? Neither was ever certain, and Eller thought that hurt. He also believed the White House took too long to devise and press for
its health-care plan, allowing its many enemies enough time to
organize and attack.

But Eller also saw a broader problem that went to the heart
of the presidency and its ability to communicate. Although
the President spoke out often and with great fanfare in places
like Providence, the public was not buying what he sold.
"The membrane is getting thicker and thicker," he explained,
and persuading the public about anything political—about
anything in Washington—was harder and harder. His decision to leave got easier and easier.

．　．　．

By June, Eller thought a decent interval had passed. He could announce his resignation and still have ample opportunity to get a first-rate job on the outside. He had worked in the White House for eighteen months, and that was about right. Furthermore, Eller was more than ready to quit. He had labored as long and as strenuously as his body and mind could endure. Even as a lower-ranking official in the health-care War Room, he was putting in fourteen-hour days. And by then his head was constantly in a fog.

But even through that haze he was beginning to sort out what went wrong. He should have been perfect for his job. Few people understood how to do it better. But technical proficiency was only the minimal requirement. He had been felled by two shortcomings, one of his own making and the other completely out of his control. His initial downfall was caused by personal weaknesses. Eller had succumbed to his appetites and made a few mistakes. And at the White House, any error, no matter how small, compounds into disaster, and Eller was never quite able to recover. But the second problem was more nettlesome. As the town hall meeting in Providence proved, even Eller's best efforts, unmarred by personal foibles, were not good enough. Health care languished, and the public was not willing to hear a different story. All the computers, faxes, and talking points in the world, Eller thought, would never get the legislation closer to law.

So on Thursday, June 23, Eller submitted his letter of resignation. The stated reason was failure by his bosses to make good on pay increases for his staff. He had promised them raises, but, despite prodding for weeks, no money was forthcoming. This wounded Eller because among the people he had told he could get more money were Lisa Mortman and Ken Chitester, two of his favorite employees. But, in truth, there were primarily personal calculations in his action.

Mark Gearan said he would not accept the letter and put it in his desk drawer. They would talk more, he said, and he would try again to shake the money loose. But he was not optimistic, and Eller turned his search for another line of work up a notch.

On Wednesday, June 29, Eller had dinner with Jack DeVore, a former aide to Lloyd Bentsen, who was working for Public Strategies, a public relations–political consulting firm based in Austin, Texas. Any close observer of Washington had to like the crusty DeVore. He loved to tell corny stories and smoke stinky cigars. He never took anything too seriously. But, like any top political aide, he could be relied upon to all but lay down his life for his boss. In that way, he and Eller had much in common, and they began to see the potential for other common interests through their mutual tobacco smoke at the Jefferson Hotel's restaurant that night.

DeVore told Eller that for the first time in his life he did not have to worry about money. He had bought a new car and was having a great time. The people he worked with were all good eggs. And, more, the firm was rich and getting richer. It was the top of the line.

So on Friday, July 29, Eller flew to Austin to visit DeVore's partners. He liked the idea of not selling out to the highest bidder in Washington, of not being just another lobbyist hanger-on. The Austin folks offered him that chance. But they also gave him his path skyward. They were a well-established campaign consulting firm.

Their offices were on the ninth floor of a building overlooking Austin's scenic river. Eller was told his space would have a window and enough ventilation to allow him to smoke cigars inside. That night he dined, drank, and slept at the luxurious Four Seasons Hotel, and he left the next day for a hunting trip on the sprawling ranch of the senior partner, Jack Martin, a longtime confidant of Lloyd Bentsen.

After resting awhile, Eller and several principals of the firm set out to tour the mesquite and cactus scrubland in a souped-up pickup truck. For practice, they shot at cans with a 12-gauge shotgun, a 30-30 Winchester rifle, and a .357 magnum. They kept on shooting even after it got dark by using the truck's headlights. When that lost its allure, they returned to the ranch house, ate a hearty meal, and sat on rocking chairs on the porch until 3:00 A.M. discussing the hottest election contests across the nation.

They got up at 9:30 the next morning and went hunting for real game. Eller saw deer, quail, doves, and roadrunners. Mark McKinnon, who headed the consulting part of the firm Eller might join, shot a rabbit. They drove with the catch farther into the brush until they came upon a large holding tank. There they did something Eller had only seen done symbolically before: they fed the dead rabbit to an alligator in the tank and watched it eat.

It was at that moment, beers in hand, that McKinnon laid out the job offer. Eller would become a name partner— McKinnon, Eller, Ranne—and stood, eventually, to double his $100,000 income from the White House with a combination of salary and performance bonus. Eller would not have to lobby and would get ready access to the ranch, among other perks.

Eller liked what he heard. His route was clear, his ambition sated. His time in the White House had done the trick. But before he said yes, he telephoned Myers in Washington. As soon as she heard about the alligator, the cigar smoking, and the beers, she told him, "They have you," and she experienced an enormous letdown. She was happy for Eller, but she felt a tightness in her throat and a flush around her eyes whenever she tried to think about the White House without him.

On Monday morning, August 1, Eller walked into Myers's office and closed the door. He told her he was leaving and gave her a hug. An era was ending.

Later, Eller telephoned Nancy Hernreich, Clinton's scheduling assistant, and said he had to talk to the President about something personal. At about 7:30, after the President finished meeting with some lawmakers, Eller found him at Hernreich's desk just outside the Oval Office, and they walked down the colonnade past the Rose Garden to an elevator in the White House residence.

"I'm leaving to take a job in Austin with Jack Martin and Mark McKinnon," Eller said, screwing up his courage.

"Yeah," the President replied, "I know them."

"Over the last six months I wanted different things—more of a personal life," Eller explained. "And I thought it was time to get on with it."

Clinton said he understood and asked Eller if he would still help him out from time to time. Eller said, "Of course," and allowed the President the last word. "I'll miss having you around," he said. "You've done a good job."

The next day Eller received a box of Dominican Republic–made cigars from his new partners. And on Wednesday morning, August 3, he attended an 8:00 A.M. communications meeting in Mark Gearan's office and, for the first time ever, sat on the couch and slept the entire time. "I'm a basket case," he confessed to a friend. He knew his time inside the madhouse was over.

Down in Austin, Eller went through a kind of White House withdrawal, as if his labors there had been an addiction. McKinnon described the process as "getting some oxygen into Jeff's brain." And, in fact, Eller was shocked by how long it took to recover from the pounding he had taken. For three or four months after his White House stint, Eller found himself at home and in bed by 8:30 most nights. He gained weight. He also found himself marveling at otherwise simple pleasures he had once taken for granted, like reading non-work-related books. "I could actually sit and think about things," he said, with a sense of awe. And, most of all, he was surprised how happy he was to be away from the place he had once wanted to come to so badly.

RIGHT: BRUCE REED

BELOW: GENE
SPERLING WITH
PRESIDENT CLINTON

3

Good Policy Is
Not Good Politics

ON HIS FIRST DAY IN THE WHITE HOUSE, BRUCE REED HAD ONLY
the vaguest notion where to find his office. He knew it was
somewhere in the Old Executive Office Building, the weathered granite structure across an alley from the West Wing
where, in fact, most aides worked. But once inside, he was
completely lost. The ceilings were high, the hallway floors
were marble, and the lighting was dim. The building had once
housed the departments of State, War, and Navy. Yet its odd,
institutional odor and its air of constant confusion reminded
him of another sort of place entirely: an elementary school.

He was told his office was Room 215. When he got there,
he found a men's room. Eventually he figured out he should
really go next door to Room 216, and he could hardly have
been more pleased. The corner office was spacious, with a
view of the Washington Monument. But that turned out not
to be his office either. That one belonged to Ira Magaziner,
the head of the President's health-care task force. Reed's of-

fice was across a reception area in a somewhat smaller room with a window overlooking a driveway.

Reed was not disappointed, however. He and his fellow White House staffer, Gene Sperling, had more on their minds than office space. Unlike so many others who were joining the new administration straight from the campaign, they were serious about government policy. They understood that they had more to do in their new jobs than posture and pretend, as they had for the past several months in the campaign. They thought they had a rare chance to actually *do* something—maybe even change the world.

"I never really thought I'd be in a winning campaign, let alone be in a position to have a say in what the government does," Reed said. And with evident delight he added, "Now I will spend most of my time thinking about what would be the best way to try to point the country." So when Reed got settled in his office, he did not make a round of phone calls to his friends and relatives the way some of his more showy, and less serious-minded, colleagues did. Instead, he took the advice of a friend who had worked in the White House of George Bush: "You'd better write down the three or four things that you really want to accomplish, otherwise the paper pushing will entirely consume you and four years will pass and you'll wonder what you've done." So Reed hung on his wall a complete list of Clinton's campaign promises and attached to it a small yellow note detailing the four promises he personally was determined to achieve. It read:

Goals for the Next Four Years
1. End welfare as we know it.
2. Cut 100,000 bureaucrats.
3. Put 100,000 cops on the street.
4. Take government away from the lobbyists and
   special interests and give it back to the people.
                    Signed,
                    Bruce Reed

He then set to work trying to figure out how to make those
things happen.

Most people dismiss the sincere beliefs held by government
officials as meaningless posing for public consumption. But
Reed and Sperling were not what people expect. They were
honest, dedicated policy experts—wonks in the vernacular—
who knew all about appearance politics but were far more interested in bringing their ideas about government, and
government service, to life. They helped formulate and refine
the President's policies, and thus spent most of their time im-
mersed in the drudgery of developing the fine points of legislation the public would never see. They sat through countless,
boring meetings on the details of little-understood programs
for the sake of advancing a broader cause or an important
policy that they thought—indeed, they believed deep inside
themselves—would make a tangible improvement in the daily
lives of real people.

As a resident liberal in the Clinton White House, Sperling
thought the way to help people was to fight for spending increases. But for him, this work was more than a job. It was a
personal passion, especially in the case of one policy that most
people had never heard of: the earned income tax credit. The
EITC is an antipoverty program that provides cash to families
with low incomes even though someone in the family is working. Sperling had never needed the EITC; he had grown up
the son of an affluent attorney. But he knew the program first-
hand. His girlfriend, Heidi Chapman, had survived—and
eventually succeeded—because of it. As a result, Sperling was
the EITC's most fervent backer.

When Sperling met her, Chapman was a twenty-four-year-
old courier for the Clinton campaign in Little Rock, working
to support a nine-year-old daughter and a two-year-old son.
She was the product of a broken and dysfunctional home.
Chapman gave birth to her first child at age fourteen, was
placed in a girls' home at age fifteen, and struggled to make

ends meet at age eighteen by flipping burgers at a fast-food restaurant. In her early twenties, she got married and pregnant, only to have the marriage fall apart not long after her sister was killed in an automobile accident.

To say the least, the highly educated Sperling and Chapman were a strange combination. But he was devoted to her. He all but adopted her children. He helped her financially. He also became a believer in the other main source of subsidy to her family: the EITC. "She's such a survivor," Sperling said with admiration.

After Clinton won, Chapman was rewarded with a $33,000-a-year political appointment to the Department of Housing and Urban Development. And the EITC helped her make the transition. She used her last check from the program to finance her family's move to Washington.

Sperling never mentioned his personal connection to the EITC to the other aides debating the budget. But he fought for it zealously, and he used the President's campaign promises as cover. Every chance he got, he reminded the room that Clinton had said working families should not have to live below the poverty line. The only problem was that keeping the promise with the EITC cost about $3 billion a year more than Lloyd Bentsen's Treasury Department was willing to spend, especially given the widening budget deficit.

For many days, Sperling made his case and Clinton listened sympathetically. After each plea, Bentsen would come back with slightly more money for the EITC. But Sperling remained frustrated. He was getting nowhere fast. Surely, raising the EITC was a wonderfully good idea, but the imperative at the moment was *reducing* the budget, not *increasing* it. And that was a tough lesson for the young ideologue.

Then luck intervened. Sperling considered his quest largely failed until, ironically, Bentsen got his way on a tax increase. The Treasury secretary thought a broad-based energy tax was the most equitable—and politically palatable—way to raise large sums of money, which the President needed for his plan.

Ultimately, Clinton bought the idea. But in order to meet the President's "fairness" test, Bentsen had to find ways to offset the extra burden the energy tax would impose on low-income people. The best solution: give Sperling the massive boost he wanted in the earned income tax credit.

When the numbers were finalized, Sperling's thoughts were of Heidi Chapman. He felt an enormous sense of accomplishment. But, on another level, the whole process gave him pause. His good deed had been done almost by accident. And he might not be so lucky the next time.

Reed was feeling run over by the budget juggernaut. Its confusing mixture of spending cuts and increases, and its neglect of the cultural issues he cared most about—especially welfare reform and anticrime efforts—were galling and troubling. Reed was part of the moderate, "New Democratic" wing of the party, and he did not see many types of spending increases as "good" policy at all. He and his fellow moderates were beginning to think Clinton had fallen off the New Democratic bandwagon that had brought him to the White House.

On Tuesday, February 16, Reed took on the issue directly. That morning John Podesta, the staff secretary, called a meeting in his basement office to make final decisions about the budget. To Reed's eye, the entire document was a disaster. For one thing, its beginning was all about spending *increases.* Reed wanted to know why a document describing a deficit-reduction bill started with a large section about making the deficit *bigger.* He got some sympathy for his view from Laura Tyson, who chaired the Council of Economic Advisers. But he ran into resistance from Alice Rivlin, the deputy budget director and the person in charge of the document. Almost everybody who had worked in the campaign disliked Rivlin, a career budgetary expert. They considered her inflexible and almost completely uninterested in anyone's opinions but her own, including at times the President's.

After a while of circular conversation, Reed came to believe the ordering of the document, as wrong-headed as it was, already was a foregone conclusion. So he decided to fight for something he thought was even more important: the inclusion of welfare reform. He argued that the budget was the ultimate expression of the President's priorities. Leaving out welfare reform would be tantamount to trashing one of his campaign's central themes. But Rivlin was adamantly against it. She argued the President's welfare proposal would pay for itself and therefore was not a deficit-related issue. And, anyway, the welfare plan was not yet completed.

"That argument is completely specious," the usually mild-mannered Reed shouted—but, again, to no avail. Good policy, again, was getting nowhere.

Matters got worse the next morning, when Reed read a draft of the President's budget address to Congress, which Clinton would deliver as the document was released. Reed sat at a table in the West Wing with his boss, Carol Rasco, the domestic policy adviser, and his colleague, Bill Galston, and read the speech closely. "It's terrible," he concluded. "It reads like a mediocre State of the State Address." Reed was amply qualified to make the judgment. He was an accomplished speechwriter as well as one of the architects of New Democratic thinking. To his horror, the speech, like the budget document itself, started off with spending increases. "First we'll spend x billion on this, and then we'll spend x billion on that" was his lampoon of the text.

Reed was about to throw up his hands in despair when, at 9:30, he got a call from George Stephanopoulos. "Can you come over to the Roosevelt Room?" he asked. And Reed hurried over. "We need a New Democrat vetting," Michael Waldman, a communications aide, told Reed as he entered. And Reed agreed. "It implies we're going to spend our way out of the problem," he observed.

The Roosevelt Room was packed with the best writers on

the staff as well as Hillary Clinton, Vice President Gore, and the President himself. Everyone agreed a new draft was needed, and Clinton directed his aides to disperse for two hours and return with something better. For a new opening, he turned to Reed and two others, who went back to Reed's office.

In the end, Reed was able to put more about the spending cuts in the beginning of the speech and, in a small but important victory over Rivlin, got the President to mention welfare reform. "Later this year, we will offer a plan to end welfare as we know it," Clinton intoned to the televised audience. "I know from personal conversations with many people that no one, no one wants to change the welfare system as badly as those who are trapped in it."

Reed applauded when he heard the President speak those words from his vantage point in the West Wing, but he also knew they were just that: words. He feared the harder battles still lay ahead.

If nothing else, these early budget clashes made clear to Reed and Sperling that "good" is an extremely fluid concept in Washington. Senate Majority Leader George Mitchell liked to say, "Good policy is good politics." But, in practice, things were not that easy. Especially in the Clinton White House, right and wrong were more debating points than moral constructs. The best either aide could achieve, they came to understand, was movement in the direction of "good" policy, and only then when they could find a consensus among a range of people with different views.

On most topics, in fact, President Clinton was of two minds. Symbolically, at least, one mind belonged to Sperling and the other to Reed. Sperling was the liberal, Reed was the moderate, and together they represented the blend that was the President's ideology. But the notion that two so different aides could oversee a single philosophy was evidence that Clintonism was inherently at odds with itself.

"He looks for things that government can do," Reed said

of Sperling. "I look for things that government ought to stop doing."

"Bruce would like to take down government more," Sperling agreed. "I would like to find more money to improve investment in families and children."

Those positions were expressed out of earnest conviction by both men. Reed, who hailed from conservative Idaho, had worked in Congress for southern moderates as well as the centrist Democratic Leadership Council, an offshoot of the Democratic party. Sperling, in contrast, came from the labor state of Michigan and had worked for two of the Democratic party's most liberal governors from the Northeast: Michael Dukakis of Massachusetts and Mario Cuomo of New York.

The two men were just as different in style as they were in substance. The tall, thin Reed was an organized and sharply attired thirty-three-year-old whose unlined face made him look much younger. Quiet and reserved, he enjoyed few things more than going home to be with his wife, Bonnie LePard, a well-regarded environmental crimes prosecutor at the Justice Department who had been his childhood sweetheart.

Sperling was a year older than Reed but appeared far more senior thanks to a sallow complexion (the result of overwork and lack of sleep) that gave him the look of a pale hound dog. He also was short and a little rumpled. He liked nothing more than work and made his hours at the office even longer by talking constantly. He also was the kind of fellow others liked to tease. In keeping with that tradition, Sperling kept near his desk a note from his friend and mentor Robert Reich, then secretary of labor. It read: "Gene—This office must be kept neat. You are now in the White House." Of course, Sperling never heeded the advice.

On a personal level, the opposites attracted. Reed and Sperling became fast friends the moment they met in Little Rock during the campaign. Thanks to a screwup, they had to stay in the same hotel room during Sperling's first night in town, and, true to form, Sperling kept Reed up most of the night with his incessant chatter. Even though they often disagreed, they promised never to keep professional secrets from each other and, more important, to work together whenever they could.

That pledge turned out to come in handy in the whatever-works Clinton White House. It was painful at first. But Reed and Sperling, who shared the rank of deputy assistant to the President, soon came to accept that they would do better working together than against each other, even though they had to bend their beliefs to make common cause.

Such accommodation was possible on the issues Reed pressed for that also entailed higher government expenditures. One was his pet project to put 100,000 more cops on the street. After the stimulus package failed, the White House began to craft a scaled-down version, and, thanks to Sperling, a few thousand cops were included in it. In late April, Reed was unable to attend an Oval Office meeting about the alternative, so he flashed a brief reminder—"ask for $200 million"—about the provision onto Sperling's pager, which was able to display full-sentence messages as well as telephone numbers.

Sperling already was well aware of Reed's interest. Reed was so obsessed with the cop issue that other friends had given him a toy police car for his birthday. And Sperling and Reed had discussed the matter many times. During one of those talks, Sperling advised Reed to think big, not to be shy. "Don't just ask for fifty million dollars," Sperling said. "Be candid about what you need." That was liberal advice if Reed had ever heard it. But, then again, he knew the optimal number for his goal of 100,000 cops was closer to $2 billion, and the chance of getting that anytime soon was remote.

So when Sperling got the beeper message, he went to work immediately, asking the President to include at least $200 million worth of cops in the trimmed-down stimulus bill. And, thanks to his persuasion, Clinton agreed. Afterward, Sperling chided Reed, "You owe me a *liberal* program next time." And Reed teased back that Sperling had seemed to be advocating more and more "sensible ideas" lately. "I can't tell which of us is the New Democrat sometimes," Reed said. From then on, the two aides happily referred to the extra police officers as beeper cops. Congress eventually allocated $150 million for the effort.

Reed knew the appropriation was a huge victory. But it was seen as small consolation by the ever-agitating New Democrats. Reed fielded phone calls constantly from moderates upset by the direction of the Clinton administration, ranging from Al From of the Democratic Leadership Council to E. J. Dionne of *The Washington Post*. Some still thought the budget contained too large a tax increase; others believed it stressed spending reductions to the exclusion of more positive, New Democratic initiatives, such as welfare reform and a children's tax credit. In any case, the whole right wing of the Democratic party, of which Clinton was supposed to be a part, was up in arms, and Reed was their sounding board. He tried to placate them. He knew he was laboring as hard as he could to get more of what they wanted. But he also saw, to his own regret, that he simply could not get everything.

The frustration sometimes poured out into the open. At one White House meeting, From berated lobbyist Howard Paster for working too closely with the liberal Democratic leadership in Congress. In fact, outbreaks of dissent from moderate Democrats on Capitol Hill were more and more frequent, including a reasonable-sounding but largely unworkable proposal by Congressman Dave McCurdy of Oklahoma to limit spending on Medicare and Social Security each year. And it fell to Reed to explain to McCurdy why the President could not endorse as his own a measure that simply would not do the job.

For help, he turned to his fellow policy expert. In May,

Reed paged Sperling to talk about the McCurdy proposal. As it turned out, Sperling already was in Reed's suite of offices, visiting health aide Ira Magaziner. So he walked across the reception area and into Reed's office.

"Isn't there some way of appeasing the moderates without accepting their stupid idea?" Reed asked.

Sperling took a deep breath and spoke academically. One alternative would be to propose additional and specific spending reductions. Another might be to buy them off by embracing some other New Democratic idea, such as welfare reform. Reed thanked Sperling for both suggestions. One or the other might actually work.

"See," Sperling joked, "at most things I'm a DLCer at heart."

"Yeah, sure," Reed teased in return.

In fact, the months *had* changed Sperling, and in much the same way they had changed Reed. Sperling also began to accept that good policy is not an absolute. The inevitable interplay of ideas and interests in the White House had thoroughly leavened that ideal. Moreover, he started to see the wisdom of compromise. Although he had come to Washington as a die-hard liberal, Sperling could no longer accept that ideology undiluted. Deficit reduction was a reality he had to face. All his best ideas to help people would come to naught, he now believed, unless he worked to conquer that issue first. Despite his personal preference to start *new* programs, he gradually understood that he could not achieve his desires in a vacuum. The budget had to be cut. And if the President did not do so, his credibility as a leader was in serious doubt. Sperling still wanted to do more with government, but he could not. At least not yet. And that view increasingly got him in trouble with his own left wing of the party.

The White House held a meeting on the politics of pending issues at 5:00 P.M. each day in the West Wing. During one of those meetings, Stan Greenberg, the pollster, and Mandy

Grunwald, the media adviser, spouted off angrily about the message being used to market the budget. They contended it was wrong to emphasize painful deficit reduction. Instead, they said, the President should sell optimism and investment. They were particularly upset by a document Sperling had sent to Capitol Hill that dwelt mostly on the budget-*cutting* parts of the President's economic plan.

After a time, they summoned Sperling to explain himself. He showed up unshaven and looking even more tired than usual. He also was not in any mood to be second-guessed. But that was exactly what the consultants did.

"I feel like I'm living in the movie *Invasion of the Body Snatchers*," Grunwald told him. After all, she said, here was one of the administration's leading liberals talking as tough on spending as such administration fiscal conservatives as Leon Panetta or Lloyd Bentsen.

At that Sperling exploded. "We don't have a choice. We have to keep a simple message on the deficit," he insisted. He said that was the only way to win any increased spending of the kind they all really wanted—a little sweetness with the bitter medicine. "I have fought my heart and soul out every single moment. If there were any other way, I'd do it. But we can't."

After the meeting, Sperling took Reed aside and vented some more. Every morning he came to work early, and he did not leave until after midnight. He was beyond tired. Yet at times he felt as if he were all there was between the President and chaos on the economic front. "These guys just don't understand," he said, and he knew Reed did. Surely the words *optimism* and *investment* sounded more appealing to the public. But makers of policy could not content themselves with nice-sounding words. The deficit was an issue that worried lawmakers and therefore had to worry Sperling as well. Referring to the lawmakers, he told Reed, "They are fanatical up there about deficit reduction. It's vital to our survival on Capitol Hill."

Even a true believer like Sperling could not ignore that fact.

Sperling will probably be remembered as one of the most obsessive workaholics ever on staff at the White House, a place legendary for overwork anyway. He labored in his cramped, messy office until 1:00 A.M. on most nights and woke up before dawn. The only way he could be sure to rouse himself was to set two alarm clocks: one near his bed and the other across the room that he would have to stand up to turn off. He did not even have time to find his own apartment; his mother did that for him.

"Unlike most people in the city of Washington, Gene does not have delusions of grandeur," political consultant Paul Begala once said of his friend. "He doesn't even have delusions of normalcy." To say he acted like an absentminded professor would be to give him more credit than he was due. During the campaign he became instantly famous for failing to notice his pen had broken during one of his first meetings with Clinton, splattering blue ink all over his face and shirt. He worked so hard that months passed before he even bothered to cash a paycheck. His motto: "I may not be particularly good, but I'm always there."

Some saw Sperling as inconsiderate and arrogant, and, certainly, he did not lack confidence. He also was congenitally late for meetings and appointments. And, judging by his hours in the office, one could not be blamed for thinking that he was simply nuts. But his colleagues saw in him an enthusiasm so uncontrived they came to accept that his craziness was not simple at all. Underlying it was a dedication to public policy and the advancement of his boss's goals that only a real student of Washington could fully appreciate.

Sperling was raised in Ann Arbor, Michigan. His mother was a teacher and his father a successful lawyer who, among other things, incorporated Domino's Pizza. Sperling majored in political science and captained the tennis team at the University of Minnesota. At Yale Law School, he jettisoned most athletic interests and paid near-constant attention to his studies. "He basically never left his library cubicle," said Christian Merkling, a classmate. "He was obsessed with policy to an extent that made it difficult for even those of us interested in policy to talk to him."

Instead of joining a big-bucks law firm like most of his classmates, Sperling worked summers for political economist Robert Reich at Harvard and at the NAACP Legal Defense Fund. He also worked briefly for the pro-abortion-rights lobby, the National Abortion Rights Action League. To get a business degree, he attended the Wharton School at the University of Pennsylvania, but left before graduating to volunteer for the Dukakis campaign in 1988.

At Dukakis headquarters, Sperling bonded with people who would later play major roles in the Clinton campaign, including George Stephanopoulos and Robert Rubin, Sperling's boss. After the Dukakis debacle, Sperling returned to Harvard for a while, but he kept his eye on the next presidential campaign. In 1990 he joined the staff of Mario Cuomo in Albany, hoping the New York governor would enter the 1992 race. But when Cuomo decided not to run, Sperling was at loose ends. Stephanopoulos sought him out, and in June of 1992, Sperling joined the Clinton campaign as its economic policy director.

By the time Sperling came to Little Rock, Reed was already an old-timer. He had helped draft Clinton's announcement speech in 1991 and served as policy director for the entire election effort. While most of the campaign staff was located in Little Rock, Reed spent a large part of his time in Washington and on the campaign plane, trying to keep what facts there were straight for both the candidate and the traveling press corps.

He was born in scenically beautiful Coeur d'Alene, Idaho, not far from less scenic Spokane, Washington. His mother was an active politician in town, and a devoted Democrat. Reed grew up working in a succession of campaigns and never shed the election bug. He went to Princeton, class of 1982, then moved on, in true Clintonian fashion, to be a Rhodes scholar at Oxford.

Politically, Reed's views were formed during the election of 1980, which swept Ronald Reagan into the White House and swept out of Congress one of Reed's heroes, Senator Frank Church of his home state. He saw that election as "a shot across the bow at liberalism," Reed said. "I'm not sure how well I understood it at the time, but I remember thinking sometime in the early eighties that I was tired of defending what was wrong about government and that I wanted to fight for something new."

His status in the administration was noteworthy because of his close ties to both Clinton and Gore. Reed had worked as a staffer for Gore from 1985 to 1989 and served as his chief speechwriter for the 1988 presidential campaign. Afterward, Reed attempted to get out of politics briefly and wrote freelance articles. He then found a job where he could combine his search for a new kind of Democratic politics with writing—at the Democratic Leadership Council. The next year, Clinton, then governor of Arkansas, became DLC chairman.

A little over a year after that, Reed moved from the DLC to the nascent Clinton campaign and helped write Clinton's decidedly New Democratic announcement speech. Through it all, he retained a wry humor that made him well liked by almost everyone who encountered him. Reed's intelligence and insight were admired even by people many years his senior. And his humility and candor were endearing. He once told *The Washington Post,* "People tend to think being a Rhodes scholar is a bigger deal than it really is."

But when it came to his beloved ideas, Reed was not so underspoken. And he was beginning to sound off. By June, welfare reform still had gone nowhere, and the crime bill remained a nonstarter. Worse yet, Reed and the liberal attorney general, Janet Reno, were beginning to look like adversaries on the crime issue. Reed wanted more cops on the street, but Reno sought to emphasize prevention rather than cops. Her resistance was impeding progress.

"There hasn't been an idea that hasn't run into a red flag, and there's no referee," Reed complained. "We run this place like the U.N. Security Council: every member has a veto."

While Reed wished for more progress on crime and welfare, Sperling and the rest of the White House staff threw themselves into the budget debate. Sperling's assignment was to cast aside all pretense of ideology and work even harder than he had already as the budget project's chief detail man. He was told to sell the plan on its merits—whether he agreed with them or not. And he devoted himself entirely to the task. For two straight nights, Sunday, July 11, and Monday, July 12, he stayed up until 4:00 A.M. drafting what turned out to be a treatise on the reasons for enacting the budget plan. Using narrative, charts, and graphs, he laid out the plan's main elements and explained why each was necessary for effective deficit reduction yet also was fair to the middle class. He accomplished that feat and also woke up both mornings in time to attend the 7:45 senior staff meeting.

Only one Republican attack seemed to be breaking through: the notion that a tax increase was a "job killer." Sperling knew more work was needed to counter that thrust, so he began to pester the Treasury Department to use its huge computing ability to show, state by state, just how many jobs the Clinton bill would *create*. Alicia Munnell, an assistant secretary at the Treasury, initially resisted. How could such estimates be verifiable and statistically sound? But after much agonizing, Sperling convinced her to run the numbers using as conservative a formula as she could find.

To him, the pulling and tugging illustrated "all of the tension that exists between political necessity and economic methodology"—in other words, all the tension that was playing out in his own mind. In the end, he chose to press the political aim first. "It was better," he said, "than leaving our people out to dry."

Sperling felt a twinge of guilt doing all this political message work after months of developing policy. "But when you give them ways to attack the other side," he said about members of Congress, "they all love you." Policy makes enemies, he concluded, propaganda makes friends. It was an unusual statement for a true believer. Then again, Sperling had changed.

More proof of that came in the midst of the budget battle, when Sperling and Heidi Chapman broke up. She was still young and eager to explore the world. But, more to the point, Sperling, while enduringly devoted to her children, was working almost all the time and was unavailable to the relationship. Although Sperling continues to this day to visit her children on weekends, he and Chapman stopped seeing each other romantically.

On the rebound, he turned to Reed and LePard to help him find someone to fill the void in his love life. LePard replied, "I'm sure a lot of my friends are looking for a boyfriend who is only available between 2:00 A.M. and 6:00 A.M."

Reed hoped that once the budget passed he might get more attention for the New Democratic agenda. But that did not happen. In fact, he had to struggle mightily just to get a crime bill *introduced*. In this case, its adversaries were not warring factions with high-minded differences of opinion but people from the same party with niggling tactical disagreements.

The controversy of the moment was this: should the Brady Bill, requiring a five-day waiting period before a handgun could be purchased, be part of the anticrime measure, or should it be introduced as a separate piece of legislation?

Joseph Biden, Democratic chairman of the Senate Judiciary Committee, wanted it included, and Jack Brooks, Democratic chairman of the House Judiciary Committee, wanted it separate. Then, at the last moment, they switched positions after reassessing the relative clout of the anti-gun-control National Rifle Association in each of their chambers. The result was a complete mess, and an increased chance that the anticrime bill would not get unveiled at all. It was to be scheduled for a Wednesday in mid-August.

Reed spent almost every moment until then fighting to make sure the bill did not disintegrate. Throughout, he felt more like a cruise director than a policy expert. But that was what he had to do to achieve what he wanted. At one point Biden threatened to press forward with a version of the crime bill that New York congressman Charles Schumer, a major player in the House, had vowed to oppose. By unhappy coincidence, on that day Reed had charge of his infant daughter, Julia, and had to cart her from one office to another while he worked to persuade the lawmakers to back off. On and off throughout the day, Reed talked with a lisp because Julia playfully grabbed his lower lip and would not let go. He wondered how anyone could take him seriously.

There were also crime bill detractors within the Clinton circle. The political consultants, for example, did not like the idea of holding any event that distracted from the recent budget victory. Winning was worth flaunting, they reasoned. Besides, the President's agenda already was too crowded, and health care was the next priority. Why drag in crime? And why now? Clinton was planning a vacation.

And there were the last-minute details to iron out. Biden was insisting that the bill be introduced before Clinton left town on Thursday. But Brooks said *he* was leaving town Wednesday morning. "The event was so precarious that anytime anyone got nervous, everyone else assumed it wasn't going to happen," Reed recalled. "We had to spend all our time calming people down."

To finally bring things together, Reed followed what he called the Gene Sperling rule: the key to a successful public event is to write a four-page summary. He wrote one and on Tuesday morning compelled the staffs of the principals in Congress to approve it line by line. That way, he thought, he would force a consensus. And, to a large extent, he did. But he had to keep the controversy of the hour vague. The President would say he supported the Brady Bill, but he would not make clear whether he wanted it introduced as part of or alongside the crime bill itself.

The reluctant lawmakers bought the formulation. But then the attorney general weighed in. After Reed sent the four-page summary to her, Reno telephoned David Gergen to ask where the numbers in the bill came from. She still was balking, at least indirectly, about the promise of 100,000 cops. To erase that objection, Reed convened yet another meeting at 5:30 that evening in the West Wing with the attorney general's staff. He explained that the bill was definite about funding 55,000 cops, because that was how much money was absolutely available. The remainder could be funded with incentives from other places. But even that did not satisfy. He had to get Reno on a conference call before she would agree.

Just as Reno seemed settled, Biden's staff got nervous and started talking to the attorney general's staff. Then they both got nervous together. News of the skittishness reached the White House scheduling office, which refused to put the Rose Garden bill unveiling on the President's itinerary. But Reed could not wait any longer. Assuming that somehow the event would happen, he drafted the President's remarks anyway and read them to Justice Department aides over the telephone from midnight until 1:00 A.M. In the meantime, the rest of the event was slapped together. One of Reed's aides, Jose Cerda, got police groups to come. Communications aide Rahm Emanuel persuaded some mayors to attend. And Reed chipped in, directing a White House fellow to call Boston's police chief late in the evening to invite him to hurry down for the morning event.

Reed left his office at 3:00 A.M. and returned at seven. He gave Dee Dee Myers's office the four-page summary and went off to put the finishing touches on the President's remarks. It was threatening rain that morning, but Reed felt glad just to be entering the Oval Office to give the President a briefing on the event. At last! It was scheduled. It would happen.

Even at that eleventh hour, however, there was a spat. Reed and Reno, who was also in the meeting, had one more argument about how many police could be put on the streets under the proposal. Reed thought the numbers were clear and solid. Reno still did not. "Just don't make me answer any questions about the police," she concluded, to the nervous laughter of others in the room.

Luckily, the tussle was not apparent to anyone who witnessed the public address that followed the briefing. The President, surrounded by police and fawning politicians, read Reed's words with confidence and evident approval. But afterward, reporters cornered Clinton and asked, "Would you do the Brady Bill separately or as part of the crime bill?" to which he answered evasively, "I would prefer to get it as quickly as possible." Reed told a friend, "I'm going to Idaho and never coming back."

One reason Reed did not leave forever was another upcoming announcement, and the start of another initiative he had posted on his wall: Vice President Gore's program to "reinvent government" and reduce the size of the federal workforce. To Reed, deciding how to trim the bureaucracy was just as important as health care. In fact, he rightly worried that the health-care issue might degenerate in the public mind into a debate about big government, and that could only hurt the Democrats and Clinton. So for many hours late that summer, Reed devoted himself to "re-go," reviewing three thousand pages of recommended program cuts. He also wrote a memo to Gore suggesting that in his final report he highlight a specific personnel reduction goal, between 200,000 and 300,000. "Most of the rest is hard for the average taxpayer to understand," Reed reasoned.

The specifics of reinventing government were cobbled together in a series of meetings, some of which Sperling also attended. During one, Gore's staff raised the possibility of paring the Supplemental Security Income program, which aids injured workers. Sperling knew more about the program than most of the people in the room realized. When he was growing up, his father had told him horror stories about how some of his badly disabled clients were tossed off the rolls for no good reason. So Sperling raised his hand and started his argument to spare the program from cuts by saying, "I have to disclose that, because of my father, I never saw such cruelty from the federal government."

During a later meeting in the Oval Office with the President, the Supplemental Security Income program was raised again. Only this time, Clinton spoke first. "It was a terrible thing that Reagan kicked people off the rolls," he said. "I will never forget a guy who had his arm crushed, and they threw him off saying he could do secretarial work. I swear they did that." Afterward, Sperling could not wait to call his father and tell him the program was saved.

But Reed knew the whole purpose of the reinventing government effort was to find places that could be cut. And that proved heavy going at almost every turn. During one typical conference call, a staffer voiced concerns about Congress's reaction to violating existing labor laws, and Stephanopoulos fretted that some of the plan's specifics hurt interest groups so badly they might threaten other Clinton programs. To Reed it began to look like Clinton might end up reinventing government in its own image.

It was not long before Reed and Sperling were dueling. Reed wanted to use any savings that reinventing government produced to reduce taxes on families with children—the middle-class tax cut Clinton had promised during the campaign but dropped when he came to Washington. Sperling wanted to take the same money and put it into government job-training programs—a liberal idea that a big booster of education like Clinton would also approve of. Either way, Reed was determined that no money be spent until it actually had been saved. To do otherwise, he thought, would only make things worse with the anti-Washington public.

In the end, as usual, Clinton ducked the issue entirely. On Tuesday, September 7, Gore and Clinton unveiled their reinventing government report, which called for a 12 percent reduction in the federal workforce; that amounted to 252,000 people, the midpoint of Reed's recommendation. But the report did not specify where its savings would go. Reed and Sperling would have to battle that one out later. "We're putting you out of business," Reed teased his colleague. But they both knew that was not true. The two staffers decided the Clinton administration needed to think of itself as a crusade. Only they could not agree on what that crusade should be about.

On Capitol Hill, in the meantime, the crime bill was floundering, and Reed and Reno continued to feud. Although the administration proposal had been finalized the month before, the attorney general still wanted to reopen the question of how many more police it would put on the street. Reed could only hang his head in frustration. "There are infinite appeals on decisions here in the White House," he said. "That's what makes life so difficult. You need to keep an eye on everyone to make sure they don't undo the deal you just forged."

Reno added to the insult by inviting Biden and Brooks to a meeting *at the White House* without first asking Reed or anyone else who worked there whether she could. When Reed and Gergen heard this, Gergen phoned Reno to ask if they could have a "premeeting." She agreed.

They convened on Tuesday, September 14, in the Roosevelt

Room, and the dialogue was like a broken record. "We need to know who to talk to around here," Reno complained. "The White House needs to speak with one voice." And she suggested that a cabinet-level group convene to find that voice.

The others at the table had a different idea. One aide recommended she talk to the White House lobbying office about legislative strategy and to Reed about policy. In fact, though, Reed knew she preferred to talk to Gergen if she had to talk to anyone at all. And that was fine with him. He joked that Gergen was the only person in the White House who was taller than she. They remained in stalemate.

But nothing stood still at the White House for long. Despite Reno's reluctance, the crime bill began to take off. All of a sudden, polls showed crime to be the chief concern of the American people. Apparently the passage of the budget bill and the appearance of a strong economy left room for citizens to worry about other things. And number one turned out to be Reed's issue.

Republicans were moving in Congress to add all the money they could find to make the Clinton bill tougher on crime. Biden and other senators tried to toughen up the bill themselves so as not to be left behind. One night, Reed got a cryptic call from Biden's top aide to say the senator was working on a bill to expand the Clinton measure. The next thing he knew, not only was it expanded but it included all 100,000 of his cops on the street—paid for by trimming 252,000 employees from the federal payroll. Reed was overwhelmed, and then he got worried. The price tag for the entire crime bill was a whopping $22.3 billion. On Thursday, November 4, the Senate, in a rush of bipartisanship, approved the plan 94–4. As Reed and Jose Cerda watched it happen on C-SPAN, they thought how right they had been about the issue but how unpopular they would be with their colleagues in the White House.

At around ten o'clock that night, Reed brought some talking points about the new, expanded crime bill to Mark

Gearan and Dee Dee Myers. And in the West Wing lobby, he ran into Sperling.

"Gene, did you hear what the Senate did?" Reed asked with feeling.

"No," Sperling replied, eager and hesitant at the same time.

"They agreed to give us 100,000 cops and get rid of the bureaucrats to pay for it. Twenty-two billion dollars!"

Sperling could only shake his head. "I go to these budget meetings day in and day out. Fight for $100 million for technology, another $100 million for children. And you don't go to a budget meeting in nine months and walk off with $22 billion."

The next morning, Reed was asked to attend the senior staff meeting, and he discovered how right he and Cerda had been about their colleagues. Although the Senate had just passed the largest single domestic initiative of the President's first year, no one even mentioned it during the first fifteen minutes. When they did get around to the crime bill, it was only grudgingly. Stephanopoulos said in jest that budget director Leon Panetta should move his office from the Old EOB to the Justice Department because crime had just become the entire Clinton domestic agenda.

At a later meeting in Mack McLarty's office, Reed pleaded the case for the President to voice strong support for the Senate bill. He reminded everyone that Clinton had campaigned in 1992 for both more cops on the street and fewer federal workers. It had even been in his manifesto, *Putting People First*. "This is a historic agreement," Reed implored. Referring to the senators who passed the bill, he said, "We ought to bring everyone down to the White House and let the public know what happened." But that idea was rejected, and Reed was distraught.

On Sunday, November 7, he got his revenge. William Schneider, the political analyst, published an opinion piece in

the "Outlook" section of *The Washington Post* that was an answer to Reed's prayers. It pointed out at great length how important the crime issue had become with the public. But it
said Clinton was mostly an outsider to the trend. "The public
gives him worse ratings on crime than on any other issue—
including foreign policy, where he has been taking a lot of hits
lately," Schneider wrote.

Reed was irate, but how could he disagree? He had been
working for months to get Clinton on the forefront of the
crime issue, but he had been blocked at every turn. Now that
the public was demanding a government solution, the President was too far behind other politicians to get credit for trying. "It was obvious what was happening," Reed fumed. "He
wasn't getting credit for his own idea."

The next morning, Reed took a copy of the article to Carol
Rasco and asked her to give it to the President. "He ought to
know," Reed said, "that while we were debating among ourselves about whether to accept the inevitable, he was suffering around the country because we weren't giving him a
chance to talk about the issue he's been saying is so hot."
Reed also wrote a one-page memo to Clinton that said in part,
"If we continue to pursue an inside strategy for this, we'll get
nothing but grief and none of the credit."

After Rasco gave Clinton the article and he had a chance to
read the memo, the President erupted. He called McLarty
into the Oval Office and yelled at him for a while. Then others got a piece of his mind. That night Reed was paged by
Gergen, who said, "Let's talk more on this. Get the word
out." Gergen suggested that a press conference the next day
would be a good time for Clinton to elevate the issue. And
there was also a speech on Saturday at a church in Memphis.
They agreed that the crime issue should be part of that as
well, and Reed quietly rejoiced.

On Saturday, November 13, the President gave his now-
famous speech in Memphis, and it was more than Reed could

have hoped for. Clinton, a religious man, always gave his most emotional addresses in churches, usually predominantly black churches. And as the fate of the Brady Bill hung in the balance on Capitol Hill, he delivered one of the most powerful speeches of his term.

Speaking from the pulpit where Martin Luther King, Jr., had delivered his last sermon the night before he was assassinated twenty-five years before, Clinton said, if King were to "reappear by my side today . . . he would say, 'I did not live and die to see the American family destroyed. I did not live and die to see thirteen-year-old boys get automatic weapons and gun down nine-year-olds just for the kick of it. I did not live and die to see young people destroy their own lives with drugs and then build fortunes destroying the lives of others. . . . This is not what I have lived and died for.' "

Clinton's words were trumpeted on the front pages of both *The New York Times* and *The Washington Post*. As Reed waited for his wife and daughter to get ready for church, he read both articles, and his eyes brimmed with tears.

Remarkably, even that speech was not enough. Senate Republicans, instigated by the National Rifle Association, filibustered the Brady Bill. On the night of Friday, November 19, Reed visited Stephanopoulos, and they both were pessimistic.

"We don't have the votes, do we?" Stephanopoulos asked.

"I don't think so," Reed answered, "unless the Republicans get embarrassed."

In the meantime, Reed and Sperling were assigned to attend a meeting on, of all subjects, welfare reform. To make the gathering even odder, it was being held in a local Holiday Inn because of a quirk in federal rules that prevented staffers from different agencies from meeting in a government building.

Needless to say, neither Sperling nor Reed gave much of his attention to welfare that day. Sperling spent a lot of time watching the University of Michigan–Ohio State football game in the hotel lobby and returning frequent pages from Stephanopoulos on a nearby pay telephone. Reed cared a good deal about welfare reform, but the setting for the meeting was so bizarre that even he had trouble concentrating.

That evening at home, Reed got bored watching *The McLaughlin Group* and switched to CNN. And the news nearly knocked him off his feet. The announcer said the Brady Bill had just passed the Senate, 63–36. Reed could not believe it, but a few minutes later someone from the Justice Department called to confirm the news. Then it was time for Reed to make some calls. He telephoned the White House operator and asked her to send pages to Jose Cerda and to George Stephanopoulos. He told her the pages should say, "The Brady Bill passed."

"Oh good," the operator said, and Reed could not have agreed more. But he was too stunned—and surprised—to thank her for the thought.

Final work on the crime bill did not begin until early the next year, 1994. And given the whipsaw he had gone through to get the bill as far it was, Reed decided to step back further from his policy development role and, like Sperling, become more of a policy marketer. He assembled a team of staffers to press the issue forward. They were himself, Rahm Emanuel, and Ron Klain, a rising star of the Democratic party who had worked for Senator Biden before moving to the White House and was about to move again to a top slot at the Justice Department.

Both Reed and Sperling became salesmen for the party as well. At the request of the Democratic National Committee, they went to the Boca Raton Resort and Beach Club in Florida during the last weekend in February to serve as celebrities in residence for some of the biggest campaign contributors of the party. The few hundred business executives in attendance had forked over at least $1,000 each to the DNC's coffers to get the chance to sit at poolside with the Clinton staffers.

Neither aide was overjoyed at the prospect. The President had come to Washington vowing to end the city's notorious laxity in ethical standards. But his administration turned out to be mostly business as usual. Without public notice, big campaign contributors were routinely given special access to top Clinton officials. They were once treated to speeches at Washington's Madison Hotel by top Clinton officials ranging from McLarty to Rubin. Afterward, each giver had his photograph taken with the Vice President. At the time, Reed and Sperling had been revolted by the scene.

But now it was their turn to woo the party faithful, and they used a variety of self-deluding arguments to justify it. One was that they were exhausted and deserved a break. Another was that they were not really listening to the big-money lobbyists who were paying them court. Also, they were not the big draws. Other attendees included Gore, Secretary of Commerce Ronald Brown, House Majority Leader Richard Gephardt, and Congressman Sam Gejdenson of Connecticut, who, ironically, was the prime author of the House's campaign-finance overhaul bill. In such company, Reed and Sperling tried to think of themselves as invisible, even though each had to give a little speech as part of his stay in the sandy hideaway.

"I don't know how we keep our hands clean," Sperling said later, resignedly. "Fund-raising is the dirty part that leads to everything else happening." So they spent a weekend in a lovely spot—for the cause. And Sperling admitted it was "an unbelievably nice break." One reason: he went with his new girlfriend, Kim O'Neill, a young economist at the President's Council of Economic Advisers whom he had met, of course, at work.

Back in Washington, the wind howled through the low-slung buildings of downtown, producing a sound reminiscent of baying wolves. And on a Tuesday in the beginning of March, no one at the White House doubted that they were the prey that day. Reed suspected it when he found an urgent memo in his office from McLarty, instructing him to report to the East Room. He knew for sure when he walked by the briefing room and saw reporters packed in there, cheek by jowl.

The gilt-edged East Room on the White House mansion's first floor was usually the scene of presidential press conferences. But when Reed arrived, the room was filled with fellow White House staffers, many of whom maneuvered for position in front of a television set. They strained to see the latest chapter in the rapidly unfolding Whitewater saga: the naming of a new White House counsel, Lloyd Cutler.

For Reed, it was a strange moment in a stranger week. The White House was under attack from all quarters, and some of the stalwarts of the administration were in the crosshairs: Roger Altman, George Stephanopoulos, Mark Gearan, Maggie Williams, Bruce Lindsey, Harold Ickes, all were part of ongoing inquiries in courts of law and in the court of public opinion on Capitol Hill. The President's poll ratings were falling fast. And the mood in the East Room was ugly.

Reed disliked what he was hearing from his colleagues. Their tone was bitter; they wanted to lash out. They blamed their woes on Republicans and the press. While some tried to deny there was any real problem, most talked of hunkering down and fighting back against the forces arrayed against them. "The feeling in the room," Reed said, "was of 'us versus them.' "

After the announcement in the briefing room, the President, the First Lady, Al Gore, Mack McLarty, and Lloyd Cutler came to the East Room to try to reassure their staff. Each took a turn at urging a longer view of the situation and asking everyone to concentrate not on the diversion of Whitewater but on the good works they had come to the White House to achieve. Clinton in particular insisted the current troubles were just politics—the price that must be paid for the privilege of public service. He even related a story he and the First Lady had read to their daughter, Chelsea, when she was a child to emphasize their belief that things would turn out well in the end.

Reed appreciated the pep talk. It was badly needed. Still, he worried. The partisanship Whitewater had stirred could only hurt his issues—crime and welfare reform—because both required Republican support to succeed. On their way back to their offices, he and Rahm Emanuel agreed that the whole Whitewater issue should have been better handled. The people whose job it was to protect the President from incendiary side issues like this had failed completely. And the result, Reed and Emanuel feared, would be more "blood in the water" and a harder time getting done what really mattered.

Next Reed faced another nemesis: the press. He was intent on trying to keep White House deliberations on welfare reform secret. But every time a large meeting was held on the subject, its outcome made its way into the newspapers, particularly *The New York Times*. Carol Rasco, Reed's boss, referred to these leaks as "a dagger in the President's heart," and she was determined to plug them by whatever means necessary. Lately that meant telling fewer people what the President was really thinking.

Reed was not suspected of leaking and for good reason: he did not. So he knew—while others did not—that the President's decision on welfare boiled down to a single issue: the gambling tax. Two alternative welfare packages were in play: one, with the gambling tax, which cost $12.6 billion over five years, and a second, without the tax, which cost $9.5 billion over the same period. Reed and Panetta argued strenuously against the inclusion of any tax. The last thing the Clinton administration needed was a revolt on taxes that alienated lawmakers from such large and largely Democratic states as Nevada and New Jersey.

Reed knew it was just a matter of time before Clinton chose

the no-tax route. Chairman Dan Rostenkowski of the House Ways and Means Committee was opposing any new taxes. Chairman Daniel Moynihan of the Senate Finance Committee was sure a gambling tax could not pass the Senate. And there was also what Clinton called the Tim Valentine problem—named for the congressman from eastern North Carolina who had once asked the President, "If we're going to end welfare, why does it cost more money?" A tax increase would make the Valentine problem even worse.

All these factors coalesced at the end of April to kill the gambling tax. But the decision was slow to be made official. The paranoia about leaks compelled the White House to keep ever fewer officials informed. The handful of White House officials who knew about the plan's final details included Mack McLarty, Leon Panetta, Carol Rasco, and Reed. But now it was necessary to orchestrate the announcement, and to get as much mileage as they could out of dropping the idea of the gambling tax. So the White House lobbying office got ready to involve the lawmakers from Nevada and New Jersey so they could claim victory in simultaneous press conferences.

But on Monday, April 25, welfare sprang its biggest leak, and the leaker was the President himself. Without informing his staff, he telephoned Nevada governor Bob Miller and told him the gambling tax was not going to be in his welfare proposal. Within what seemed like minutes, Miller called a press conference and announced it to the world. The problem was that not only were other elected officials unaware of the decision but some senior people in the Clinton administration, including Secretary Donna Shalala of the Department of Health and Human Services, did not know either. The result was a Keystone Kops–like scramble. One moment Reed was moving through his day unhurried, and the next he was being summoned to the Roosevelt Room for an emergency meeting of the Domestic Policy Council.

Reed was asked to chair the impromptu gathering, even

though Rasco was not present and he did not know why the meeting had been called. But his innate good manners prompted him to begin by apologizing on his boss's behalf. Someone managed to find a printed agenda for the meeting, and Reed dutifully started to follow it. Then, not long after he began, Rasco popped into the room, grabbed Secretary Shalala, and disappeared down the hallway with her in tow. Reed tried to keep his mind on the agenda. But that was hard. At one point he called on an assistant secretary of the Department of the Interior to make a presentation—even though he was not there.

After a while, Reed's pager went off. It read: "Come to Rasco's office ASAP. She will explain the ins and outs." As calmly as he could, Reed turned the meeting over to his colleague Bill Galston and left the room. When he learned about the leak—this time from the highest level—he went immediately to Emanuel and Stephanopoulos to discuss how to contain the damage.

Rather than go back to the meeting, Reed picked up the telephone and called several reporters, including Wolf Blitzer, whose Cable News Network had been the first national outlet to air the story on the gambling tax. For some reason, *The New York Times* did not call back. And the next day, Reed did not feel guilty when he saw that the paper did not have much of a story. They had missed one leak—and it was the big one.

Bob Rubin wanted to keep Sperling to himself, confined to the economic policy that he oversaw. But Roger Altman had been so impressed with Sperling's marketing efforts on behalf of the budget that he told Hillary Clinton she should not even try to sell health care without him. So Sperling was added to the health-care team. Sperling liked the diversion, at least in part because his new girlfriend specialized in health policy. He also was getting smarter about delegating. He no longer did all the work himself but instead formed a unit of four or five younger aides in the War Room who helped him make the case for health reform.

One project was to draft a series of op-ed articles to be placed under the bylines of more senior Clinton officials. The first drafts were written by his "kids" in the War Room, but it was Sperling's job to edit them and coordinate their publication with the higher-ups whose names were to be attached. This was a delicate political task. Sometimes he did it through intermediaries: for Secretary Bentsen he spoke to Marina Weiss, Bentsen's top health adviser. But he talked directly to others, including Secretary Ron Brown of Commerce, with whom he started his negotiations at the black-tie White House Correspondents Association dinner. Sperling was hitting the big time, and he liked it.

He also was relied on inside the White House to play a larger role in pressing issues for his allies, particularly his old boss, Secretary of Labor Robert Reich. In early May, for instance, Reich asked Sperling to persuade the President to push for full funding of Reich's job-retraining programs when Clinton spoke with Congressman David Obey, chairman of the House Appropriations Committee.

"He's really got to drum this home," Reich told Sperling on the phone.

"Don't worry," Sperling replied. "Leon's going to stress that with him," referring to Leon Panetta, then of the White House Budget Office.

"But he's going to have fifteen things to stress with him," Reich complained. So Sperling agreed to do more lobbying on Reich's behalf.

The first thing he did was go to Stephanopoulos. "George, you've really got to make sure he's fired up about this," Sperling urged. So Stephanopoulos got aboard too. In the end, the Sperling-Stephanopoulos axis was strong enough to convince Bob Rubin to sit in the Oval Office while Clinton telephoned Obey and, by his mere presence, help reinforce the importance of Reich's request.

.   .   .

But most of Sperling's working life was not so well orchestrated. On Tuesday, May 10, he had to situate himself by Clinton's side during two presidential speeches just in case something unexpected happened. And, true to form, something did. During the first speech—to the executive council of the AFL-CIO in the Diplomatic Reception Room—the blue-chip forecast came out showing very little inflation for the next two years, and the bond market started to rally.

After Clinton's statement to the group, Sperling caught the President's attention and told him both pieces of good news. "Why is the bond market doing this?" the President asked. And since Sperling was not certain, he went back to his office to find out.

By two o'clock he met Clinton outside the Oval Office and accompanied him to his second speech in the Old EOB. Sperling and two other aides briefed the President as they walked. Michael Waldman, the speechwriter, suggested some themes the President might hit. Fellow staffer Robert Kyle talked about some encouraging new trade numbers, which had helped cause the bond market to rally. And then Sperling raised the rally as a way for Clinton to tout his economic accomplishments.

"I just wanted to remind you there was a huge bond rally today," Sperling said, "down sixteen basis points."

The aides tried to blend inconspicuously into the rear of the ornate Indian Treaty Room, where the speech was being held. But before Clinton began, Waldman leaned over to Sperling and said, "When you were a little kid watching Bobby Kennedy and dreaming of social justice, did you ever imagine whispering in the President's ear, 'Sir, there was a big bond rally today'?" The two laughed so hard they had to turn their backs to avoid causing a scene.

After a while, Sperling lapsed into almost complete salesmanship. He began Sunday, July 10, with a 7:30 A.M. breakfast at the Jefferson Hotel with his boss, Rubin, and a television consultant named Michael Sheehan. Rubin, who had been an investment banker his whole career, was not comfortable in public settings, but later that morning he was going very public—on *Meet the Press*. He needed Sperling to help him phrase the good economic news he wanted to present, and he wanted Sheehan to help him smooth his television persona.

Sperling had gone through ten hours of briefings with Rubin the day before, so all he had to do was update him on the morning newspapers. Sheehan had the larger task. He wanted to transform the mumbly, almost shy Rubin into someone who appeared both comfortable and confident on television. So he suggested ways for him to hold his hands, how he could look serious, and what tone to take when he answered questions. Morning shows require a gentler approach, he explained, much different than the faster-paced, harder-hitting shows that air at night.

Rubin's appearance was slated as the kickoff of a week of economic boasting by the White House—all directed by Sperling. His idea was to take a usually boring and forgettable document called the midsession review and use its findings to show how wonderfully Clinton's budget was working.

And the strategy succeeded. Stories appeared in *The Wall Street Journal, The New York Times,* and the *Los Angeles Times.* Sperling did not have long to savor his triumph, however. He already was planning a series of luncheon briefings by Secretary Bentsen, Rubin, and others to make the President's case for universal health-care coverage—events Bentsen dubbed the Sperling lunch.

Reed also took a detour into marketing, even when he was home in Idaho. With the crime bill finally picking up momentum in Congress, he took every opportunity to lobby for it. So when he saw his congressman, Larry LaRocco, in Coeur d'Alene, he pressed him for a yes vote when the time came. LaRocco said he could not promise; the National Rifle Association was prominent in that part of the West, and gun control was part of the bill.

Reed even worked on Sunday. On July 17, he was invited to make his case to a broader audience—via NBC's Sunday *Today* show—and he was loath to turn it down. When he agreed to go on, however, he did not consider how early he would have to wake up. But he understood pretty fast when his father, Scott Reed, roused him at 3:30 A.M. Outside, on the narrow, dirt road on the outskirts of town, was a white stretch limousine. Reed was certain it was the largest car ever to visit the vicinity. At least the neighbors' dogs must have thought so; they could not seem to stop barking.

Reed and his father were greeted by a chauffeur, complete with driver's cap, and drank deeply from a thermos of coffee as they were driven to Spokane, where the interview was to be beamed live to New York. Reed's segment, at 5:00 A.M. Pacific time, was shoehorned between a sports story and a retrospective on an Apollo moon landing. He was interviewed for five minutes, mostly about the virtues of changing the welfare system. The show did not bother to explain why a White House aide was talking from Washington State.

When father and son returned home at six o'clock, Scott Reed woke his wife to show her the car. At 6:15, Reed's sister called to say she had seen her brother on television and was so proud. But Reed was not sure anyone else in the country had tuned in. Certainly *he* would not have. But every chance to make the case was worth taking.

But the Republicans had other plans. Eager to capitalize on Whitewater, the GOP tried to block every bill Clinton advocated. If they succeeded, they gambled voters would penalize the President and his party in the upcoming elections. They reasoned that a President who had come to Washington to end gridlock would be unable to explain why he could not get his agenda off the ground. So the drumbeat of opposition, even to the popular crime bill, began. Republicans started to say the bill was actually wasteful spending rather than a legitimate effort to fight crime.

Still, Reed believed they were very close to passing the bill in the House. But looking up at the television at yet another Whitewater hearing, he said aloud, "I don't know what to make of this whole thing." What he meant was he knew the implications all too well. Clinton was vulnerable, and so was his project.

To fight back, the President scheduled a press conference, and beforehand he shuttled aides in and out to brief him on specific topics. First was health care. Then came crime—and Reed, Emanuel, and Klain marched into the Cabinet Room. They urged the President to say the bill would pass and to dismiss Republican opposition as merely a sour grapes effort to trash a good bill. Then they began to go through the legislation point by point.

The aides had decided in advance that they did not want to talk about the complicated procedural battle going on behind the scenes in Congress. There was no need to burden the President with those details—at least on that day. The National Rifle Association opposed the assault weapons ban, and its strategy was to kill the bill by defeating the so-called rule. That was the motion that would allow the bill to come up for debate and a vote.

But after a half hour of briefing on the substance of the bill, Clinton stopped them. "I gather by the fact that we haven't brought it up that we're OK on the rule," he said.

"Oh no, Mr. President," Reed replied, and everyone laughed.

"Let's not get into that now," Stephanopoulos insisted and shook his head.

Then Sperling walked in to give his own briefing on the economy. But before he started, he noted how wonderful it was that Clinton was on the verge of making good on his promise, made during his acceptance speech at the Democratic National Convention, to put 100,000 more cops on the street and to get rid of thousands of bureaucrats—separate provisions in the crime bill. The crime team then left feeling upbeat—except they knew they still needed thirty or forty more votes to pass the rule.

By now, Reed was almost a full-time lobbyist, and he lobbied everyone he could. He saw Larry LaRocco and pressed him again to vote yes on the rule. LaRocco said he would not be the vote to sink the bill, but he also made clear he would be the very last vote for the rule. The NRA was just too strong in Idaho. Reed also pressed a fellow moderate Democrat, Congressman Glen Browder of Alabama. But Browder said he had no leeway on the rule.

Every day since the press conference had been essentially the same for Reed and his crime team. Democratic leaders expressed confidence that the bill would pass, asserting it could not lose in an election year in which crime was the issue most on voters' minds. But every day they also said they had not yet secured enough votes to win.

The House vote was scheduled for Thursday, August 11, and that morning it was still too close to call. Reed's best information from Democratic vote counters was that the White House had between 216 and 218 votes; it needed 218 to win. Reed was not optimistic.

But the Democratic leadership did not think delay would improve the bill's prospects, so late that afternoon they agreed to commence the vote on the rule. An hour before that, Reed tried LaRocco one more time. He told the congressman he was about to make a big mistake. He predicted LaRocco would pay a higher price at the polls if his own party lost a vote as big as this one. "Anybody who thinks they could lose votes by supporting a bill with 100,000 cops, more prison cells for violent criminals, and three strikes and you're out, isn't paying any attention to what's going on in the country," he admonished. But LaRocco still said no.

Reed and Jonathan Prince, a speechwriter, made several attempts to draft a presidential statement for use if the crime bill passed. But they could not bring themselves to finish it. Instead, Reed walked over to Emanuel's office. The hyperactive Emanuel stayed on the phone almost constantly, fishing for the latest vote count. As the vote approached, the whip's office said there were 206 absolutely solid Democratic votes in favor. "How many leaning yes?" Emanuel asked. Reed could see the answer in Emanuel's face. There were none. Everyone's mind was made up. There was nothing more Reed could do.

Reed and Jose Cerda watched the vote on the television in Emanuel's office. Emanuel himself watched in the Oval Office, where he strode back and forth nervously. He paced so much, in fact, that Andrew Friendly, Clinton's personal aide, had to ask him to stop. The motion was setting off alarms and driving the Secret Service crazy.

Emanuel's office was too small for pacing. Every Clinton adviser, including Stan Greenberg and Mandy Grunwald, was desperate to learn the outcome of the vote, and they wedged themselves into the tiny office too. It was a grim scene. Sensing calamity, CNN's cameras trained on Emanuel's window to try to get some candid shots. Michael Waldman stood in front of the window to block them, and it was a good thing he did. When the rule was defeated, by a humiliating vote of 210–225, the room went quiet and people's expressions went blank. They did not know what to say.

The Republicans had exercised extraordinary discipline; only eleven of them voted in favor of the rule. And Democrats abandoned Clinton with unanticipated fervor. Fifty-eight of them defied their leadership and voted to block the bill from coming to the floor. It was the President's worst loss and a crippling blow to the administration.

Stephanopoulos and Gearan came into Emanuel's office and said the President was going to make a statement in the briefing room. Reed and Prince immediately sat down at

Emanuel's computer to draft it. Now they had no choice. The next several days, Reed knew, would be a living hell.

Things got worse for Sperling as well. To remove some of the underbrush of the Whitewater controversy from the legislative landscape, Roger Altman resigned as deputy secretary of the Treasury on Wednesday, August 17. In his resignation letter, he wrote, "I regret any mistakes or errors of judgment I may have made. For them, I apologize. And, hopefully, my stepping down will help to diminish the controversy." Clinton termed the departure "the right step under the circumstances."

But Sperling did not take it so lightly. He took it on himself to spend the day telephoning reporters and backgrounding them on his mentor's many virtues, particularly Altman's selflessness and integrity under fire. He acknowledged that Altman had made mistakes by not being forthright at a Whitewater hearing in Congress but insisted his friend had done nothing *intentionally* wrong. And that, to Sperling, made a difference. Still, for the good of the President—and the country—Altman resigned, making him more a martyr than a miscreant. Given an extra moment to talk, Sperling also raged about the unfairness of Washington and its piranha culture.

Few versions of the Altman resignation carried in the press that evening and the next day included much of Sperling's rendition of the facts. And probably for good reason. Anyone who had enough time to hear him out readily understood that concerning Altman he could not be completely believed. The policy aide had become a publicist, and a ranting publicist at that. Sperling had gone too far.

While Sperling bloviated, Reed kept on lobbying. He and his team continued to meet each morning and tried to think of yet another venue for the President to say, "Pass the crime bill." And they came up with several good ones. One was at a predominantly black church in the Maryland suburbs of Washington. Another was the President's Saturday radio address. They also stirred the President to say those words many more times on the telephone from the Oval Office, mostly to swing Republican moderates.

Ultimately, those were the calls that made the difference. A marathon bargaining session over the weekend produced a new version of the bill. And this time it had enough votes to pass the House. The key to its success was the involvement of a sizable group of pro-gun-control Republicans. They could accept the assault weapons ban, but they wanted the whole pricey bill trimmed back. And Clinton readily agreed. The new version cost $3.3 billion less than the original, and the House passed it 235–195.

But the Senate remained a problem. Clinton needed sixty votes to get the bill beyond the obstacle of a filibuster led by western-state senators who supported the National Rifle Association. It was impossible to say exactly where the votes were.

For that reason and others, it could hardly have been a more trying week for Reed and his colleagues. Ever since the first crime-bill vote two weeks before, Reed had been trying to get out of town for a prearranged and expenses-paid trip with his family to Australia. Unless the bill was resolved that week, the trip was off. Ron Klain was having an even more stressful time. He and his family were moving to the suburbs and were supposed to sign the purchase contract. But at the last minute there was a glitch, and the settlement was postponed. And that, Klain told Reed, was the story of his life in crime. He had started with the issue as Joe Biden's staffer many years earlier. "But every time we got to the brink of something happening, everyone would back away," he said.

On Wednesday, the sale did go through, and the Democratic leadership decided to try for a vote the next day, Thursday, August 25. That morning, Reed and Jonathan Prince once again started to draft a presidential statement. This time they tried to write a version for use if the bill died. "The American people will not forget what a few in Congress did to them today," it read. "They care more about their political interests . . ." But they could not finish that one either. It was too disturbing to contemplate.

Instead, they opted to sit and watch Emanuel pace. At about four o'clock, Reed got the first solid indication that the vote might actually succeed. Senate Minority Leader Bob Dole was reported to have left his office and given a thumbs-down. At about 5:30, Emanuel was still pacing, and Reed and Prince started drafting a victory statement. CNN's cameras were again directed at the window, and Emanuel gave strict orders to the ten or so aides sitting around not to show any emotion if the vote was positive. He wanted nothing to jinx the bill. A little later, when the key procedural vote came, Reed and the others could not help but give a stifled whoop when the yes votes hit sixty-one. Dee Dee Myers, who was not part of the no-cheering conspiracy, walked into the room and gave Emanuel a pat on the head. Footage of that scene made the national news.

Reed went home to pack. There, his wife gave him a photograph taken earlier in the day. Their little daughter, Julia, had been eating her lunch with the television tuned to the Senate's crime debate. During one particularly droning speech, she fell fast asleep in midchew, and her head dropped right into her plate of baby food. Her mother took the picture of the sleeping child angled so the senators could be seen in the background. When he heard the story, Reed under-stood—and agreed with—the sentiment. Good policy finally became law, but at a horrible price.

Passage of the crime bill, while a great triumph, was not the big news. The most significant fact was that the President agreed to allow Congress to go home without passing health reform. The concession was part of the deal he'd cut to sal-vage his anticrime legislation. It also was a recognition of re-ality. Health reform was in mortal danger, and everyone knew it. Sending Congress home was tantamount to admitting that a comprehensive health bill—Clinton's top priority—was dead.

Reed's mind spun back nearly eighteen months to the innocent days at the beginning of the administration. How hopeful he had been. How promising things had seemed. How much fun it was going to be. And how rewarding! He remembered arriving late on the inaugural platform and being forced to sit quickly in a section filled mostly with senators. When Sperling saw the maneuver, he stood up and shouted, "Senator Reed! Senator Reed!" to the giggling delight of their friends and the embarrassment of the adults within earshot.

After the inauguration, when the President had left the platform, Reed and Sperling rushed together around the podium where Clinton had just given his speech. They stared in disbelief at the crowds. And then, Reed recalled, they play-acted their favorite fantasy, becoming President. Sperling and Reed snapped photos of each other sitting in Clinton's big leather chair. Then they took pictures of each other pretending to give their own inaugural addresses. What rubes-come-to-the-big-city they had been. And, Reed thought, if only he could live those moments again.

But he could not. The Republican strategy worked, and the next few weeks were a frantic dash to try to stem the electoral losses. Sperling buried his sadness over the loss of health reform in an all-out effort to discredit Newt Gingrich's Contract with America. He conspired with Democratic staffers on Capitol Hill to claim that the ten-point program would cost billions of dollars in lost revenue from tax cuts for rich people. He also argued that the contract would hurt two programs especially sacred to Democrats: Medicare and Social Security. In a manner that had by then become rote, Sperling worked up the numbers and spread them around, hoping if enough Democrats used them, voters might turn against what was clearly a Republican tide. He threw himself over completely to being a political operative.

Reed became a policy promoter and arranged anticrime events for the President to buttress his tough-on-crime image. But he also tried to keep at least part of his mind on the substance of the message. He and Emanuel wrote a New Democratic manifesto of sorts, laying out a course the President might take after the Republicans won in November. The components were not surprising: tax cuts for working families with children, welfare reform, and additional anticrime legislation. In other words, the initiatives Reed had already pressed for but had had decidedly mixed success in getting through the morass of the White House. Unfortunately for Reed—but not unexpectedly—a rival memo, which gave very different advice, was written by two Old Democratic staffers, John Podesta and David Dreyer. Both the Old and New Democratic memos were part of the 472 Group, which was named for the room in the Old EOB where senior staffers met, obviously in disarray, to plan for the postelection carnage.

On the evening of Wednesday, October 19, Clinton traveled to New York City to attend a fund-raising dinner for Democratic governor Mario Cuomo. As a former aide to Cuomo, Sperling got to tag along and fiddle with Clinton's speech. On the way up on *Air Force One,* Sperling telephoned Reed to see if he could "toughen up" the language the President was using to announce a waiver he was giving the governor so New York could pursue its own welfare reform. Both aides relished the irony of the call: the liberal wanted tougher language on the moderate's issue. To complete the reversal, Reed told Sperling the President could not make a bigger deal of the waiver, given what he was waiving. The two also realized the conversation was, in microcosm, a study in how the policies they had loved so dearly when they arrived at the White House were no longer cherished goals but merely another set of plays on the political field.

. . .

On the day before the election, Monday, November 7, Reed got an inkling of just how bad it was going to be. He received a phone call from Peter Fenn, a former aide to Idaho senator Frank Church who was now running the Senate campaign of Democrat Ann Wynia in Minnesota. Fenn told Reed he saw a lot of similarities between 1994 and 1980, when Church had been defeated in a Republican sweep. Wynia's polls had collapsed the night before, Fenn said, and it did not look like she was going to make it. Still, he invited Reed to his election-night party but added, "You probably won't want to come. It's not going to be a lot of fun." Reed agreed and did not attend.

In the White House on election day, Reed and Sperling tried to busy themselves with nonelectoral matters. They attended a meeting in the Old EOB about job-retraining proposals. In the midst of it, Sperling leaned over to tell Reed about the one-stop career centers located in the basement of a government building in Albany, the capital of New York State. All someone had to do to find employment options was push a computer button. Sperling noted that the White House might need a machine like that soon.

Later in the day, after some devastating exit poll results began to make the rounds, Sperling was in a health-care meeting in the West Wing. The numbers indicated that Republican gains might be even larger than anticipated, and Sperling was trying to digest that fact. Bob Rubin asked Sperling a question but got only a blank stare in reply. "I think Gene is somewhere else now," Rubin said, and the meeting went on without him.

As the real polls were about to close that evening, many staffers, including Myers and Sperling, went downstairs in the West Wing to Mark Gearan's new office. Reed went home. He could not bear the thought of spending the night in so gloomy a place. At least he could play with little Julia before he had to face the television returns again.

Four televisions were on in Gearan's office, and everyone was depressed from about eight o'clock on. By then exit polls showed the House would fall to the GOP. The only hope was the Senate. And there was a ray of sunshine at about 10:30, when someone said the Associated Press had predicted Democrat Harris Wofford would win in Pennsylvania. But fifteen minutes later the networks began predicting Republican Rick Santorum would win instead. Paul Begala, who was staying in steady contact from the Wofford campaign in Philadelphia, told George Stephanopoulos the networks were right. "It's gone," Stephanopoulos reported to the others. "It's gone. I just talked to Paulie. . . . It's gone."

Almost at the moment Stephanopoulos finished his sentence, Mario Cuomo was declared the loser in New York. Sperling, who was sitting on the floor in front of Gearan's desk, was unprepared for that. He knew his old boss had a tough race, but the exit polls had had him two percentage points ahead all day. He did not think Cuomo would lose. When he did, Sperling was overcome. He hung his head and began to cry. Myers, who was sitting next to him on the floor, put her hand over his. She thought, This is unimaginable.

The wreckage of that election for the Democrats—and for Reed and Sperling—was almost total. The two once-idealistic aides realized their own spat over ideology, clouded as it was by relentless kowtowing to interests along the way, was a sideshow to the rest of the country. Reed recalled that David Ellwood, a liberal staffer at the Department of Health and Human Services, had once referred to him as "a right-wing hack." In fact, Reed now realized that, judged against the average person on the street, he was barely holding his own as a moderate. Sperling was even further afield.

When Clinton began what he hoped would be a comeback a month later, he borrowed a page straight from the Reed playbook. On Thursday, December 15, after an extended and, as usual, agonizing debate inside the White House, the

President called for a tax cut, much of it targeted to working families with children. But Reed did not say, I told you so. Instead, he was candid enough to worry aloud that the whole new tack to the right might simply be coming too late to do much good. "I had hoped that we could do more to affect the climate of the country," he reflected. "But the political system is a machine that doesn't work very efficiently." And in the end, Reed and Sperling fully understood that they were just two more cogs in those creaky old gears.

In the meantime, Reed no longer looked as boyish; lines had begun to creep into the corners of his eyes. And at the end of 1994, Sperling and his girlfriend, Kim O'Neill, broke up. Sperling grieved, but he understood why she had left. "If only I could have trimmed back to eighty hours a week," he said. "I could have done a lot with those extra twenty hours." And then he went back to work.

DEE DEE MYERS

4

The White Boys' Club

WHEN SHE WAS THIRTY-ONE YEARS OLD, THE ENTIRE NATION knew her name and could recognize her face. Maître d's would rush her to the best tables in their restaurants. Flight attendants would put her in first class if there were an available seat. People on the street would ask for her autograph and, sometimes, break into applause at the mere sight of her. Dee Dee Myers was the first woman ever to hold the title of White House press secretary, and, for a time, she was one of our most celebrated personalities. Yet glamour was only part of her story.

To Myers and many of her female colleagues, the Clinton White House, despite its rhetoric about the virtues of diversity, was a boys' club of the most awful kind. Whenever big decisions were made, it was a group of white men who made them. And even when women were invited to attend, they had to struggle to be heard. In sheer numbers, the Clinton White House was awash in female employees, especially on the staff of Hillary Clinton. But when it counted, very few if any of them were brought into the circle of power. Women on the

White House staff used the term *white boys* to describe this masculine cabal and, in shorthand, to deride their domination.

Few women were as hampered by the white boys' club as Dee Dee Myers. In 1993, she was given the title of press secretary but not its duties. Those belonged to the quintessential "white boy" George Stephanopoulos, the White House communications director. He was slated to do the daily press briefings, the traditional task of press secretaries. He also occupied the larger press secretary's office, which features a famous horseshoe-shaped desk. Myers was two doors down in a cubbyhole-size office usually reserved for a lowly deputy. And, true to form, Stephanopoulos was paid a higher salary: $125,000 compared with Myers's $100,000.

Later that year, when Myers finally did move up to do the briefings, she was overshadowed by not one but two white boys: Mark Gearan, the new communications director, and, most of all, David Gergen, the veteran White House Press Office hand who was inserted above Gearan in the hierarchy. (Aides derisively called the very tall Gergen "the Cat in the Hat," after the Dr. Seuss children's book about a lanky feline. A sequel is named *The Cat in the Hat Comes Back,* just as Gergen did to the White House.) Stephanopoulos also kept a hand in the communications pie. With such talkative aides all around her, Myers, justifiably, continued to feel shut out.

Ironically, it was a woman who made sure Myers was put in a subservient role at the start. During the transition period between the election and the inauguration, Myers made the mistake of crossing Hillary Clinton's friend and close adviser Susan Thomases. Thomases had coveted Myers's office at transition headquarters in Little Rock, but Myers did not want to give it up. The ensuing fight, which Thomases won, led eventually not only to Myers's tiny office in the West Wing but also to her diminished role on the White House staff. In addition, Hillary Clinton remained one of her most persistent behind-the-scenes critics.

Myers tried to be philosophical. She was glad to be at the White House, grateful in fact. Yet she knew it was not going to be easy. She thought she would have to put up with a lot. But she had no way of guessing just how much.

Few people would have guessed Myers would rise to such prominence. She was the much-traveled daughter of a military man who chose a career that made her just as rootless. She was a political nomad who moved from one campaign to the next. When she finally came to rest, she found herself, to her own astonishment, in, of all places, Washington and at the White House.

Her father was a Navy pilot who did two tours of duty in Vietnam. His family moved seven times until he took a job as a test pilot for Lockheed Corporation, settling in the Southern California suburb of Valencia when Myers was in second grade. There she led a comfortable, even sheltered existence. Steve Myers was a Catholic and a Republican. And Dee Dee, the middle of his three daughters, was very close to him. "She was my boy," he recalled, with the same sly sarcasm for which his daughter became known. "She was always good at guy stuff," he continued. "When she was in grade school and maybe the first year or two of junior high, she was the ten-speed bike expert, and all the little boys used to come over to get their bikes fixed." She also was athletic, a broad-shouldered swimmer in the California sun.

The three Myers girls hung out together and were the best of friends: Betsy, a financial planner, who also got a job in Washington with the Small Business Administration; JoJo, a hairdresser and makeup artist; and Dee Dee, who was born Margaret Jane but who became forever Dee Dee because her older sister couldn't say *baby* when she was young. "She was the most flexible, malleable, pleasant little child that I ever saw," Steve Myers remembered, characteristics that certainly came in handy in her professional career.

Myers got her start in politics in the 1984 Mondale presidential campaign, when she worked as a gofer in California under Mickey Kantor, a Los Angeles lawyer and Democratic politico. The experience hooked her on campaigning—the thrill of it and the challenge—and she abandoned thoughts of attending graduate school in foreign affairs. Instead, she found work as press secretary in a succession of campaigns in California: for Los Angeles politicians Art Torres and Tom Bradley, for the ill-fated Dukakis campaign in 1988, and for Dianne Feinstein in her unsuccessful run for governor. She learned what it was like to lose—and how important it was not to give up.

In 1991 Myers joined Frank Jordan's run for mayor of San Francisco and added toughness to her tenacity. Jordan, a former police chief, was relatively conservative and was once forced to flee a campaign event by an angry crowd of gay-rights activists. In the melee, Jordan lost a shoe, and Myers tried to retrieve it. When she found the man who had taken it, she demanded, "Can I have that shoe, please?" The answer was no, and, later, it was burned in effigy. After Jordan won, his staff mounted the remaining shoe on a plaque with the inscription: LISTEN CAREFULLY AND YOU'LL HEAR THE SOUND OF ONE SHOE KICKING BUTT.

In the midst of that campaign, Myers got a phone call from Kantor. She feared her old boss was going to berate her for picking Jordan as her candidate—Kantor was backing his opponent—so she delayed calling back for twenty-four hours. When she did, Kantor surprised her by asking, "Are you with anybody in '92?"

"What?" she replied, a little confused.

"My friend Bill Clinton is looking for a press secretary."

"I don't know," Myers said, pretending to sound more confident. "I think I'm going to sit this cycle out."

Kantor begged her not to say no and to make time to meet Clinton when he was in Los Angeles in mid-October. Myers, who had met the candidate briefly earlier in the year, agreed to fly down to see him again.

She was impressed. Clinton was his most ingratiating self. She thought he was smart and full of ideas on such cutting-edge issues as welfare reform and deadbeat dads. He was not the kind of traditional Democrat who had lost national elections with such painful regularity. She thought he would be a good boss. But Myers was part of a campaign in progress, and she flew back to San Francisco uncommitted to Clinton.

The next day she received another call, this time from Eli Segal, a senior Clinton campaign staffer. "If you are offered this job, would you take it?" he asked.

She said she would not leave the Jordan campaign. She would not betray her employer. Segal called back and said Clinton would wait. And wait he did. Seven weeks later, on December 10, Jordan won. And three days after that, Friday the thirteenth, Myers flew to Orlando to start work as Clinton's traveling press secretary. One of the first people she met in Florida was Jeff Eller. He wore no tie and had a fat cigar in his mouth. Myers knew instantly they would get along. Their friendship deepened when she learned he was a military buff. Almost from then on, Eller handled the local press while Myers took care of the nationals.

For more than a year, Myers lived out of a suitcase as she flew around the country at Clinton's elbow. Along the way she became a favorite not just of Clinton but also of the national press corps. Her calmness, quick wit, and good nature were tonics both to the candidate and to the reporters who followed him. She once turned cartwheels on a lonely airport tarmac to entertain bored journalists—and herself.

When she joined the campaign, no one believed George Bush could be beaten. And even when it became clear Clinton would win, Myers could never quite get her mind around it. She had not wanted to leave California, certainly not to set down roots in Washington. She had never given much thought to governing; politics was her profession. In general, she was not a deep thinker about anything. She rarely read books. Once over lightly was about as thorough as she could manage. "I'm wider than I am deep," she admitted. "Jack of all trades, master of none, that's me." But, then again, her job was to be glib, not intellectual. She certainly was capable of being the White House press secretary.

When she started with Clinton, she told her friends in Los Angeles, "I'll see you in three months—or three years," and they all laughed. It seemed to make little difference. Even when her candidate won the election, she said, "I could never think beyond the end of the campaign. Government was never something I aspired to."

But once she was in the government—in the White House, no less—she thought it was certainly worth a try. Her reasoning was just that simple. "I gotta tell you," she confided. "I'm thirty-one years old, and I'm pretty damn happy with where I am right now. I would be happy to take more money. I would be happy to take a promotion in title. But if anyone had told me a year ago that I would be sitting where I am, I wouldn't have believed it."

Although she played second fiddle to Stephanopoulos, Myers did her own job as well as she could. She was, by all measures, a model employee. She retained her good-natured self-irony, in sharp contrast to the sometimes condescending and mostly humorless Stephanopoulos.

Even as, in effect, *deputy* press secretary, Myers's life was incredibly hectic—and exciting. She received as many as fifty phone calls a day. But her main chore was dealing with reporters face to face, often in the White House briefing room, when Stephanopoulos was not around. To prepare, she awoke at 5:30 A.M. and spent an hour reading *The Wall Street Journal, The New York Times,* and *The Washington Post* in her one-bedroom brownstone apartment in a downtown neighborhood near DuPont Circle. She took a cab to her West Wing office for a round of meetings that began at 7:15. And from there, it was a wild rush just to keep up with events.

She kept two or three television sets on in her office so as never to be out of touch.

Myers also had the privilege of seeing Clinton several times a day, and she was routinely briefed by his top aides, including National Security Adviser Tony Lake. But she also knew—and resented—that she did not have as much access to the higher-ups as previous press secretaries. She was not in the meetings where decisions were made, as previous people with her title had been. Certainly Stephanopoulos was almost always there—with the other white boys.

Still, Myers lived in hope that, in time, that would change.

The job was not easy. During one of his first days as President, Clinton made clear that of all the groups the White House had to deal with, the national press corps—the group Myers was supposed to look after—was his least favorite.

He made his disdain known in a speech to the entire staff, which gathered for the purpose in the elegant East Room. Clinton began by thanking everyone and urging them on. But then he issued a warning: do not leak to the press. Such leaks, he said, might help the leaker, but they would not enhance the greater glory of the Clinton administration, and that was what they were all there for. "We don't want to get caught up in the same old Washington games that paralyzed past administrations," he emphasized, referring to damage caused by unwanted disclosures. He did not point out, though many aides were well aware, that he was making the plea in the very room where presidential press conferences were routinely held.

From that moment on, everyone understood it was OK to disdain the Washington press corps. So another obstacle was thrown in the way of Dee Dee Myers.

A further problem was Clinton's own fiery temper, and his tendency to blame bad news stories on his press office staff. On the morning of Tuesday, February 16, the President snapped at aides who prevented two local politicians from joining him in front of the cameras. "Listen, goddamnit, you can't do that!" he screamed during the designed-for-television meeting with construction workers. "You can't bring me out here with the mayor and the congressman and push them back."

The outburst was a shock to outsiders. In public, Clinton showed only his huggable side. But people who knew him well, especially his staff, were also well acquainted with—and were often the brunt of—his considerable wrath. They called it Clinton's purple rage. In the hard days since the inauguration, such blowups had become commonplace. He roared over a premature leak about a proposal to limit the automatic rise in Social Security benefits. He berated Secret Service agents for restricting his freedom. And he could not stop shouting about media accounts that he had actually chosen federal judge Kimba Wood as attorney general, only to back away later. "The press appointed Kimba Wood," he exclaimed. "Not me!"

Luckily for the staff, the flare-ups quickly subsided. One veteran of Clintonian eruptions explained, "You would be fired at 8:00, be horsewhipped at 8:05, get a talking to at 8:10, and be a good guy by 8:15." The episodes of temper, aides were glad to learn, passed like summer storms.

But that did not mean the staff did not feel thoroughly drenched by them. No aide was ever fully prepared to be verbally thrashed by the President of the United States, no matter how often it happened. Stephanopoulos usually got the worst of it, and he had started to become immune. But Myers also was whacked regularly, and she did not wear it as well. She tried to take it in stride but always emerged from the sessions with that strained, slit-eyed look that said, You know, that really hurt.

Still, Myers understood and remained loyal. The President had plenty of reason to shout during his first few months in office. The early Clinton White House made many, many mistakes. Adjustments were inevitable. But, as usual, she did not know anything for sure. On Friday, May 28, she was traveling with the President in Philadelphia when Wolf Blitzer of CNN found her in the press center and confronted her with what he had been hearing.

"What do you think about Gergen?" Blitzer asked.

"Oh no" was all Myers was able to say in reply.

Blitzer told her Stephanopoulos was to be removed from his communications post and replaced by, of all people, David Gergen, the high-level operative for Republican presidents Nixon and Reagan. Myers could not believe it. She shook her head, declined to say anything more, and, as soon as she was able, telephoned Stephanopoulos in Washington.

"Is it true?" she asked.

"It's not a done deal, but they've been talking," he responded with dejection in his voice. "They have to meet again tonight."

The presidential entourage got back to the White House after 11:30 P.M., and Clinton went to the residence to meet with Gergen. Myers went home "pretty bummed out," she recalled. The white boys had struck again. Although the change affected her deeply, she was one of the last insiders to know.

Early the next morning, Myers, Stephanopoulos, Paul Begala, Mark Gearan, and Vice President Gore gathered in Gearan's office. Gore himself was functioning as a staffer, writing the statement Clinton was going to deliver. Everyone else in the room was traumatized, and Gore, who was far less stiff than his public image would indicate, sensed the tension.

Sitting at Gearan's computer, the Vice President read aloud what Gergen's new job as counselor to the President entailed: "He's going to advise on political strategy"—a comment that gave Begala a jolt. "He's going to do communications strategy"—a comment that saddened everyone else. Then, without missing beat, Gore added, "He's going to be Vice President."

Everyone laughed, easing the pressure a little. But Myers was still far from satisfied, and Gore knew it. "I think we had better have a talk," he told her, and took her into his own office down the hall.

"Are you OK?" he asked. "It's a good move," he added reassuringly.

But Myers was not so sure. Why did a Democratic outsider like Clinton have to hire a Republican insider like Gergen? "And what really made me nuts was what they did to George," she said. Although Stephanopoulos upstaged her all the time, she knew that was not his fault. It was his job. She believed there was no one more hardworking or more loyal to the President than Stephanopoulos. Those were two virtues she held dear and strove to practice herself. And because of his dedication, she thought Stephanopoulos deserved better than she knew he would get in the press that weekend.

The next morning, everyone suffered through the Rose Garden announcement, during which Stephanopoulos was named a senior adviser. Then, almost immediately, the President and Myers flew off to West Point for a previously scheduled speech.

Mack McLarty, then chief of staff, knew Myers was troubled. She blamed him for what had happened to Stephanopoulos. After all, it had been McLarty's idea to hire Gergen to try to right the listing White House. But she did not tell him so. She maintained herself as a model employee. And, to his credit, McLarty did not let the issue lay idle. He tracked Myers down at West Point and told her, "I'm sorry about the way this all came together, but you're going to be OK." Then he added, ominously, "The way you handle this incident will have a lot to do with how it turns out for you."

Myers got the hint. So when she calmed down she telephoned Gergen, only to be put on hold for fifteen long minutes. Here she was, the White House press secretary, a veteran of the Clinton campaign, the loyal soldier, being put on hold by a Reagan apologist. A Reagan apologist who apparently had just become her boss! How bad could it get? Finally she tired of waiting and hung up. Typical, she thought. White-boy typical.

Still, she soldiered on.

A full week later, on Saturday, June 5, Myers was at work, as usual, and Stephanopoulos, who was busy moving out of his office in the same suite, came by to do something no one else had bothered to do: tell Myers what was about to happen to her. In his familiar, clipped fashion, he explained that the communications director job—the one he was vacating—would go to Mark Gearan. And the daily briefings, at last, would be her responsibility.

Myers felt better. At least someone had said *something*. And she was getting part of what she wanted. True, she did not get a raise or a better title or even the press secretary's office. But she did get the briefings, and surely that would be an improvement. Still, she had reservations. "I knew it wasn't as easy as Gergen waving his hand and saying, 'It's all going to be fixed,' " she said. "I wasn't sure I was going to have the authority inside."

She was right to worry. Moving higher in the White House pecking order, while an honor, also put her more in the line of fire. She needed the extra access to decision makers that Stephanopoulos and now Gergen had, but she did not get it. And that hurt, causing embarrassment to her and the entire White House.

On Friday, June 25, news stories revealed that former president Bush might have been the target of an assassination attempt by Iraq's Saddam Hussein during a recent visit to the Middle East. The Clinton administration expressed indignation that any former president could be threatened in that way and said they were looking into it. At the briefing that af-

ternoon, Myers was asked the status of a report on the allega-
tion by the FBI, and she gave an offhand answer. "We hear
that it's in its final phases," she said, "but it's not complete."

In fact, not only was the report finished but it had been
given to the President the night before. By the time Myers
was commenting, he was well on the way to making a decision
to retaliate against the Iraqis. But no one had bothered to tell
Myers anything about it. "I don't think I was lied to," she said
later. "It was just that nobody thought to tell me."

Without a word to the public, Clinton ordered a targeted
attack on Iraq's capital. And the next day Navy ships carried
out the order by launching twenty-three Tomahawk missiles
that all but destroyed the headquarters of the Iraqi Intelligence Service. The President went on national television that
evening to defend the action as a "firm and commensurate"
response to the assassination attempt.

Myers was anguished about having been kept so far out of
the loop. Even on the day of Clinton's nationally televised address, she was not told what was happening until late in the
afternoon. So on Sunday she vented her anger to Gergen and
Tony Lake, the national security adviser. Please, she said, this
cannot happen again. It does not serve the President. And
they agreed. Lake apologized, and Gergen said he would try
to keep her informed about similar events. He also advised
her to find a few trustworthy souls in the White House who
could keep her up-to-date. In other words, she had to become more like the people she served—reporters—and check
with a range of sources to make sure she was not missing
things. It was an odd state of affairs, but she had no choice
but to accept it. It was the best they were offering. She also
began to cultivate Lake as a primary informant.

But first Myers had to face the wrath of the press corps. On
Monday, June 28, reporters demanded to know why she had
lied to them. It became the first of a long series of briefings
that degenerated into what one reporter called "Dee Dee
abuse."

"Dee Dee, you've been reported to be concerned about the impact of the weekend on your credibility," one questioner began. "Can you talk about that a little bit, your concerns?"

"Well," she replied, "it was an honest mistake, something that we've had a number of conversations about here and something that we'll try to change in the future."

But that was not the end of it. Reporters hurled question after question about her faulty answer on Friday. Myers stood for it all, maintaining some semblance of composure. But it was a distasteful experience she vowed never to repeat if she could help it.

Privately, she could not get over the vitriol with which she had to deal routinely. "There are a lot of things about Washington that are very mean-spirited," she said. "There isn't a culture here that reinforces people's success. It's always at somebody's expense."

Through it all, Myers was still able to find—and enjoy—those few, special White House moments she knew would always glow in memory. The brightest was on Wednesday, September 1, her thirty-second birthday. She was working in her office when Ricki Seidman marched in with a surprise guest. General Colin Powell was in the building for a meeting and had agreed to stop by to wish the press secretary well. Like all of Myers's friends, Seidman knew what a crush she had on Powell. He was, after all, a military brat's dreamboat. So it was one of Myers's best days when the handsome chairman of the Joint Chiefs of Staff sang "Happy Birthday" to her.

She also cherished other times, such as when, before the Middle East treaty signing, she watched Clinton talk by telephone to Syria's President Assad while simultaneously reviewing his mail and signing letters, all with a cigar in his mouth. And there was the look on her sister's face while she took part in what was by then routine—a conference call that included the secretary of state, the secretary of defense, and the national security adviser. "It goes by so fast you hardly have time to see it," she marveled.

But she also realized this was not the job she wanted to be in when she was fifty years old. It took almost everything she had just to keep track of the volume of events of the day. During the presidential campaign, she had been able to let down a little, turn off the world every once in a while. But at the White House, she did not get a minute to breathe. "One day we have to deal with Somalia, and tomorrow it's something else," she said. "It's relentless."

It also was a lonely life, especially for someone accustomed to having lots of friends around. It was hard to work so many hours, often to such little effect and in such cold isolation. Although she was deluged with invitations to official events around Washington, Myers disliked attending them and rarely did. She was not a party person. In fact, she did not much enjoy going out at all, except with close friends, and did not have much time to even do that. She had taken advantage only once of the free tickets to the Kennedy Center that were available to White House aides. And on many nights her recreation was pulling a cap over her head and jogging up Massachusetts Avenue, hoping no one would recognize her. "She's personally unhappy," Jeff Eller reported after a long talk with his friend. "And she doesn't know what to do about it." In that she was not alone.

Myers's chores became even harder under the pall of the Whitewater scandal in 1994. While she traveled with the President on a series of state visits in Europe that January, even the Democrats started to speak out with ominous regularity about the need for Clinton to name a special counsel. These included such mainstays as Senators Daniel Moynihan of New York and Charles Robb of Virginia. The senior staff at the White House had to field dozens of calls from worried friends, including Jody Powell, the press secretary to President Carter. The questions were pretty much the same:

"What are you guys doing?" The Clintons were refusing to budge on an issue that was obviously a no-winner for them.

Myers reluctantly agreed with those who called for a special counsel. But she was powerless to change the President's mind, and the President, of course, did not ask her view. So she tried to make the best of her stay in Europe. On Tuesday night, January 11, she and a few fellow staff geeks—as she liked to call them—visited the Old City of Prague, drank beer, and listened to live jazz. It was one of those rare and glorious times on the road when all the cares of the world, which were usually her staple, were laid aside. She just had fun. "The whole night," she said, "was like I was in someone else's night."

Later, while Myers was asleep, Clinton conducted a conference call with others at the White House, including Stephanopoulos and Begala. The aides beseeched the President to agree to a special counsel. And he came close to accepting, only to pull back in his usual fashion. He said he wanted to sleep on it. On Wednesday, January 12, he bowed to reality and gave his assent for a statement to be prepared.

Myers found out about the decision late—when she got to the ambassador's residence that morning. And if she had not been told, she would have guessed. Clinton was at his surliest, and even though his press secretary had not been given the courtesy of sitting in on the calls that decided the issue, she bore the brunt of his reaction to their outcome. The President was about to shoot the messenger again.

Myers arranged television interviews with the President later that day, but she had reached an understanding with the reporters that they would ask about a new denuclearization pact and not anything else, including Whitewater. The Whitewater news was so big, however, that NBC could not resist. Afterward, Myers caught hell. Out of camera range, Clinton launched into one of his yelling fits.

Clearly, Myers knew, the outburst was part of his larger anger—at Washington and his own loss of privacy to what would surely become a major investigation. But, as the nearest staffer at the moment, she had to take the heat. As he shouted, Clinton thrust his finger at her with that nasty twist of the wrist she had come to dread. "That's my life," she said, still trying to keep in her mind the glorious night before, "swinging between extreme highs and lows." And her eyes turned to slits again.

Myers struggled to keep as even a keel as she could. On Monday, February 14, she spent the morning taking phone calls, watching television out of the corner of an eye, and reading through her constantly growing stack of memos informing her about what was happening throughout the White House. She kept three folders of memos on her desk. One was about foreign policy, the second dealt with domestic issues, and the third with administrative matters. She plowed through a few issue papers, including a draft decision memo on welfare reform, which she sardonically marveled had not yet leaked to the press, as many earlier versions had.

Since the debacle of the Iraqi attack, she had worked hard to stay better informed. And thanks to Tony Lake, she had done especially well with foreign affairs. After their collision in June, the two had struck up a working friendship that allowed them to remain in steady and largely informal contact during the course of every day. Sometimes Myers would walk the few steps to Lake's office or he would drop by hers. He also would insist she sit in on many important meetings. In just the previous week, she had observed a meeting on Bosnia in the Oval Office that included both Lake and Secretary of State Warren Christopher. With the blessing of Lake and McLarty, who also had developed into an ally, Myers became a frequent participant in more and more high-level meetings.

She attributed the change in part to Lake's guilt over having failed to keep her informed about the President's decision to bomb Baghdad. But over time, she and Lake also struck up a rapport. Unlike other men in the White House, he was accustomed to dealing with women in the normal course of business; he had taught at the all-female Mt. Holyoke College for years. Myers also believed they had a lot in common that helped them communicate. He was the father of two daughters; she had two sisters. In any case, she found herself better informed.

She also was better liked, not just by the press corps, who sensed she had a somewhat better understanding of events inside the White House, but also within the government itself. And it was true. That afternoon, for instance, she was visited by Lieutenant General Barry McCaffrey, the flag rank officer who had been snubbed early in the Clinton administration by a young White House staffer who told him she did not talk to anyone from the military. After that incident, Myers sought him out and discussed the problem. To help make amends, Myers also gave McCaffrey's daughter a job in her office over the summer. Both actions helped repair troubled relations between the White House and the Pentagon, and also made Myers a good friend in McCaffrey. "He's one of my favorite characters," she said lightheartedly, thinking that, maybe, things were beginning to look up.

A lot of people work Saturdays. But when shopkeepers, for instance, go to work, the most exciting thing that happens is a sale. In contrast, when Myers worked on the weekend, it was usually because some part of the world was about to change forever, and the most powerful nation on earth needed to comment. Saturday, May 7, was one of those days. A new mass exodus from the impoverished island nation of Haiti required the attention of all the top policy makers at the White House. And, thanks to Lake, Myers was included in the 9:30 A.M. meeting in the White House residence to discuss the options.

The President had worried for weeks about reports of increased violence in Haiti as well as the exile of its democratically elected leader, Jean-Bertrand Aristide. Now, the outpouring of boat people was forcing him to act. So he met with his top national security advisers for two hours and decided to start a new effort to manage the influx of Haitian refugees by establishing immigration centers on ships and in cooperative third-party countries.

Myers was not an important voice in determining the policy; in fact, she had no voice in that at all. But she did recommend how to disseminate the policy makers' decisions. "It will leak," she warned, and, for once, they listened. She advised them to disclose the new policy selectively by giving the details to the major newspapers that publish on weekends: *The New York Times, The Washington Post,* and the *Los Angeles Times.* Their Sunday editions print what amounts to the weekend gospel in national news, and their reporters could be counted on to get the facts right and to place them in context. The national security aides agreed.

So Myers asked her assistant, David Leavy, to contact the White House reporters from each publication. When he reached them, Myers told them there had been a change in policy on Haiti, and Lake would fill them in on background. The stories in the papers the next day carefully outlined the new policy in the same straightforward way Lake had described it to the reporters. And they helped form the basis for questions to Sandy Berger, his deputy, who appeared on *Meet the Press.*

What Myers knew, but did not tell the reporters, was that former congressman William Gray of Pennsylvania was under consideration as special envoy to Haiti. She had seen Gray on the White House grounds late Saturday afternoon and asked him if he had decided to accept the post. Gray, a Baptist minister, said he had not. "I'm going home to talk to my wife and pray," he said. So she stayed mum about his role. When he accepted the next day, she arranged a Rose Garden announcement and, to follow, a larger briefing on the new policy she already had planted in the morning newspapers. In Monday's *Washington Post,* reporter Ann Devroy wrote, "Clinton's announcements accomplished the immediate political goal of quieting the intense criticism of his policies at home, primarily from Democrats." For once, and with enough help from the rest of the staff, Myers had done her job well.

But she was still not in the first tier. The white boys' club would not let her in. Proof came on Monday, June 27, which began like any other day for Myers. She came in for the early-morning meetings, talked afterward to the few reporters who were hanging around, and began to prepare for her afternoon briefing. But there was something more in the air; she could sense it. The extra phone calls. The furtive shuttling between offices that usually were not so active so early. Something in the tightened way McLarty was sitting during one meeting they both attended. Still, she did not know for sure. And, as in the old days, nobody was confiding in her. She had to wait until whatever was going to happen, happened.

She waited all morning. She waited into the afternoon. No one told her anything, so she went out to do her regular briefing soon after one o'clock ignorant of what she felt sure was a major change in the offing. And, of course, she could say nothing to the reporters. It was not until after she finished that Gergen came into Gearan's office. To Myers, Gergen looked like the Cat in the Hat who ate the canary. The expression on his face said to her that he knew a big secret everyone was going to find hard to believe.

Gergen escorted Myers and Gearan to McLarty's office, where McLarty explained the news: he was stepping down as chief of staff and was going to be replaced by Leon Panetta. The air seemed to go out of the sunny, light-carpeted room. Somehow, Myers maintained her composure. She felt bad for McLarty, who spoke with confidence but, to her eye, seemed ambivalent at best about the change. She had only good feelings for Panetta, whom she respected as a straight shooter. And, despite his failure to give her the support she needed to do her job, she had a warm spot for McLarty as well. She liked him even though she remained one of the last to know.

At the moment, though, the main issue was not personal but professional: how should the White House announce the change? Myers thought that doing her job well, and without fuss, was the best response she could offer. Vice President Gore, who was also in the meeting, urged rapid dissemination. President Clinton was scheduled to go to New York to give a speech later in the day, so the announcement should come before that. "I can feel this thing is about to go," Gore said. "It's going to leak, let's announce it." So Myers and her staff dutifully arranged for cameras to be carted into the Oval Office for an impromptu announcement of the biggest change in the White House staff since the start of the administration.

For the rest of the day, Myers coordinated media appearances for McLarty and Panetta. She was flooded with requests and, in consultation with both men, agreed that most of them should be honored. "We decided to put our people out there at every opportunity, fill up the space. That would leave less time for pundits," she said. The best shot that night for McLarty and Panetta, she believed, was on *Larry King Live,* never heavy going for Clinton officials. Under the show's format, McLarty and Panetta would be allowed to appear together, sitting side by side, which was just the image Myers wanted to project. She was unable to watch them, though, because she had to appear on a different show to tout the virtues of the new arrangement, ambiguous though they might be.

The interview bumped along uneventfully until King asked a surprisingly pointed question: "All management brings changes. Can we expect to see some changes in the press office and other places?"

"Well, as I indicated today, there will be more changes," Panetta replied, tellingly. "But I want a few weeks to be able to review the operation there. I want to look at every office. And I then want to make recommendations to the President."

"Would it be likely you'd bring in your own press person?"

"It's likely, obviously," Panetta said, shoving the knife in deeper. "I'm going to bring in some of my own people to try to assist me in that effort, sure."

"Now," King bore in, "let's say if Dee Dee Myers moves, would you make another place for her in the White House?"

But before Panetta could answer, McLarty interrupted with some of his usual drivel. The damage already was done, though, and Myers's minions, who were watching the show, went into a minor panic.

The telephone rang in her apartment sometime after ten o'clock. It was Ginny Terzano.

"Did you see *Larry King*?" she asked, speaking rapidly.

"No," Myers replied mildly.

"You're going to have to look at the tape or the transcript," Terzano advised. "You'll be asked questions about it."

"What happened?"

"He talked about Dee Dee Myers."

"What about Dee Dee Myers?"

"Panetta sort of left you hanging out there."

No one bothered to comment on the oddity of finding out that Myers's job was endangered by watching the new boss on national TV. That was just the Clinton White House. And it was just as routine for Terzano to fax a copy of the *Larry King* transcript to *Air Force One* on the ground in New York.

But that was where the routine ended. Harold Ickes, the deputy chief of staff, grabbed the transcript and went to see the President. A short while later, Bruce Lindsey joined them in the flying Oval Office. After poring over Panetta's words, the President called the Vice President and then telephoned Panetta. Their decision: the new chief of staff was to call Myers that night and retract his statement. It had all been a big misunderstanding.

At midnight, Myers was awakened by a phone call. It was the White House operator calling on behalf of Panetta.

"God, I'm really sorry," he said. "I didn't mean to imply that I had anything less than full confidence in you. It's really unfortunate."

"I appreciate your calling," Myers responded. "I thought you left me hanging out there a little bit."

"Well, I didn't want to leave you hanging out there a little bit. Let's talk in the morning."

At the senior staff meeting the next day, Ickes, Lindsey, and Stephanopoulos all approached Myers separately to ask if Panetta had called. She was encouraged by the show of solidarity. She was just as pleased when, in front of the entire top echelon of the White House staff, Panetta repeated his apology. "I honestly do not believe he meant to leave the impression that he left," Myers said later. "Nonetheless, he should have seen it coming. He's a pretty savvy guy." And she wondered if there had not been a kernel of truth in the slip.

Her relatively revived spirits sank as soon as she emerged to face the scathing questions from reporters who were hovering near her office. The tone was So, when do you clean out your desk? When she was unable to answer credibly—after all, she was not her own boss—she telephoned Panetta's office and spoke to his personal press aide, Barry Toiv. "I really would appreciate it if you would call the Associated Press and knock the story down," she said. And Toiv did—which helped. But the questions persisted because Panetta had not made the call himself.

Meanwhile, McLarty invited Myers to his office. He told her he saw the problem coming on *Larry King Live* and regretted he missed his chance to correct it when he could have. According to Myers, he also told her, "I failed to promote the people who worked hard and always supported the President, and I did not punish those who supported the President only when it was to their benefit." Myers took this as a belated thank-you, and she was genuinely saddened by the thought of it.

Then she went to do her regular briefing, and it turned into another nightmare. Without Panetta defending her on the record, she was forced to defend herself—an untenable position. A few of the reporters, she believed, went out of their way to humiliate her. And afterward she was irate. She had tried to suck up her pride and go out there and do her job. But she felt abused. Making her perform in front of the heartless press corps without any tangible support was despicable, she thought. She knew it would take months to recover from the slight—if recovery were possible. And that would not serve the President well. It certainly did not serve her. She felt naked before the barbarians.

After her beating in the briefing room, Myers's friends on the staff rallied around her. Jeff Eller was one of the first to call. "I feel your pain," he said, trying to make her laugh. Terzano did more than call. She went to Stephanopoulos and started screaming that Myers deserved better treatment, and he agreed completely. The anxiety everyone was feeling over getting a new boss was being transferred onto the press secretary and her very public plight. "There's a sense," Myers said, "that nobody is safe."

Panetta tried again to apologize and made some calls to reporters himself. But the damage was done. And the story was plausible. She was still not getting the support inside she needed, and everyone knew it. "I was given responsibility that exceeded my authority, and it has put me in a continually difficult position," she said. "I think this happens to women a lot. There was a lot of chattering about this among the chick feminist types. You get the title, but you don't get the job." It looked to Myers and her friends as if the white boys were beginning to make their move.

Myers did not give up easily, though. No one becomes White House press secretary without throwing some sharp elbows every once in a while. So, she thought, maybe the blowup was the chance she needed to make her case to improve the job. Maybe she finally could make it work. "It's an opportunity for me, with some downside risk," she said. "Either things happen or they can find some other goat. I'm out of patience. I can't keep working under these circumstances." For the first time, she thought about leaving the White House.

Myers began to think of her job as "the appendix" of the White House staff—a part of the body that "once had a function but no longer does." And while it was never that bad, it was close. Although she was seen around the world as the spokesperson for the President and, in many ways, the United States, her real job most of the time was not to make news but to prevent news from being made. Not to give information but to withhold it.

Like the appendix, the worst thing she could be was a problem—by making a mistake or giving the wrong impression about the President's policy. But otherwise, like her title—indeed, like her very presence on the staff as the first woman press secretary—the entire function of the office was mostly for show. Her words were more a diversion from the real work going on behind closed doors or an elaborate excuse for the many mistakes that the White House was prone to make each day.

Myers could only shake her head at the changes she had seen. It had been just a year and a half ago that she and fellow staffer Degee Wilhelm, the wife of Democratic party chairman David Wilhelm, had been thrilled at the thought of sitting in a presidential limousine. And when they got the chance, they jumped at it. Once, while the rest of Clinton's entourage stepped into the White House, the two aides, with the winking assent of friendly Secret Service agents, ducked into the President's big black car. "We sort of like checked it out," Myers recalled gleefully. "We felt the leather on the backseat and the doors. We had a good laugh. We were like little kids, playing with things in the garage you're not supposed to touch." But now that thrill was gone.

The afternoon of Saturday, July 2, was simple and slow, two things the White House was not. The reason for the change of pace was that Myers spent the end of the day outside the White House. Diane Begala had told her husband, Paul, "We have to have Dee Dee over, she's really hurting." So, at Paul Begala's invitation, Myers made her way out to the couple's suburban home. The diversion was much appreciated—by everyone. Begala grilled some chicken and served it cold. He drank beer. The women drank wine. They all played with little Johnny Begala on the living-room floor.

It was a time of relaxation and comradeship but also of reflection. How the world had changed for them! Here they were, two heroes of the historic, come-from-behind 1992 presidential campaign, and both were having major problems less than two years later. News stories continued to hint that Myers was a short-timer at the White House, and there were new rumblings, presumably from Panetta's office, that Begala and the other political consultants were not as welcome as they used to be. In any case, as Panetta gradually took control, he limited access to the Oval Office, and that meant even less contact with their boss for both Myers and Begala.

But neither was a quitter. Myers in particular was flattered by a surprise job offer that her friend Eller would have killed for. John Deutch, the deputy defense secretary, knowing about her family's military background and her ongoing relationship with military personnel, asked Myers to replace Kathleen deLaski, the Pentagon spokesperson, who was going on maternity leave. That, of course, was the job Eller had been hoping would be his lifeline out of the White House mess. But Myers was giving it serious consideration. She told Deutch she would think about it now that life inside had turned so mad.

· · ·

Nobody likes to confront the boss, and Myers was no different. She wanted to avoid any more harsh words. Instead, she wanted to ease the situation by directing the dispute more positively. She decided she would try to focus on making the position she held more workable. So on Thursday, July 7, when Panetta dropped by her office, she tried a friendly approach.

"The job of press secretary has to be strengthened," Myers said, a little nervous but eager to make things better. "You need to have a credible spokesman."

In White Houses past, she explained, the daily briefing was considered a strategic tool for the president, a chance for him to make news and to shape the national coverage of Washington. But for whatever reason—Clinton's disdain for the press or merely a lack of understanding of what a press secretary can accomplish—Myers was never given the chance to do that. Her briefings, she complained, were mostly pabulum and were ignored by both the press and the staff. And it did not help, she asserted, that there were so many other, better-connected sources for reporters, especially Gergen.

She refrained from making another point she often discussed with friends. "It's kind of a guy thing around here," she was wont to say, meaning women were not put on an equal footing with their male counterparts in the White House. Even Laura Tyson, chairman of the Council of Economic Advisers, confided to others that she had felt talked down to—or around—on several occasions. Myers believed she and Tyson were victims of the same problem. But she chose not to mention it to Panetta that day. She did not need any more tension between herself and her supervisor. Who does?

She did, though, make her bottom line absolutely clear. "Cut me in or cut me loose," she said. "It's not good for me, it's not good for the White House, it's not good for the President."

In response, Panetta said he was still learning how the communications department worked, what Myers did, and how her job differed from Mark Gearan's. But he agreed that the press secretary should be given more information and authority. He did not have much to say about Gergen one way or the other. He also was careful not to promise too much. "I'm not sure where this all is going to come out," he said. "Don't read too much into this; I just haven't made a decision."

In other words, he agreed that the press secretary ought to be given more opportunity to make an impact, but he did not commit to giving that chance to Myers. Still, she was encouraged. Maybe Panetta would come through where others had not. Maybe the white boys' cabal was about to be broken—at least a little. So she decided to turn down the Pentagon job and lay it all on the line. She would either secure a better situation where she was or find work elsewhere.

Myers's optimism was shaken in Naples, Italy, later that month, when she witnessed one of the worst examples of exclusion since she had come to Washington. Clinton and his team were in Europe for a meeting of the leaders of the major industrial nations. And in the middle of it, the value of the dollar dipped in a way that caused alarm and required a presidential comment.

The meeting to decide what to say and how to act included many of the biggest names on the President's economic team: Secretary of the Treasury Lloyd Bentsen and the chairman of the Council of Economic Advisers, Laura Tyson, as well as senior economic aides Larry Summers and Bo Cutter, among others. But the way the advisers were arrayed was almost a caricature of the problem Myers and her women colleagues discussed so often among themselves.

Around the table at which the President sat were all of the men, even such nonpolicy types as Gearan, the communications director. Against the wall on chairs were the women, including Myers, the trade aide Joan Spiro, and, to Myers's shock and dismay, Laura Tyson.

The situation was made worse by how the men monopolized the discussion. Tyson, who is an expert in international economic matters, tried several times to speak, but the men at the table talked over her words. Myers and Tyson had seen that happen many times before, but Myers was aghast that it would occur on an issue in which Tyson should certainly have been a major voice.

"Laura finally almost started shouting," Myers said, and Clinton recognized her to talk and, in the end, largely took her advice. But the spectacle was disconcerting, to say the least. As the two women walked out after the meeting, Myers said, "It's shocking what just happened to you," and Tyson obviously agreed. It was not the first time it had happened, and both women knew it would not be the last.

Back in Washington, from out of nowhere, Myers was handed an unlikely escape route. One morning her assistant, Dave Leavy, wandered glassy-eyed into her office and said, "Satan left a message on our voice mail." Roger Ailes, the former Republican advertising expert and then president of CNBC, the talk television network, had telephoned for Myers. He wanted to know if she was interested in leaving the White House to cohost CNBC's *Equal Time* with Mary Matalin.

Myers thought the change might be fun. She liked Matalin. She liked the idea of working less and making a huge sum of money. A new job would at least end the nagging uncertainty about her position in the White House; Panetta had still not made up his mind about how to reorganize the staff. But, on reflection, the timing did not seem right. She would call Ailes back and tell him no—for now.

On Monday, August 15, Myers was ready for another chat with Panetta. Her access to decision makers had not improved, and news stories about her imminent departure continued to appear. When they met in his office that day, she tried to be straightforward. She said she would do whatever

Panetta wanted. She would do anything the President wished. But she did not want to remain a target of damaging speculation. Please, she pleaded, let her know where she stood.

But she did not get an answer. The dire straits of the Clinton agenda, especially the crime and health bills, were more than Panetta was able to handle. Stopping the public anguish of the White House press secretary was not his top priority. So Myers tried a different approach. She began to contact her friends around Washington and ask them to make appeals to Panetta on her behalf. If he would not listen to her, maybe he would listen to them.

She called Jody Powell; Vernon Jordan, the President's confidant and golfing partner; and Mack McLarty. She asked each to deliver a message: if Panetta wanted her to leave, he should tell her so. But if she was going to stay, make the job a real one. Give her access and clout. In other words, give Myers a chance.

The tactic was very sophisticated—indeed, very Washingtonian—for someone who liked to pretend she was just another "California girl." But Myers was much more able than the men in charge of the White House were ever willing to give her credit for. The white boys always seemed so willing to underestimate her. But that had to stop. It was time—past time—for her to make clear she would not allow that to go on.

Still, the struggle was beating her down. Normally so cheery, Myers began to look tired and forlorn. Her eyes were sunken and had dark circles underneath them. She began to snap at any reporter who inquired about her future. When one reporter inquired, sympathetically, about how she was feeling, she retorted that she was "sick and tired" of being asked. "People are watching me too closely," she complained, with a new testiness in her voice. "I don't think you can argue things are going well. It's not been an easy couple of months." She did not know how much longer she could take it.

·   ·   ·

In the meantime, Myers had work to do. At that moment she was up to her ears in Haiti. At least she was supposed to be. But, despite repeated requests for help, she was often among the last staffers to know the President's plans. Even her old ally Tony Lake let her down. "He's very supportive of me personally," Myers said. "But when it comes to letting go of information, he doesn't think the press is very important." It was back to square one, again.

At the same time, she knew Panetta had talked to the State Department spokesman, Michael McCurry, about a job of some kind in the communications operation at the White House, presumably press secretary. McCurry himself had told her about his conversation with Panetta during one of their regular conference calls on the tumultuous situation in Haiti. He even wondered aloud with her whether he would accept an offer if one were made. "It's so sick," Myers reflected.

It also had been eighty endless days since Panetta took over, and still there was no word about how he might restructure the staff. "Has it served anybody?" Myers asked testily. She did not think so. "If they want someone old and more male than me, OK. I'm a big girl," she said. "I wouldn't be happy about it, but I would leave." She told friends she suspected Panetta wanted a male face and voice as the White House spokesperson, especially when an invasion of Haiti loomed. "They want an older, balder white guy," Myers said, but the longer her limbo lasted, the more she wanted to hear Panetta say so himself—while looking her in the eye.

On the day former president Carter set off on his peace mission to Haiti, Myers declared war on Leon Panetta. In a meeting in his office, he finally suggested a restructuring plan for the communications department. But it was not at all what Myers wanted. There would be a press secretary and then another person, in effect a deputy, who did briefings and traveled with the President. That second person, she guessed, would be Dee Dee Myers.

"No, Leon!" she protested, no longer reticent or nervous. Now she was angry, and she allowed her voice to rise. She had been patient and loyal enough. It was time to take a stand. "The new structure doesn't work. You can't set it up this way." Then she added, "If you're thinking I'm going to take this job, I'm not. You know what my bottom line is. I don't begrudge the President at all if he wants to make this change. But I'm not interested in doing the same job. It's not good for him. It's not good for you. It's not good for me. It's not good for the press secretary."

She said it looked to her as if Panetta were trying to fit the structure of the office around her, perhaps because the President liked having her around. Well, she said, that was what had happened to begin with. It did not work then, she said, and it did not work now. "I'm not going to let you do it," she said. "I'm not going to be party to this bad decision. You have to have one person, and it's got to be clear. You can't split this job up." Then she said boldly that if the job of press secretary were restructured in the right way, she would like to have it. "Fix the job, put me in it," she said. "Everybody wins."

"All right," Panetta replied, a little exasperated. "I get your point. I'll take this back to the President."

Myers came away thinking Panetta was no further along than he had been nearly three months before. And she started to ready herself, psychologically, to depart.

On Sunday, September 18, McCurry was in the West Wing helping to ascertain the details of President Carter's success in defusing the Haiti crisis. In the middle of the day, he propped his feet on Gearan's desk, the one usually reserved for the press secretary, and said aloud and within Myers's hearing, "I could get used to this."

A couple of days later, Dave Leavy stumbled into Myers's office with a piece of paper in his hand and a cross look on his face. The paper was McCurry's résumé. It had just been faxed to the press secretary's office from the State Department. News stories had continued to hint that more than McCurry's résumé was coming, and here was further proof— as if any were needed.

Without Myers's knowledge, McCurry was scheduled to meet with Panetta at the White House on the night of Wednesday, September 21, but when McCurry got into his car, he discovered its battery was dead. So he walked from the State Department. When he arrived, a little winded, Panetta gave him a pitch similar to the one he had given Myers. McCurry would become the real press secretary, and Myers, in effect, would be his deputy. McCurry was flattered but said he did not think Myers would play a secondary role. And if she remained in the communications department, there would be no place for him. "I don't think you've got the Dee Dee piece set yet," he told Panetta in the shorthand of Washington insiders, and he left without being offered a job.

Still, the next day produced a series of news stories saying, in effect, that McCurry was about to replace Myers. Reuters even ran a story under the headline "STATE DEPARTMENT AIDE TO BECOME CLINTON SPOKESMAN." Upon seeing it, Myers demanded to speak to Panetta, which she finally was able to do that afternoon. "I asked you two things three months ago. First, don't leave me twisting in the wind, and, second, I don't want to read about my replacement on the wires, and now I've done that," she said.

In response, Panetta began to shout. He said the problem was all her fault. He accused her of planting the story about McCurry, which she denied. He also said he had not offered any jobs to anybody. And if he wanted to talk to McCurry, so what? She knew he was talking to people.

"I'm not telling you what to do, but I don't think I'm asking too much not to read about my replacement on Reuters," she said.

After a while they both stopped yelling, and Panetta said,

"You need to meet with the President; he wants to talk to you." By then it was about two o'clock. Myers canceled her briefing and went to see the President's scheduling assistant, Nancy Hernreich. The meeting was set for 6:30.

In the interim, she sat down in Gearan's office and exclaimed, "He's screwed me, I'm dead." Several of her friends urged her to call Roger Ailes immediately. But, in a telephone conversation, Mary Matalin suggested she wait. Ailes liked to deal with people in a weakened state. Besides, Myers's women friends said she should not give up too soon. It was a matter of principle; the women finally had to be heard. Even Stephanopoulos agreed. He came into Myers's office and said, "Don't do anything. Don't do anything! You haven't talked to the President. He's not going to let you walk out of here. Don't do anything until you've talked to him."

Maggie Williams heard about the contretemps and invited Myers to come upstairs to her office. Myers slumped into a chair while Williams tried to liven her spirits with some peach schnapps she kept around for such occasions. They talked about Williams's new boyfriend, who worked elsewhere in the administration. They talked about lots of things. Myers stayed there for about two hours, trying to collect her thoughts.

How far she had come in such a short time! She thought back to her first day in the West Wing and the shock it had been. The building itself was not impressive. It was a low-slung bunker appended to the western end of the much more stately White House mansion, which contains the president's residence and a variety of lavish rooms for ceremonies of state. But the ninety-year-old West Wing was not lavish at all. It's so small! Myers thought when she stepped inside—more like a crowded old townhouse than the workplace of a president. It was clean, well appointed with lots of dark wood and walls painted white, of course. But it was tiny by modern standards, a warren of cramped spaces connected by narrow corridors and narrower stairwells. "I had no idea what connected to what," she said. "I had no idea where I was or how I was supposed to get there."

Luckily, soon after she stepped into the building's lobby, she ran into Jeff Eller, who had been casing the place for hours. He showed her down a hallway that took her past the Roosevelt Room. A right turn would have taken them to the Oval Office. Instead, they ducked left into a doorway that led straight to her office. At the sight of it, Myers took a deep breath. In her native California, brooms were given more room. If she took more than three steps after entering, she would have walked right out the window. How could this, she had wondered, be the most powerful place on earth? Maybe, in fact, it wasn't. And now she knew she was right. It was just another high-pressure workplace, and it was time for one employee to demand her due.

Myers decided she was not going to get squeezed out. If the President told her she had to find another job, she would be gone in a heartbeat. But there was no way she was going to allow Panetta and the others to decide by *not* deciding. That would be too easy for them, and too cowardly. Clearly that was what Panetta was trying to do: get her to leave without telling her to go. And Myers said to herself, Hell no!

Off and on she had tried to talk to Clinton about the problem. Just a couple of weeks earlier she had given him her rap about fixing the job and putting her in it during a flight on *Air Force One*. But his response was noncommittal. "Yeah, yeah, you're right," he said, absently. But she did not know if he meant, yeah, she should have the job, or yeah, the job should be restructured, or yeah, she should find somewhere else to work. And she did not press the point. She knew how bad he was on personnel matters and, at the time, did not want to take advantage of their friendship. She wanted him to do the right thing for himself.

But now the crunch had come. Right before the President was scheduled to attend a rhythm and blues concert on the South Lawn, Myers was ushered into the Oval Office. What was said there will always be mostly a matter of conjecture. Out of loyalty to Clinton, Myers refuses to talk publicly about their conversation. But she did tell friends what transpired between the President and herself that night.

Clinton sat behind his desk, and Myers took a small seat next to it. She began by expressing how disappointed she was. She had not asked for a lot, basically only not to be left twisting in the wind. She had given Panetta every opportunity, had even sent messengers to convey her thoughts. But nothing had worked. Now everything was out of control. She had tried to stop it but could not. She had done everything she could to protect herself—and the President—from bad publicity. But here they were anyway.

Clinton said he felt terrible about the turn the story had taken as well. He was upset about everything that had happened to Myers. He did not blame anyone; he had let the issue fester as much as anyone else had. And, in his own way, he apologized for mishandling her situation. He said he had not meant for any of it to happen. He also talked about the problems he had with communications, problems that went well beyond Myers. He talked about mistakes and worries and the need to get back on track. He spoke more frankly than Myers had heard for a long time. He acknowledged he had put people in the wrong jobs. He admitted he had spent too much time selecting his cabinet and not enough picking the more important White House staff. Some good people had gotten a bad deal.

When he returned to her, his voice turned soft. He said he got up every day and read quotations in the newspapers attributed to "senior White House officials" that invariably belittled him or his programs. But he said he knew none of those ever came from her. She was completely loyal, and that meant a lot to him. "I know in my heart and in my soul that you have never done that," he said. "You are unfailingly professional, and I feel like you're a member of my family."

At that moment, he started to cry. And so did Myers. Then, speaking as if they were family, each said, in turn, "I love you."

"I want you to be happy. I don't want this to happen," he said.

"I don't want this to happen either," she replied.

"I am so sorry for the way this has happened."

"I don't blame *you*."

In the end, they talked it through and decided she should stay. In some ways, he almost left it up to her. But, as with so much about Clinton, there remained some ambiguity. She made clear how angry she was about the way she had been treated. She also said she was going to leave—and soon. She did not think things would ever really change for her, especially with Panetta looking over her shoulder.

After the meeting, which lasted more than an hour, Myers saw Panetta. She knew her job status was up to her, but, oddly, she did not feel comfortable talking about it. She said she thought she was going to stay. And Panetta said he had thought that was how it was going to turn out.

Even before she reached her office, the wires were reporting that Myers had met with the President. When she stepped in her doorway, she saw some of her many friends—Rahm Emanuel, Mark Gearan, and George Stephanopoulos—stuffed into the tiny space, waiting eagerly for the outcome. "Good," Stephanopoulos said, reading her face. "It's done." Her job was saved.

The next day, Friday, September 23, the first day of autumn, Leon Panetta ate crow. He announced his long-awaited staff restructuring. One of the changes was the unexpected promotion of Myers. "The press secretary to the President will be Dee Dee Myers, and both the President and I have full confi-

dence in her ability to handle that role," he said, obviously
fibbing. "She will be an assistant to the President, she will
have direct access to the Oval Office, and we have full confidence that she has the ability to fulfill that responsibility." He
claimed not to have known about Myers's visit with the President, even though, of course, he did. And under intense
questioning about McCurry, Panetta retreated to this response: "The President has decided who he wants for his
press secretary, and that's Dee Dee Myers."

Myers was not around for the press conference. With
everything else happening, she had to face a family crisis. Her
sister Betsy was in the hospital for surgery and had had a bad
reaction to the anesthesia. She wanted Dee Dee by her side,
and Myers went right away. She did not know what Panetta
was saying or doing and did not especially care. But after the
press conference, and while she was still tending to her sib-
ling, Panetta called and upbraided her—in the hospital. "I
just walked across hot coals as if it were my fault!" he shouted
and did not even ask how Myers's sister was doing. The
episode made her feel, literally, ill.

Others were far more charitable. Leavy paged Myers at the
hospital periodically. "You have thirty-seven phone calls."
"You have fifty-five phone calls," the messages read. When
she came back to her office that evening, there was no place
for her to sit. It was filled with five bouquets of flowers and
four dozen roses, not to mention telegrams, notes, and faxes
of support.

Calls of congratulations came from both ends of the political spectrum. Conservative Republican senator Orrin Hatch
of Utah telephoned to say, "I don't really know what's going
on down there, but I just want you to know that I'm thinking
about you, and I hope it all works out well for you. You have
always been kind to me personally, and you have been tough
but fair to me and my Republican colleagues professionally.
I just wanted you to know that I respect you and I hope that it
works out for you." Later she got a call from Democratic

senator Tom Harkin of Iowa. "That son of a bitch Mike McCurry, I never trusted him," he said. "I'm glad he [Clinton] did the right thing. God damn, I'm glad he knows who's loyal to him."

News accounts of Panetta's announcement said that his long-anticipated shake-up amounted to barely a vibration, and that the major happening was that the press secretary had rolled the chief of staff. That was not a good outcome for anyone. Myers was joyful she had won, but she also worried it might be a Pyrrhic victory. And already there were signs her worries were well-founded. Other staffers at the White House made sure every reporter who called about the changes knew that Myers had said she intended to leave the White House soon, certainly by year's end. So on the very day she got what she most wanted, she already was headed for the door.

At the same time, Myers became something of a folk hero, especially to women who empathized with her plight. Shortly thereafter, during a trip to New York City, she was given a high five by a woman in the street who was a perfect stranger. Whenever she ate out, her table was filled with drinks bought by worshipful fellow diners. And she began to get calls from everywhere with job offers for when she left the White House, which they knew would be soon: CNN's *Crossfire,* Warner Bros., and, once again, Roger Ailes.

Back at work, Myers became persona non grata with Panetta. If she had had limited access before her run-in with him, she had none afterward. She increasingly found it hard to get even basic information. It was obvious to everyone Panetta was determined she would make good on her intention to leave soon, perhaps by year's end—if not sooner. In the meantime, she was treated with little respect. At more than one meeting of the senior staff, Panetta would act as if Myers were not in the room, pointedly asking others to answer questions that should have been directed at the press secretary. She was not welcome, so she made plans to say good-bye. She managed to extend her tenure into December, then bowed to the pressure. Her replacement, of course, was Mike McCurry.

She began her briefing, to a packed audience, this way: "Well, this is an impressive turnout here for my final briefing, so I prepared a couple things that I thought you would— I just didn't think it would be appropriate for me to leave without going through those Clinton accomplishments one more time."

"Oh, noooo!" the reporters shouted, laughing.

A few minutes later, the President walked in without warning. "Oh, my God!" Myers exclaimed in honest surprise.

"I thought I should come in and get you out of hot water since that's what you've been doing for me for years," he said. "I just wanted to come in here and say, in front of all of you, how very grateful I am for everything Dee Dee has done for me since long before I became President, starting in our campaign. . . . We've had a wonderful professional relationship, we've had a good personal friendship. I think she is one of the best people I have ever had the privilege of working with, and I'm really going to miss her and I'm especially going to miss the card games."

The rest of the day brought a parade of visitors to Myers's office. They included all of the military representatives who worked in the White House. One even gave her his hat. A good number of the others were women, many of whom sat and commiserated with her about her fate at the hands of the white boys. One of those was Laura Tyson. The tone of her comments was this, Myers said: "We'll fight on. Don't let it get you down." And, in some ways, she was right. In 1995 Tyson, after a good deal of delay and indecision, was promoted to become Clinton's top economic adviser when Bob Rubin became secretary of the Treasury.

But in the months surrounding Myers's departure, a whole slew of midlevel White House women left as well: Joan Baggett exited her job as political director. Ricki Seidman stepped down after holding a series of responsible jobs. Maggie Williams thought about leaving but did not. And Christine Varney moved out of the post of cabinet secretary—the White House liaison with the cabinet—to become a member of the Federal Trade Commission. Varney, another veteran of the Clinton campaign, was overheard remarking bitterly at the time, "Let me get this straight. Bosnia is collapsing, Whitewater is raging, Haiti is a mess . . . so fire the girls." None of the women was fired, of course, but it was clear to plenty of women in the White House that in vital ways they were not as welcome as men.

After a vacation abroad, a round of exciting job interviews in Hollywood and elsewhere, and a satisfying number of paid speeches at $10,000 to $15,000 a shot, Myers settled down for a regular stint on Roger Ailes's CNBC, an editorship at *Vanity Fair,* and a life that allowed her to sleep most mornings until 7:30. When she did come back to visit her old haunts, early in 1995, she ran into House Speaker Newt Gingrich in the West Wing lobby. Although he had just taken his new post, he was already under fire for his book contract and various other foibles. So in Myers he recognized a kindred soul.

"You think you're ready for this, but nothing can prepare you for the spotlight," he said to Myers.

"Yeah," she said. "Tell me about it."

In a reflective mood later, Myers said, "I saw the world from a front-row seat, and I'll never regret a minute of it." But she added, "It wasn't always fun, and that's not how I want to live my life anymore. I'm sure other White Houses had different experiences, but I doubt they were any less awful."

For Myers the really awful part came six months later, when she learned that even though she had left the White House, she will never be fully detached from it. Ten days after buying a new car, a white Ford Explorer, following more than two years of not even owning a vehicle, she was arrested in the

District of Columbia for driving under the influence and related offenses. That was embarrassing enough. But because she was Dee Dee Myers, and had the misfortune of being in the car with one of the new White House reporters for *The New York Times,* Todd Purdum, her arrest became big news.

The next morning local television newscasts all over the country *led* with her arrest, or so Myers was told by a friend in network news. But she witnessed the really ghoulish, macabre part of the episode herself. On her own television, she watched in numb silence as CNN's Headline News showed footage of her stumbling out of the police station in the wee hours of the morning—*every half hour for the entire next day.*

"It's embarrassing, it's expensive, it's time-consuming, but what made it horrifying is that everybody in America knows about it," Myers said after the incident. "When I left the White House, I thought I would be anonymous, but I wasn't. I should have been more careful." Top White House aides live in peril even after they leave.

PAUL BEGALA

5

The Control of Illusion

ON INAUGURATION DAY, PAUL BEGALA WAS WIDE AWAKE AND
ready to howl. He was standing on the roof of the Labor Department overlooking the swelling crowd on the Mall, the
long ribbon of green that stretches from the Capitol to the
Lincoln Memorial. The *Today* show had jury-rigged a studio
up there, complete with a holding room, to broadcast the inaugural festivities. Begala and two of his fellow political advisers from the Clinton campaign, James Carville and Mandy
Grunwald, were about to go on the air to extol the virtues of
Clintonism, and Begala recalled, "It couldn't have been a
more exciting, or happy, or emotional day."

Then the telephone rang.

It was John Shakow, Begala's usually bubbly assistant,
bringing bad news. "You don't have podium passes," he reported. The message was cryptic, but Begala understood. It
meant he and Carville, Grunwald, and Stan Greenberg, the
pollster—Clinton's entire team of top political advisers—
were not going to get a close-up view of the inauguration they
had helped make possible. They were not going to sit on the

inaugural platform, near the podium, as they had been promised.

How could this happen? Begala wondered. Whenever he had fantasized about what it would be like if Clinton actually won, he had never thought of election day. For him, the real payoff was this day: Inauguration Day. "For me," he said, "the dream was seeing that left hand on the Bible and that right hand shooting up in the air." So now, to be thrown off the platform and placed far back into the crowd was hard for him to take. He slowly hung up the phone and managed to tell the others.

On the air a few minutes later, there was no sign of distress. The consultants were lauded for their brilliant direction of the Clinton campaign, and they accepted the accolades with grace. But like so much in their working lives, the television appearance was just that: appearance. For Begala in particular, real heartache lay behind his smile. True, he had made a name for himself by mocking other Washingtonians for the kind of pettiness and elitism he was feeling over the loss of front-row seats. But he could not help himself. He was having trouble accepting the fact that he had, for some reason, been pushed aside.

Carville refused even to acknowledge the anguish. He was in complete denial. "Oh hell," he told Begala. "I probably wasn't going to go anyway. It's too cold." It was spin unworthy of his talents, but that was the best he could do. He went back to the office of Carville & Begala, a mere four blocks from the event itself, on the other side of the Capitol. Hundreds of thousands of people blanketed the Mall to watch in person. But Carville chose his office, known as the Bat Cave, a claustrophobic hideaway in the basement of a sliver-thin red-brick row house behind the Supreme Court.

It had a small garden, a black, iron fence, and no identifying sign out front. Inside, shelves were stacked with C-SPAN videotapes; here and there were sloping piles of newspapers and magazines. The lavatory doubled as a laundry room. And it was amid this clutter that Carville and his mother silently huddled on a shabby couch in front of a television to watch the swearing-in ceremony that surely would not have happened without his help.

Begala and his wife, Diane, went to the event anyway and found their seats were so far away they could barely see Clinton at the podium. "It hurt," Begala recalled later. "Diane knew I was hurting, and she started to cry." But for the camera, he maintained the careful artifice.

Carville and Begala made different choices after the 1992 election. The older, more experienced Carville chose to avoid being appointed to any position in the new administration. He decided to remain true to the mythology of his profession. After their work was done, political hired guns like himself were supposed to ride off into the sunset. And, for the most part, that was what he did. He became an occasional consultant to the Clintons but focused on cashing in on his celebrity with other kinds of work. Carville understood that he and government service would never see eye to eye.

Begala was young and romantic enough to think otherwise. Around the time of the election, he was warned not to take a staff job at the White House by such disparate advisers as Susan Thomases, Hillary Clinton's powerful friend, and David Gergen, the Republican spokesman who later ignored his own advice. They said that working in the White House was not like working in a campaign, and that Begala could not possibly appreciate just how different it was. And, to a point, Begala agreed with them. He did not join the staff, per se. And he was never taxpayer paid. But he did become a senior adviser to the President as a consultant to the Democratic party. And, far more than Carville, he became a White House staffer in all but name. Why? Because the President of the United States asked him to, and that was reason enough.

The inaugural mix-up, though, made him question his decision. During the campaign that would not have happened.

Begala had much more control. But Clinton penned Begala a note, and the First Lady telephoned her apologies. So, overwhelmed by the attention, Begala chose to ignore the early warning signs.

To mark his acceptance, Begala was invited to a senior staff meeting in the Roosevelt Room that same week. And it seemed like old times again. He hugged Betty Curie, the President's executive secretary, who had answered phones in the Little Rock War Room. He whooped it up with Bruce Lindsey, Clinton's bespectacled right-hand man, and thanked Hillary Clinton for her kind words. Then the President walked in.

"Have you seen the Oval Office?" he asked and threw open the doors.

To Begala it was as if time froze. He could hardly move his feet. The weight of history seemed to bear down on him, and he tried to savor every detail. He looked up at the eagle embossed on the ceiling. He looked down at the carpet, embroidered with the seal of the President. The desk, Clinton explained, had been a gift from Queen Victoria. Begala noticed that the eagle design on the front of the desk was clasping arrows, not olive branches.

"Yeah," Clinton said, "Truman had that changed."

Like a tour guide, Clinton pointed out the other items of interest. Over there was an Impressionist painting called *Flag Day.* And there was a miniature of Rodin's *Thinker.* Begala did not tell him he did not like it. But he did not hold back anything about being in the Oval Office.

"This is just so great!" he said. "It's so great to see you here."

"Don't let that get to you," Clinton responded. "This is the crown jewel of the federal penal system." And both of them had to laugh. They knew, like so much else about their relationship, that the words were at least partly true, and that was their beauty.

. . .

Begala was in the business of partial truths. As a political consultant, his job was not to lie but also never to tell the whole
story. He was paid for his ability to find that precious handful of ideas and phrases that would make his candidate popular and for his willingness to ignore everything else. Spin is
what most people say political consultants do. But that is mis-
leading. What they really do is settle. They settle on a story
line and stick to it no matter what. They control the illusion.
They create a fantasy about their candidate and then must be
nimble enough to make sure it holds up. The phrase "crown
jewel of the federal penal system" was literally true: Clinton
was extremely limited in his mobility because of Secret Service protection. But what made it beautiful to Begala and to
Clinton was that it concealed how much Clinton reveled in
his new job and made him sound more like the Washington
outsider they knew was a more popular pose.

This nimbleness in defense of an image was Begala's chief
skill. And when he threw himself into that mode, he was like
a prizefighter without the gloves. And no two-bit puncher either. He could pummel his client's opponent with a barrage
of invective and innuendo. But, like that of the greatest of the
heavyweight champs, Begala's strength lay not so much in his
ferocity as in his feinting. He could give any number of looks.
He was a virtuoso of the bob and weave. He could cover up,
stick and move, and even rope a dope if he had to. But then
he could unleash a vicious assault with either hand,
whichever the opponent was least expecting. He could play
the angles until he found the right one, then move in to deliver the knockout blow. And winning, of course, is what any
boxer—and any political consultant—cherishes above all
else.

Begala even created, and defended, a story about himself. He
was the junior and lesser-known partner in the political consulting firm Carville & Begala. And to garner sympathy and

put his adversaries off guard, he loved to emphasize the junior part. "I'm usually introduced as James Carville's partner," Begala liked to say. "It's like being Dolly Parton's feet." In fact, after the 1992 election, Begala was the primary consultant in the firm, to Clinton and to any other politician. Carville spent a lot of his time being an author and speaker for hire.

The thirty-two-year-old wunderkind also fancied himself a Texan, complete with a subtle southern twang. With his red beard and piercing eyes, he looked like Vincent van Gogh in blue jeans. When he was not wearing running shoes, he sported cowboy boots. But, in fact, he was born in Montclair, New Jersey, and did not move to Texas with his four siblings until he was in sixth grade. Pretending to be a favorite son of the Lone Star State gave him a more plausible genesis for the populist rhetoric that was his trademark. "Everything I learned in politics I learned from Court's Hardware Store," Begala drawled, recalling his part-time, high-school job in Sugar Land, Texas. "I worked there every day after school and all day Saturday. People would come in there on Saturdays, especially, and stand around the nail bin drinkin' coffee and talkin' politics."

No doubt there is some truth to the story. But it is probably truer that Begala gained more knowledge about his future vocation when he ran for student body president at the University of Texas in Austin. His main rival in the 1982 contest was a pure illusion, Hank the Hallucination, an imaginary character whose ironic slogan was "Get Real." Hank won, and Begala took third place. But when the students later decided to elect a real person, Begala took control of the illusion. He carefully adopted Hank's laid-back persona and even promised to erect a (make-believe) statue to Hank. He attracted most of the hallucination's voters and won handily.

Begala became a professional political illusionist the next year, when Senate hopeful Lloyd Doggett hired Carville as his campaign manager and Begala as his travel aide and, later, speechwriter. Doggett lost the race to Phil Gramm, but the campaign was the beginning of a partnership that improbably survived years of intense, sporadic work. Carville and Begala teamed up full-time in 1989, after Begala had done a stint as a speechwriter for Richard Gephardt and finished law school, which completed his training as an unrepentant advocate.

Carville & Begala went on to engineer successful campaigns for Georgia governor Zell Miller, Kentucky governor Wallace Wilkinson, Pennsylvania governor Robert P. Casey, and, most important of all, the come-from-behind effort of Senator Harris Wofford of Pennsylvania over former Attorney General Dick Thornburgh. It was the Wofford win—and its middle-class themes—that attracted Bill Clinton to them.

The Arkansas governor met with them at the urging of Zell Miller, who was a fan of both Clinton and the consulting duo. The two were the hottest political advisers in the Democratic party at the time. And they would go on to meet with two other presidential hopefuls as well, Tom Harkin of Iowa and Bob Kerrey of Nebraska. Begala liked Harkin. Carville favored Kerrey. But both were immediately impressed by Clinton, who seemed sincerely interested in issues and "message," the overall impression he would convey to voters, which was the heart of the consultants' trade.

After their first encounter, Begala remarked to Carville about how full of ideas Clinton was. That was refreshing but also a problem, they agreed. It would be hard to narrow his many notions into a marketable sound bite or two. The potential candidate needed to find a story line. Later, after Clinton announced his intention to run, Begala read his announcement speech and thought he saw just the theme: "the forgotten middle class." Now *that* was a winning angle. Clinton did have a "message," and, in the consultants' cliché, it *resonated,* which meant it might just be popular enough to win. It also fit the view Begala had gotten over the mythical nail bin at Court's Hardware. Well, it was close enough. Soon thereafter the Clinton campaign hired Carville & Begala for a whopping $25,000 a month.

During the campaign, Carville stayed at headquarters in Little Rock, running the War Room, while Begala manned the plane alongside Dee Dee Myers and, occasionally, Bruce Reed. The only time Begala left Clinton's side for any prolonged period was when he took paternity leave to be with his wife, Diane, and their first child, John Paul. But over the entire period, he made a name for himself as a thoroughly likable, essentially good-hearted rogue and a political wit. The press dubbed his bons mots Begala-isms; his fellow Clinton aides affectionately called them Begala's bullshit. For instance, he described Clinton's nonstop campaigning as "like force-feeding sugar to an ant. He can't get enough of this." And right before election day, Begala said he was "as nervous as a porcupine in a balloon factory."

Back in Washington after the election, Carville & Begala kept their biggest clients: Miller of Georgia, Wofford of Pennsylvania, and, of course, Bill Clinton, thanks to a retainer from the National Democratic Committee that got as high as $35,000 a month.

Begala's perspective of White House work was shaped by his campaign experience and its four main tools: rhetoric, speeches, promises, and attacks. He was never more at home, and he believed Clinton was never better off, than when they were both out of Washington and speechifying to big crowds, just as they had in 1992. In February 1993, for instance, Clinton embarked on a campaign-style swing with Begala in tow. And after a speech in Detroit, Begala plunged into the crowd of reporters. The President's early problems with Zoe Baird and gays in the military, he said, had nothing to do with what real people like the ones Clinton had just spoken to really cared about. "We're back out here," Begala declared. "This is where we should be."

But the White House is more than well-chosen phrases.

The President made real news for those same real people that night, and Begala could not hide it. For the first time, Clinton confirmed he not only was breaking his campaign promise to cut taxes for the middle class but was going to raise taxes instead. "I wish I could promise you that I won't ask you to pay any more," he said. But he could not, and that, rather than Begala's line, made headlines. "In the campaign, everything you do is what you say," Begala said. "In the White House, everything you do is what you do." And that was just one of the many perils to come.

Later in February, Begala left the Bat Cave for a while and became a full-time "volunteer" in the White House—in effect, a Clinton speechwriter in residence. During that period he came face to face with another disturbing difference between the campaign and the White House: bureaucracy. Meetings concerning the politics of issues, for instance, had as many as twenty participants and had to be held in the spacious Roosevelt Room. And they sometimes dealt with the most trivial topics. There was even a meeting to decide whether the President should go to Waco, Texas, after the disastrous fire there at a cultists' compound. That meeting included the President, the Vice President, the First Lady, the chairman of the Democratic National Committee, the chief of staff, and six assistants to the President. Of course, Clinton never went on the trip.

After another such meeting, Carville complained to Hillary Clinton. "There are too many people," he said. "I can't say what I mean in [these meetings]. I've become a cheerleader." But even she could not alter the routine, at least right away. It was the method her husband liked, despite its many drawbacks, to help him find the answers he needed. Begala, too, was frustrated.

One of the highest talents of a political consultant is the ability to sense a popular movement. There is nothing tangible or logical about this gift. It is something that people have or do not. The ones who do can foresee a change in public sentiment before it comes into common view. Begala possessed this ability and during the campaign was able to act on what he saw. On the campaign plane, he would turn to Clinton and say, "Governor, why don't we try this?" and at the next stop, he would. Simple as that.

But the White House is another kind of beast. Even as the administration tumbled from one public relations disaster to another, Begala was unable to turn things around. What hurt most was that he usually could see the next crisis on the horizon, and would warn his friends that it was coming, but it still would erupt and damage the President.

In late May, Begala telephoned Senator Barbara Boxer's administrative assistant to thank her for helping confirm Roberta Achtenberg as assistant secretary for fair housing and equal opportunity. It had been a controversial appointment, because Achtenberg was a lesbian. The aide thanked Begala and returned the kindness with a message of her own. "You've got to know that Barbara can't support Lani Guinier," she said, referring to the President's freshly minted nominee for assistant attorney general for civil rights.

That was all Begala had to hear. If a lawmaker as liberal as Boxer opposed Guinier, surely the nomination was doomed. The White House simply had to know. Without missing a beat, Begala drove down to 1600 Pennsylvania from his Capitol Hill office. It was about five o'clock when he arrived. "She's gone, she's gone, croak her now!" he exclaimed to almost anyone who would listen. Mandy Grunwald and Dee Dee Myers were just as adamant. But Guinier hung on. In the White House, there was often too much happening for people to listen.

Over the next several days, every time Begala took a sounding from Democrats on Capitol Hill, he heard the same footsteps of calamity. The nominee was becoming a liability to a President who did not need any more bad news. But Begala was helpless to prevent things from getting worse. Every chance he got, he picked up the telephone and offered his opinion to his friends in the West Wing. George Stephanopoulos and Rahm Emanuel got call after call. But all they could do was commiserate. Yes, Guinier's academic writings looked like she advocated quotas. Yes, the Democrats in the Senate were losing faith. Yes, yes, yes. But the decision belonged to the President, and he had not made it yet.

By Thursday, June 3, Begala had had enough. Once again he made his way to his Bronco II for the drive to the White House. He simply had to state his case again. And they *had* to listen. He opened the door and got in.

But this time he could not go through with it. He felt woozy and feverish. He couldn't bring himself to start the engine. He went back to his office and laid down on a couch. He tried to calm himself. White House friends like Ricki Seidman started calling to console him. But nothing helped. Begala is not generally prone to depression. He was more likely to explode in a rage than to sulk if he believed his efforts were faltering. But in the White House he learned that shouting did not work. It certainly did not work in the case of Lani Guinier until well after the President's image had sustained another jolt.

Luckily, there were some venues in which Begala thought his skills were still in demand. On Thursday, June 17, Clinton reached for one of them. He was scheduled to hold a televised press conference that evening, and his political team met at noon in the Oval Office to discuss strategy. Begala, Grunwald, Gergen, Stephanopoulos, McLarty, and Greenberg were there. "We are positioned for a set of turnaround stories," Begala told them hopefully, and he set about with the others to suggest how the President should coax the press to unleash them.

Clinton was seated near the fireplace, in the gold-colored wing chair he favored. Begala and Greenberg sat on the sofa to the President's left. Gergen, Carville, and Stephanopoulos were on the sofa on the right. And McLarty sat in his own chair, set off from the group. Greenberg explained what he had learned from a recent series of focus groups he had conducted for the Democratic National Committee. But Clinton stopped him when it began to sound like little more than the whining about Washington that he had heard ever since the campaign. "I'm tired of hearing what's wrong," the President complained. And Begala tried to calm him. "The difference now," he said, "is we have a strategy."

With Greenberg's help, Begala had refined that strategy into four straightforward goals: (1) Clinton has the responsibility to fix the fiscal mess that was left by the Bush administration; (2) the budget plan he is pushing is fair; (3) it does not harm the elderly; and (4) it will work. The shorthand version, Begala suggested, was this: "It's fair and it works." The President brightened as he heard the advice. It was a story line that resonated.

"You know, Mr. President," Gergen said, "this press conference is prime time. You need to take these themes and return to them."

"What Dave is saying is enormously important here," Begala agreed. "Don't lose it."

At 6:00 P.M. the advisers reconvened in the Family Theater. Begala was wearing a tuxedo in preparation for a roast of his consulting partner. Before the President arrived, Myers, Grunwald, and David Dreyer critiqued the speech Begala was going to give, saving him from at least three clinker lines. When Clinton saw Begala all dressed up, he said he looked like a maître d'. "Soup, salad, or dinner?" Begala shot back. "Oh, it's you, I guess it's all three."

Then they got down to business. Gergen warned that if the President's opening statement was too long, the networks would be loath to grant him another free chance at prime-time television. And, sure enough, the original draft of the opening statement was far too long, at least fifteen or twenty minutes for a press conference scheduled for a half hour. "David, you're right," Begala said, bolting out of his chair. "We have to cut the shit out of this thing." "You do that," Gergen agreed. "We'll work with him." So Gergen and Stephanopoulos stayed to prepare the President for questions while Begala sat on the hallway floor in his tuxedo, beneath the silent gaze of a Secret Service agent, scratching out as much excess verbiage as he could. He dropped a digression about what opponents of the budget plan had said and tried to focus on the main message: the plan will work and it is fair.

He returned with a much abbreviated statement and handed it to Clinton. "What's this?" the President asked.

"We cut it down," Begala replied.

"Why?"

"It was too long. It would embarrass us," Begala answered.

"OK," Clinton said simply, and read it over.

Begala had to leave before the eight o'clock press conference, but he listened to it on the radio as he drove to the hotel where the roast was being held. The first thing he noticed was that Clinton started on time. And then he watched the digital clock in his Bronco. The President's opening was seven and a half minutes! Just right. Begala felt pumped, and he went into the roast confident that Clinton would do fine for the rest of his performance.

A few days later, as a reward for his labors, Begala and his wife watched basketball and ate dinner at the White House. The other guests included singer Liza Minnelli and her boyfriend and accompanist, Billy Stritch, who was a boyhood friend of Begala. At the end of the evening, they sat on the Truman Balcony, and Begala marveled at the scene: a cloudless night overlooking the White House grounds and the Washington Monument with the Jefferson Memorial in the background. "It was magical, a once in a lifetime thing," he said. "We were pinching ourselves."

. . .

But nothing stays still at the White House for long. Certainly not the good things. The issues that besieged the West Wing were just too complex to survive under the banner of a single story line, no matter how well crafted. And it was not long before Begala found himself in another collision, this time with Bob Rubin.

As part of the budget plan, Begala, the populist rhetorician, wanted to include a provision that would prevent corporations from deducting from their taxes the salaries they pay to their top executives. Such a provision, he knew, would make Clinton wildly popular, especially with the working-class base of the Democratic party. But Rubin, who had received more than $20 million when he left his Wall Street company, Goldman Sachs, vehemently disagreed. And prior to a scheduled presidential speech before the U.S. Chamber of Commerce, Rubin and Begala met in Ricki Seidman's office to argue about it.

Rubin thought the idea was senseless. It would inflame the many upper-class Democrats Clinton also attracted. But more, it made no economic sense; the measure was demagogic politics and nothing else. Besides, Rubin contended, it was unworkable. He said, "You either cap the salary deduction at one million dollars for no particular reason or tie it to performance, which is impossible to measure."

"I'll take either option," Begala replied. "We cap lots of things."

"The business community will hate this," Rubin said. "They'll hate the President."

"I just don't believe that," Begala said. "They'll just pay their own money. This is welfare for the rich."

After a while they realized they were going nowhere. So Rubin made a suggestion. "I'm going to check with Roger," he said, referring to Roger Altman, the deputy secretary of the Treasury who, like Rubin, was a recent expatriate of Wall Street. He left the room to make the call.

About five minutes later, Rubin returned. "He says you're right. The business community doesn't care about it," Rubin reported dutifully. "But I'm still going to make my case to the President."

The two then marched over to the Oval Office. Rubin called the proposal "dumb," "stupid," and "unwise." Begala said it had been a signature part of the presidential campaign and would be conspicuous in its absence.

After hearing both out, Clinton sided with Begala—and Rubin. "I am for limiting the deductibility of CEO pay when it's a problem," he said. But he added he was not in favor of an arbitrary cap. And so it was in the world of Clinton compromise, a place where Begala was feeling increasingly lost.

The contretemps on executive pay was only part of the ongoing battle between the political advisers and the economic aides. The economic team thought deficit reduction was essential. Period. The political team did not so much disagree as think that talking about the policy in terms of pain rather than benefit to the middle class was electoral suicide. It was not a story line they could sell.

Much to the chagrin of the political consultants who had been so close to Clinton for so long, the President was mostly a policy wonk. And he found himself agreeing more and more with the economic advisers. It hurt Begala to realize that those economic establishmentarians were the ones who had the President's ear. He felt cut out. And worse, his old campaign pal Gene Sperling, who was Rubin's deputy, seemed to be siding with them.

To Begala, some of the disagreement was nothing less than disloyalty to the President. He once overheard Bo Cutter, an economic aide to Rubin, say aloud, "I don't know if the President will want to do health care if he knows it would hurt GATT and NAFTA," the two big trade agreements that were Cutter's chief responsibility. So incensed was Begala at the comment that he met with the President in the Oval Office and told him, "You have people who work for you who don't know what you stand for. How can you expect the American people to?"

The showdown between the politicos and the economists came on Friday, June 25. John Shakow, Begala's assistant, called Rubin's office to set a time when they could meet. "July 17 looks good," Shakow reported. "No, now!" Begala demanded, and he and Carville headed straight to the White House.

They met in Rubin's wood-paneled office on the second floor of the West Wing. Rubin and Sperling sat across a conference table from Carville and Begala.

"We're going on two tracks now," Begala began. "We have to put an end to this." Rubin and Sperling agreed—and listened.

"We're far too driven by the deficit," Begala said. He accused them of being "economic Calvinists preaching pain to atone for sins." Instead, he suggested, "We think we should be economic evangelists preaching eternal life."

More to the point, Begala argued that the whole strategy was too closely tied to the Democrats on Capitol Hill. Howard Paster and the other Washington types were bogging down the President's message with legislative jargon and other minutiae. "The American people are optimists, and Bill Clinton is the ultimate optimist," he asserted. Even if the policy is deficit reduction, the message has to be optimistic. "Presidential advisers go on TV," he complained, "and look like they just sucked a lemon."

Then the warring aides got down to basics. Carville and Begala accused Rubin and Sperling of refusing to give them information they needed to do their job defending President Clinton. They wanted a breakdown of the economic plan's spending increases and cuts but did not get it. Shouting, they accused the economists of playing power games.

Sperling could not believe what he was hearing. Here were

his two old allies saying he was sabotaging their own boss. It was just incredible! He was more than upset; he was offended, and hurt. Yes, Carville and Begala had asked for some numbers, but so had a dozen other people: in the White House, on the Hill, in the Treasury. Sperling had been doing more than he thought was possible already. The notion that he was stiffing these two friends was absurdly self-centered and lacked any comprehension of what was going on.

"How can you say that?" he demanded. "That's absolutely, one hundred percent untrue. It's outrageous that you could say such a thing to me."

After the shouting subsided, Rubin, who managed to keep some distance, suggested there must be a solution. The President's policy was at stake. Each side, he said, must agree to keep the other better informed. Sperling would act as liaison. He would try to make the substantive arguments more politically marketable—and the other way around. And, yes, Carville and Begala would get their numbers.

But Sperling did not know if the breach would ever mend. He also saw more clearly than ever how much more was involved in governing than in the illusions Begala and Carville spun during their campaigns. Governing was much harder, more meaningful and multidimensional. It was not pretty, but he was struggling to make it work day to day.

Begala took away some lessons as well. His father used to joke that he could argue with a chair, and that trait suited him to the heavy verbal combat of elections. But it did not prepare him well for the compromises and accommodations that were essential to governing. "Campaigns are life or death. I want total victory," Begala said. "I have to adjust to government. It's hard for me to see compromise, because it's not the way campaigns work." He was beginning to wonder if he could ever make the transition.

One of the things Begala missed most about campaign life was its sense of family. The campaign workers were not just employees, they were brothers and sisters at arms. Outsiders could never completely believe what Begala said. But inside the campaign Begala's word was golden. He made the best friends of his life during the grueling election of 1992. When they did disagree, they did so openly. Time was too short to harbor a grudge.

But in the White House, the work was just as arduous if not more so, yet the familial feeling was gone. One reason was the sheer number of people. The White House is a much more impersonal place. Another reason was raw ambition. A campaign is so short-lived there is little opportunity for advancement before it ends. A presidency is four years long—at least—and the chance to get ahead is the reason a lot of people take their jobs. Begala was not seized by any such personal drive, but he soon suspected that others around him were.

As part of the final push to pass the deficit-reduction bill in August, the President planned to give a brief, nationally televised speech, and Begala took part in writing it. Drafts were circulated methodically to important people in the West Wing and the Old Executive Office Building. To Begala, all that bureaucracy was a terrible inconvenience. But at least, he thought, things appeared to be organized. That was some solace.

After six days of tortuous give-and-take, he and others brought a well-developed version of the address to the Oval Office for Clinton's perusal. Begala was seated across from the President when Gergen came in and interrupted the flow of the meeting. "Here are some suggestions," he said and handed the President a partial new draft of the speech that he had prepared. Begala went slack-jawed and red with anger at the power play. He turned his chair so he faced Gergen, away from Clinton's view, and stared at him with his most searing gaze until the meeting was over.

Afterward he stomped out—not just out of the Oval Office but out of the White House—and drove home. He had had it. Everything he had heard about Gergen and his reputation for self-promotion, he thought, was true. Gergen, seeing Begala's anguish before he left, tried to catch him and explain that his intentions were only the best—he wanted to help the President. After Begala was gone, Gergen started telephoning his home. But Begala refused to talk to him. He estimated Gergen tried a dozen times before, late that night, he finally agreed to take the call. By then he had cooled down. And when he picked up the phone, he heard Gergen apologize profusely. He even offered to resign, Begala recalled. "You don't mean that, so don't even bother saying it," Begala told Gergen. But while Gergen managed to keep a mild tone, Begala's words were pointed. "I'm going to work with you," he said. "But I can never trust you again."

Begala began to spend less time at the White House. But he could not avoid the big speeches. Those were still his territory, and the Clinton health address to Congress on Wednesday, September 22, was one Begala absolutely refused to miss. Health reform was the one issue Clinton had been pressing that fit with Begala's political vision of the man.

Finishing the speech was just as long and hassled a process as with any other Clinton address. The President edited a second draft the night before the speech and began practicing that afternoon in front of a video crew in the Family Theater. He made more changes as he talked, and Begala and the rest of the staff struggled to keep up with them. As late as one hour before the address, Gergen and Vice President Gore worked at a computer in the communications director's office, wedging in the new words. David Dreyer added the latest changes by 8:30, thirty minutes before the speech, copying the text onto three diskettes and the hard drive of his laptop computer. Clinton made even more changes, which Stephanopoulos typed directly into the TelePrompTer, during his limousine ride to Capitol Hill.

To the casual observer, everything was going smoothly. The President was announced and received a thunderous ovation.

When he got to the podium, he shook hands as was custom-
ary with the Speaker of the House and the Vice President,
who sat above and behind him. But when he turned to look
at the audience and at his speech on the TelePrompTer
screens, he saw a familiar—but only distantly familiar—text.
It was the last speech he had given to a joint session of Congress, seven months earlier, entitled, "A New Direction."

In front of 100 million viewers, Clinton turned around and
told the bad news to Gore. At first, the Vice President did not
believe him. "Read it yourself!" the President admonished.
Gore did and hastily called aside for Stephanopoulos.

Begala was in the cloakroom. He and Rahm Emanuel were
on the telephone with Stan Greenberg, who was monitoring
reactions to the speech from a group of swing voters he had assembled in Dayton, Ohio. But as Clinton commenced, Begala
noted a choppiness that had not been evident during re-
hearsals. He thought it might just be a southern cadence—
starting slow and then building, like a train engine. But soon it
was obvious something else was going on. "The Tele-
PrompTer's down!" someone shouted. Clinton was reading his
speech—intermittently—from the copy he held in his hand.
And Begala became as frightened as he had ever been.

The willy-nilly management style of the Clinton White
House had finally come home. The last-minute speechwriting
had forced the TelePrompTer operator to do a dry run without the proper text. Instead, he used the President's last big
speech before Congress about the need for deficit reduction.
In the rush to put the new speech into the machine, he and
Stephanopoulos had forgotten to erase the old text first. As a
result, the health address was merely appended to the existing file, meaning that the speech at the top—and the one dis-
played on the screens in front of the President—was the old
one. The TelePrompTer operator had no reason to guess the
latest address was not titled "A New Direction." Couldn't
that title serve every speech in Washington?

Stephanopoulos said the crisis was like a "near-death experience," with "all the blood draining from my body." It also reminded him of an old nightmare in which he missed his eighth-grade graduation. It surely was the biggest foul-up any staffer could imagine. It was even beyond imagining, but it was happening nonetheless.

Begala's mind started to work overtime. After he got over the initial shock, he began to wonder, How can I convert this disaster into something positive for Clinton? He found just what he wanted at the end of that long night. After he was persuaded Clinton did not intend to blame him for the mistake, Begala asked the President what it had been like to stand in front of the country without a text. "I gotta know," he said.

No one will ever know for sure Clinton's real answer. But Begala's rendition was heroic and probably exaggerated. First, he said, Clinton explained how he had alerted Gore to the problem. Then, according to Begala, the President said, "I turned around and shrugged and saw it was time. I thought, Well, Lord, I guess you're testing me. Here it goes."

Begala breathed with relief. That answer, he would recall later, could well become "the stuff of legend." At least it was a story he could sell.

In mid-October, Begala left his White House duties to help the President from the periphery. He all but took up residence in New Jersey to serve as Governor Jim Florio's political consultant. One reason for the switch was that the race was almost as important to Clinton as it was to Florio. The contest was the only one of the three major off-year elections being held in November in which the Democrats had a shot: the New York mayor's race and the Virginia governor's race were long shots.

The New Jersey election was extra-important because if Florio survived, it would prove a Democrat could increase taxes—as Clinton had—and still get reelected. Like Clinton, Florio had raised taxes in his first year in office. Only in New Jersey, Florio's popularity sank into the twenties, and, as a result, he had been given up for dead for the longest time. But Begala got Florio to talk up Bruce Reed's favorite issue, crime. He asserted that his opponent, Christine Todd Whitman, was soft on crime and managed to revive Florio's chances.

Begala had won the reputation of miracle worker in such come-from-behind races. He had done it with Wofford. He had done it with Clinton. And he began to feel confident he could do it almost whenever he tried. Too confident. Usually, on election day political consultants do nothing rash. The superstitious Begala had been known to wear the same underwear for several days leading up to an election if he thought it would bring his candidate luck. But this time Begala and Carville succumbed to the blandishments of celebrity and broke their routine.

They had been lunching regularly at Dan's Glatt Kosher Deli in New Brunswick. Begala religiously had a tuna sandwich and Snapple iced tea. But on Tuesday, November 2, they accepted an invitation to dine at The Palm in Manhattan with the cream of New York journalists, including Tom Brokaw, Peter Jennings, Jeff Greenfield, and Ken Auletta.

On the way into the city from New Jersey, Begala telephoned Florio headquarters from his Bronco for the latest poll numbers. "It's 51 to 49 Florio," a staffer reported, and Begala's stomach tightened. That was closer than either he or Carville thought it would be. But neither said anything. "OK, we'll be there in a minute" was all Begala could manage.

As sport everyone around the lunch table placed twenty-dollar bets on the races that day. And everyone bet on Florio. Begala pretended he was absolutely sure Florio would win. "I'm ten on a scale of ten," he boasted, trying not to think about how tight the race really was.

When he got back to New Jersey, Begala telephoned Stephanopoulos at regular intervals with updates. And he went out with pollster Geoff Garin first to hit baseballs at a mechanical pitching machine and then to hit a bucket of golf balls at a driving range. He just felt like hitting things. "Maybe we will win," Begala said hopefully.

But they did not. With 98 percent of the vote in, it was close, but the wrong way. Florio had lost by a whisker to Christine Todd Whitman, and Begala picked up the phone to tell Stephanopoulos the bad news. "This is it," he said. "We're not going to catch her." Stephanopoulos was dejected. The Democrats lost in New York City and Virginia as well. The day was a blot not just on Begala's record but on the President's.

The next day Begala telephoned Stephanopoulos again and tried to make amends by asking to get back into the flow of events at the White House. NAFTA was heating up, and Ross Perot, Clinton's third-party adversary in 1992, was opposing it and the President. Begala suggested that Lee Iacocca, the former Chrysler Corporation chairman and NAFTA advocate, debate Perot on *Larry King Live.*

"I don't think that's going to be possible," Stephanopoulos said. "I think Gore is going to do it."

"Oh my," Begala said.

"It's too late," Stephanopoulos warned, sensing Begala's concern. "It's gone." He explained that the President and Vice President had cooked up the arrangement themselves.

"Wow," Begala said. "I can't believe it."

Begala was worried. He already was a well-known opponent of pressing the free-trade agreement too hard. That had been his position during the campaign. And putting the Vice President up against Perot clearly elevated the battle higher than he would have liked. But then again, Clinton had decided—a noteworthy state of affairs in itself. And Begala, the political pugilist, needed another fight, even one he did not fully believe in. So he strode into the NAFTA battle.

Friday, November 5, was Begala's chance to try to make peace with Clinton and the rest of the White House staff for the

Florio defeat. That evening the consultants and a few outside political experts were invited to dinner with the President and First Lady. And Begala made clear to everyone how penitent he was.

"I'm really sorry I let you down," he told Clinton as they shook hands before the meal. "I can't believe we lost that thing."

"How's Florio doing?" the President asked.

"It's rough," Begala said. "He wasn't prepared to lose."

"I know what that's like."

Begala said he wanted to talk to Clinton about Florio soon. Then Clinton asked, "What are you going to do?"

"I'm going to dive into NAFTA," Begala said with energy. "You need a fight, and you need a win."

On the evening of Monday, November 8, Begala helped prepare Gore for his debate with Perot. The Vice President had secretly invited some advisers and friends to his official residence off Massachusetts Avenue. In addition to Begala, there were Oklahoma congressman Mike Synar, former New York congressman Tom Downey, Leon Fuerth and Lorraine Voles of Gore's staff, and George Stephanopoulos. David Gergen also came, but two hours late. When he walked in, the Gores' Labrador retriever growled at him. Begala and Voles looked at each other and tried to keep from laughing. "Clearly," Begala chuckled to himself, "it's a Democratic dog."

Congressman Synar was there to play Perot in a mock debate in front of a camera, just as he had done for Clinton during the presidential campaign. And the others tried to pitch in with arguments along the way. As always Begala counseled that the best tack was to attack. "If you shine a bright light on Ross Perot, he will melt," Begala said. In a memo to Gore, he also suggested, "We can't let Perot be the tribune of working people."

As the evening wore on, the group devised a long list of exploitable Perot weaknesses. Aided by research from the

Democratic National Committee, they noted that two of Perot's own senior executives supported NAFTA and that, despite his anti-Washington rhetoric, Perot was an active user of both lobbyists and government services. His family even had an interest in an airport with a free-trade zone that took in goods from Mexico and distributed them duty free in the United States. Downey recommended Gore emphasize how forward looking and optimistic NAFTA was, and how backward and pessimistic was Perot's opposition.

At one point, Fuerth, Gore's foreign policy aide, summed up the evening with military language. "Mr. Vice President, you don't have a single detonation device," he said. "You have several of them." So armed, Gore braced for the big debate.

As is now well known, the Vice President clearly won. The next day, Wednesday, November 10, Bruce Reed and Begala were among the staffers who briefed the President for a victory press conference. Reed could not help teasing Begala about his role in pushing NAFTA. In 1988 Reed had been a Gore speechwriter and free-trade advocate while Begala worked for the free-trade opponent and Gore rival for the presidency Richard Gephardt.

"Do you remember how we discredited your position as Smoot-Hawley-Gephardt in '88?" Reed asked, mischievously.

"Well, Smoot and Hawley did have their good points," Begala replied, obviously more interested in winning than in what was won.

Begala was looking forward to a quiet start to the new year, 1994. Nothing much was supposed to happen: another presidential trip to Europe, that was about all. But the madhouse refused to be tranquil. Newspapers kept writing about a variety of federal probes into the growing Whitewater scandal. And with each new story came another call from a member of Congress for a special counsel.

Republicans, of course, yelled the loudest. In separate television interviews on Sunday, January 2, Senate Minority Leader Robert Dole and House GOP whip Newt Gingrich called for the attorney general to appoint a special counsel to examine the Clintons' Whitewater investment.

"There's no need at this time for an independent counsel," Stephanopoulos said on the same program, mouthing the White House position.

But behind the scenes the White House was a caldron of debate. There commenced a kind of rolling scrum of people who met and remet to chew the issue over. The group included Begala, Myers, McLarty, Gergen, Stephanopoulos, Harold Ickes, Maggie Williams, Bernie Nussbaum, Bruce Lindsey, and Mark Gearan.

In short order almost everyone concluded that the President had no choice but to give in. Begala and Myers disliked that option but understood why it had to happen. Once Congress came back to town, Republicans would force a vote on a special counsel, and the measure would pass. They all felt it was inevitable.

All, that is, but Nussbaum. The White House counsel said once the administration gave a special counsel the documents, the lawyers would look for something illegal until they found it—no matter what the facts. No one believed the argument on the merits; many suspected Nussbaum was merely making noise to justify the view of his mentor, Hillary Clinton.

That guess was given credence when, at the end of one of the Whitewater meetings, the First Lady walked in and sat down. It fell to Stephanopoulos to lay out what was by then the staff recommendation to call for a special counsel. Her reaction was swift and sharp. "No!" she said, and left. She believed she and her husband had done nothing wrong, deserved privacy, and already were doing more than was necessary.

The staff was left with no alternative but to stand and fight.

They had to take on the allegations whenever they arose—
and to defend the President's position, no matter what they
really thought. And who was better to lead the effort than
Begala?

On Monday, January 4, he agreed to appear on CNN's *Inside
Politics* to debate Iowa congressman Jim Leach, one of the
President's leading Republican accusers. Before Begala went
to the studio that afternoon, Carville pulled him aside to offer advice.

"Do you know Leach?" Carville asked.

"No."

"He's a good guy; he's a moderate," Carville said. "Don't
go after this guy."

So Begala decided to be polite. He would try to kill him
with kindness. But Leach did not act as Carville expected. He
opened by saying flatly, "Very serious questions have arisen
involving the public trust."

"But, Congressman, with respect," Begala said, gently.
"They haven't. The questions have been about a man named
Jim McDougal, and the Justice Department is investigating
him."

Leach then rattled off the full set of accusations against the
President. He alleged that Clinton had issued questionable
statements about Whitewater, used a thrift's taxpayer-
insured funds as "a private piggy bank," and allowed
McDougal, the thrift's owner, to "pick up a disproportionate
part" of the Whitewater investment.

"Excuse me, Congressman," Begala began, with a bit less
civility this time. "There's no question of wrongdoing on the
part of Bill Clinton."

But Leach did not let up. "Character is an issue in political
life. Conflicts of interest are an issue in political life," he said.
"This is a conflict of interest of extraordinary proportions."
He also began to attack the late Vince Foster.

Begala felt like grabbing Leach by the throat. He was literally shaking with anger when he took off his makeup and was still furious when he got back to the office and vented at Carville. He decided he would devote himself entirely to defending the President on Whitewater and even canceled a trip planned for him by the pro-Israel lobby to see the Middle East.

Three days later, on Friday, January 7, Begala was given another chance to face off on television against Leach on Whitewater, and he jumped at it. This time he did not restrain himself. After Leach's first allegations, Begala looked straight into the camera, said, "That's another lie, America," and went on the attack.

But all the rage in the world could not stop the controversy. Stephanopoulos appeared on *The Capital Gang* the next night and was harangued from both the left and right about the President's reluctance to seek a special counsel. After the show Stephanopoulos telephoned Begala and said, "They all think we're idiots" not to give in.

On *Meet the Press* the next day, Democratic senator Daniel Patrick Moynihan of New York said he thought a special counsel would be a good idea. And several other Democrats followed suit. Just as most of the staff had predicted, the result was all but inevitable.

Stephanopoulos recruited Begala to help draft the statement calling for a special counsel. But Begala was troubled. What irritated him was the way Democrats had treated their own President. "Reagan broke the law, and the Republicans stood with him; Bush clearly lied about his role in arming the Iranians, and perhaps the Iraqis, and the Republicans stood with him," he said in his usual hyperbole. "Clinton is not accused of doing anything wrong—his friend is—and his party runs away from him like the devil runs away from holy water."

When Begala had left campaigns for government, he had felt out of place and enfeebled. And now he knew another reason why. It was as if he had exchanged his hunter's gun for a pair of antlers, he said. In government, the hunter becomes the hunted.

Soon there was even more reason for unhappiness at the White House. On Saturday, March 5, Bernie Nussbaum resigned after *The Washington Post* revealed that he had taken part in a series of meetings about the Whitewater scandal that recalled President Nixon's widely condemned meddling into the workings of independent federal agencies. And even more trouble was brewing down the road. Whitewater was beginning to undermine the President's already shaky credibility and to hurt his prospects for success on Capitol Hill.

But Begala kept plugging away. "What are we going to do?" he asked. "Resign in disgrace and go home?" Never! There was still so much to do, and health-care reform was atop the list.

But just as he began to get up some steam for health reform, Begala awoke to a front-page article in *The Washington Post* with a headline that felt like a shiv in his ribs: "CAMPAIGN COWBOYS STILL LEARNING TO TREAD WHITEWATER." The piece included a blind quotation from a senior administration official: "In a campaign, you can afford to be a cowboy, you're even expected to be a cowboy. In the White House, you have to keep your gun in the holster a lot of the time."

Begala's reaction was a single word: "Gergen." Someone had told Begala that Gergen had been a source for the story, so he wasted not a minute. He telephoned Gergen to confront him about what he considered this hostile piece.

"What is this front-page story?" Begala asked.

"I don't think it was fair to you," Gergen replied sympathetically.

"There are some pretty damaging quotes in there," Begala continued, getting closer to the point.

"You don't think I said that?" Gergen inquired.

"Oh yes I do," Begala said. "I think you did this."

"No," Gergen protested. "I didn't." He said he had spoken to the *Post*'s reporter but claimed to have made very different points. "I hope you believe me," Gergen concluded.

"I do," Begala said, but he did not fully.

Gergen did not end the issue there. He later had Vicky Radd telephone Begala. Radd had been Begala's lawyer in private practice before she joined the White House staff. And she happened to have been in Gergen's office when Gergen talked to the *Post*. She told Begala Gergen was telling the truth. "He was being a good soldier," she said. And Begala believed her. But he would never completely lose his suspicions of the Republican in their midst.

Begala was, in effect, a political grifter, always playing a new con. And for him there was nothing worse than when one of his own people crumbed the play.

In the meantime Whitewater kept getting more problematic. The issue fed the public's already nagging doubts about Clinton's trustworthiness and character. The President's approval rating skidded in March to 47 percent, according to the *Washington Post*–ABC News survey. And, indirectly, Whitewater was helping to undercut the President's policies, especially health care. The same poll found that only 50 percent of those surveyed believed they would be better off in a reformed health-care system, which was a drop of 22 percentage points since Clinton's September speech on health to Congress.

It was time for Begala to step in. He had been with Clinton the last time his popularity fell so precipitously—during the New Hampshire primary in early 1992. News stories about Gennifer Flowers and the military draft had nearly killed Clinton's presidential hopes. And what made things worse, Begala recalled, was that Clinton went home to Arkansas for a few days to nurse the flu rather than stay and face the charges. In just two days' absence, Begala remembered, Clinton's favorability rating in New Hampshire dropped 17 percentage points—"like a rock in a well." This time Begala urged him—and everyone else who would listen—that it would be wrong to hide. The other outside advisers joined in the appeal; Grunwald and Greenberg were passionate on the subject. But people inside the White House, especially Bruce Lindsey, resisted. The whole Whitewater transaction had happened so long ago, and it was nothing—really, he said. The disagreement became so heated Begala and Lindsey had at least one shouting match.

But the President did not resist Begala's advice. Clinton remembered New Hampshire all too well and also knew how much better it had made him feel when he fought back. Begala came across the President in the West Wing on Monday, March 21, after a brief public event where he had talked about Whitewater just a little. Clinton seemed unusually buoyant, Begala thought, and he asked him why.

"Because I finally got a chance to answer some questions," the President replied. "I finally had a chance to defend myself."

Begala did not let the moment die. He leveraged the President's reaction to help make the case to schedule a prime-time news conference—only the second of Clinton's tenure —for Thursday, March 24. As it turned out, running the gauntlet served the President well. For forty minutes he took question after question about the Whitewater mess, and overall he looked sincere. Afterward Begala told him, "You did a terrific job," and Clinton obviously agreed. As the rest of the staff gathered around, the President told them, "Let the thing speak for itself," and directed that no one return reporters' phone calls. Stephanopoulos told Begala, "For once in your life, don't spin." So even the garrulous Begala complied.

But the tactic did not work for long. Mere words never do.

Clinton tried to break free from the Whitewater pall in early April by embarking on a whirlwind spree for health reform.

One day he visited a hospital in North Carolina to talk about rural health care, the next day he went to Kansas to talk to small-business owners, and on Friday, April 8, he held a campaign-style health-care rally in Minneapolis. Begala and Myers went along, but Begala, as an outside consultant, had an option Myers did not. He was able to drop off the trip when he wanted to, and he did in Minneapolis. He headed home to Washington after telling Myers there were more than enough advisers around.

Besides, Begala believed that the President was "on message," and that he did not need any more prodding. So it was with only a twinge of guilt that he abandoned *Air Force One* to attend what he knew was an elitist, inside-the-Beltway event: a dinner party at the home of Peter Hart, the Democratic pollster. Hart had helped Carville get his first two jobs in politics, and both Paul and Diane Begala liked him enormously. They also considered the party a big event and were looking forward to going together. The well-traveled Begala no longer had his old thirst for the road. He was looking forward to a relaxed evening out.

But the White House would not cooperate. Almost as soon as Begala landed, he heard from his office about a soon-to-be published article in the *American Spectator* about Clinton's alleged use of Arkansas state troopers to help him procure women while he was governor. Begala cursed under his breath and knew yet another scandal was about to be placed under the Whitewater umbrella. As he drove his Bronco to Hart's house, he telephoned the White House operator and asked her to page Myers. When she got on the line from Minneapolis, she immediately started digging in.

"I can't believe you'd leave us to go to some social dinner," Myers said, and then she handed the phone to Clinton. "I can't believe you'd leave us to go to some Georgetown dinner party with all those people who are beating my brains in," the President said. He obviously was joshing, but Begala turned red with embarrassment anyway.

"Well, boss," he stammered. "I'm going to defend you."

"Oh, that's OK," Clinton said and hung up.

Begala knew it was not OK. At the White House there is never a good time just to slip away. And, for perhaps the first time, he started to wish there were.

Begala was more than a little worried about health-care reform. So before Congress recessed at the end of May, he met with a roomful of press secretaries on the second floor of the Senate and gave a tutorial on how to boost the Clinton health-care plan. It was classic Begala bullshit.

"There are two great myths about health reform," he began. "One, it's dead. Two, it's too complicated." In fact, he asserted, "It's moving along quite nicely. And, two, it's important to talk about the bill's principles, not its details."

To help the aides and their bosses do that, Begala distributed a document prepared by the War Room entitled "Delivering the Message." It opened with a phone number for what it called the "Memorial Day recess hotline," which was the War Room itself. It then reprinted an optimistic article from *The Wall Street Journal* and went on for fifty-two more pages to tout a variety of suggested health-care events.

In the section "Health Benefits Guaranteed at Work," it recommended that lawmakers walk through a local business district, visit a grocery store, and conduct a roundtable discussion with business owners. The section called "Preserving and Improving Medicare" urged lawmakers to visit a pharmacy, conduct a conference call with adult children of elderly parents, visit "an adult or intergenerational day care center," and "speak to older Americans."

The press secretaries were decorous enough not to laugh out loud. In the first place, very few of their bosses were willing to go all-out for such an increasingly unpopular plan. Not many were even willing to mention they were in the same party as Clinton, given all his Whitewater woes. But some of the aides did give a second thought to Begala's final, patently political warning about the health-care bill: "If it fails, it will be unshirted hell. It will kill 1994. A lot of the [Democratic] members who are now swinging gavels will be swinging golf clubs instead."

That was the one part of the talk that was not just a partial truth.

But while he gave pep talks to Democrats outside the White House, Democrats inside the White House were giving Begala fits. On Thursday, June 9, Joel Klein, the deputy White House counsel, called the office of Carville & Begala to say Mack McLarty was going to issue a directive the next day requiring Begala, Carville, Grunwald, and Greenberg to disclose their assets and sources of income. They would have to meet that condition to continue to advise the President.

Begala's story about the directive was that he was not surprised. Republicans had been grousing for some time that the outside consultants were effectively working as Clinton aides but were not subject to the same disclosure laws as government employees. There was even a bill pending in Congress to force the disclosure, and the four of them had written an op-ed piece for *The Washington Post* defending their integrity.

But, in fact, Begala was hurt—deeply—and his friends knew it. Calls of support came from David Dreyer and Doug Sosnik, soon to be the White House political director. But the directive was a slap at Begala and an implicit rejection of his band of political consultants. Like so many Clinton advisers before him, he was becoming a target. His high profile in the White House had made him one. And it looked like he was going to be a victim as well. He had seen the pattern so often, but it still hurt when it hit. "I know that this is motivated by politics," he said. "But my reputation is more important than my privacy." He would comply.

It was not long before his reputation got soiled as well. One of Leon Panetta's first acts as chief of staff was to limit access to the Oval Office. And that meant less contact between Begala and the boss. Panetta asserted he was simply trying to get control over the unwieldy White House. But he also was making it clear that Begala and the other political consultants were no longer so welcome. Begala was paying a price for having been quoted calling Panetta "the Poster Boy of Economic Constipation" in Bob Woodward's book *The Agenda.*

Begala again pretended he did not mind. That was the story line. He said he had plenty to do besides assist the President. He had two big statewide races to advise, Senator Wofford's in Pennsylvania and Governor Miller's in Georgia. Besides, he said, "The White House has been too demanding, frankly, particularly for what they are paying me"—an astonishing statement given the huge amount he was contracted to get from the Democratic National Committee. He claimed he was not unhappy that the White House did not call him every day. In fact, he asserted, going to the White House too often reduced his effectiveness. He even liked to quote Carville: "We're the only people in the White House who want *less* juice, not more." But no one who knew him believed the protestations.

The next few weeks were crunch time for the staff. It was a period no less important, and perhaps even more important, than the year earlier, when the presidency had been riding on the fate of the budget bill. Now the crime and health-care bills were on the line. But this time Begala feared Clinton had gone to the well too often, and it was dry. The Whitewater scandal had taken the zing out of the Clinton presidency. Maybe this time, as in the Florio campaign, there was no coming back.

Begala kept punching—and feinting—anyway. With the help of the staff of the Democratic National Committee, he distributed to the public the amount of total health benefits paid to members of Congress as a way to show how much better off they are than average Americans. He hoped this might shame some opponents into supporting reform. His proudest total belonged to Bob Dole: $61,329.

He and Carville also devised another ploy, one their client Wofford could use to help himself *and* the President. One of the arguments Republicans used to delay health reform was that more studies were needed. Begala thought that was ridiculous; the health system was one of the most studied problems ever. So he urged Wofford and other Democrats to pile dozens of studies on their desks in the Senate chamber— in front of the cameras.

On Tuesday, August 16, Begala was sitting in his office on the second floor of his Capitol Hill town house (Carville & Begala had long since moved upstairs from the Bat Cave) when his assistant pushed a story from the Associated Press in front of him. He read it and knew immediately that he was in trouble. He ended a telephone call midsentence and plotted how best to make amends. "I better call Harold," he said. "He's going to think I did this. Shit!" He reread the story as he put in a call to Harold Ickes at the White House.

Crunch Time for Health Care and Crime, Consultants Offer Advice Aplenty

By John King
AP Political Writer

WASHINGTON (AP) In the shadow of the Capitol, two Democratic senators use towering piles of studies and reports to ridicule Senate GOP leader Bob Dole's suggestion that more time is needed to weigh the impact of health care reform.

Paul Begala is nowhere in sight, which is just fine by him. But the compelling visual prop was his idea, the product of one of the populist outbursts that Begala is famous for at meetings in the White House health care "War Room."

Begala holds no elected office, nor is he on any government payroll. Instead, he is one of a small cadre of political consultants who operate behind the scenes, putting their stamp on the contentious health care reform and crime debates in Congress.

Luckily for Begala, Ickes was not upset with the leak. "He knew I didn't have anything to do with it; he knows I'm not that stupid," Begala reported. At the same time, he was furious someone at the White House had snitched on him. "That was a Carville idea that I brought to the War Room," he said. "God, I go down there every day and trust a hundred people." Someone on his own team, he fumed, had crumbed another play.

Soon thereafter the bottom fell out on health reform, and no illusion could save it. On a Monday at the end of September, Senate Majority Leader George Mitchell announced the cause was dead. The centerpiece of his agenda became the President's most humiliating defeat. It was a victim of Clinton's own falling popularity; Whitewater was its undertow. Although the tragedy had been coming for a long while, it still stunned the White House staff. Dee Dee Myers tried to keep up a brave front, asserting in the briefing room that there was always next year. But privately she knew better. Begala was so sorrowful, both for himself and his clients Clinton and Wofford, he did not even return reporters' phone calls seeking comment on that fateful day.

Begala knew the next casualty might be the entire Democratic party. It already was clear the Senate probably would fall into Republican hands. But now it began to look like the unthinkable might also happen: the House could go Republican for the first time in forty years. Newt Gingrich, the number two Republican in that chamber, held a press conference to stake his claim to that ambition on the day after Mitchell's announcement. On the steps of the Capitol, Gingrich unveiled his Contract with America and his plan to win the House.

In early October the four horsemen of the Clinton campaign—Begala, Carville, Mandy Grunwald, and Stan Greenberg—ate dinner at Galileo Restaurant in downtown Washington and bemoaned their situation. Begala knew the Republican wave was about to hit, and he said, "We're going to lose the House and the Senate, and I'm moving my ass back to Texas." Everyone laughed. Just more Begala bullshit, they thought.

As the election neared, Begala was spending no time at all in the White House. His hands were more than full trying to get Wofford reelected in Pennsylvania. He used Gene Sperling's attacks on the Contract with America as often as he could. He had little choice. His main issue, health reform, was completely discredited. At least he was back to campaigning again, which he much preferred to the chronic indecision, backbiting, and bureaucracy that was the White House's daily fare. But the scent of defeat was too rancid for him to like being anywhere but home with his family anymore.

In the days leading up to the election, Begala took no chances. No dilettantism this year, he vowed. Several days out he put on a denim work shirt promoted by the radio talk-show host Don Imus and did not take it off. He considered it good luck. He even bought ten of the shirts and gave them to youngsters on the Wofford staff. When tracking poll numbers in the last week showed Wofford gaining on his opponent, Congressman Rick Santorum, Begala said, "It's got to be the shirt." But not even a dirty shirt was enough to pull off a miracle.

At ten o'clock the night before the election, Monday, November 7, Clinton returned from his last campaign trip and turned to Dee Dee Myers. "Where's Paulie?" he asked. "Let's get Paulie on the phone." Myers didn't know exactly where

Begala was, so she tried Wofford headquarters in Philadelphia. An officious young staffer answered. "He's out" was all the aide would say. She repeated her request, and the aide said, "He's busy." By then Myers had had enough. "Would you tell him, please, that the President of the United States would like to talk to him?" A few minutes later Begala returned the call.

Clinton and Begala talked privately for a long while, about the state of the races not just in Pennsylvania but around the country. Begala said he thought Wofford might pull the election out. But he did not promise. Both men knew the next day was going to be a rough one.

In the morning Begala woke up in his hotel room and got on the phone with Don Imus for his radio broadcast. He regaled the talk-show host with his litany of Clinton administration accomplishments, but Imus interrupted. "You know that's all true, you did all those things," he said. "But we're going to vote against you anyway." And Begala thought, You're right. Instead of saying that or something more clever, though, he began to shout into the phone. "You know what our message is going to be in '96? 'What the hell do you want, America? What the hell do you want!' " The image maker had allowed his mask to slip.

Afterward Begala went for as long a run as his legs would carry him—two hours—and he returned to the couch in his hotel room to await the exit polls. He got them from his White House friends and from friends of friends who worked for the networks. In midafternoon Carville called and said, "It's meltdown, disaster." And Begala curled up and tried to avoid his unease by watching a James Bond movie on television. But even that was little solace. One of the characters was lowered into a tank and got half his body eaten off by a shark. Begala felt a lot like that.

Zell Miller squeaked by, but Harris Wofford was defeated. Facing Wofford that night, Begala said, was one of the hardest things he ever had to do. It was a performance he never wanted to repeat. But the problem was far larger than that. The Democrats were devastated around the country, and Begala felt personally humiliated. The Republicans had won in large part by ridiculing the visage of Bill Clinton, the man whose image Begala was supposed to protect. He had tried mightily, but the White House was too tough a client to serve. As a result, Begala was questioning anew his choice of career and the wisdom of working at the White House.

The White House began to question his work there too. The Democratic National Committee put his retainer under review and, eventually, renewed it. But that was almost a consolation prize. Clinton started to increase his contacts with another political consultant, Dick Morris. And soon Morris was clearly the man who had the President's ear. Mandy Grunwald was dropped entirely, and Stan Greenberg was trimmed back. Morris's choice for pollster, Doug Schoen, got more and more of Clinton's attention. Carville made plans to write a book, and Begala tried to regain his composure and refashion his mask.

Begala prepared the new story line carefully. It just made sense for the President, or any politician for that matter, to change consultants every once in a while. In fact, it was healthy, he said. That's what he would do if he were in Clinton's shoes, given the immensity of the loss he had just suffered. And remember, he said, the politician is the organ grinder and the consultant is the monkey. Not the other way around.

It was a good line, and he was sticking to it. But his friends sensed a deepening bitterness in him. He began to spend more time at home. He certainly was not consulting at the White House as much. As the Clinton reelection team started to be assembled, rumors swirled that he might become campaign manager. Yet people close to the discussions knew that could not be true.

And Begala did not want it to be true. He became nauseated at the thought of having to clear even the most minor new piece of rhetoric with some assistant secretary for soybeans. He cringed at the dangers of testing new ideas in the vast bureaucracy, and seeing them spew out in haphazard leaks, probably with decidedly negative spins. And, most of all, he did not want to face the snake pit of personal ambition that the White House had become.

Two years earlier he had reached the apex of his profession. But since then he had learned, as he put it, "There are no condos on the top of the mountain." He had tasted his fill of White House politics, and it was sour. He was ready to ride off into the sunset.

In February 1995, the issue was brought to a head. Diane Begala informed her husband that they were going to have their second child, and they had to make some choices. She recommended, and not for the first time, that they move to Austin, Texas, where they had gone to school and near where most of their family members lived. When they had last been there over Christmas, she had taken out the real estate listings as a hint, and now Begala thought he might be smart to take another look.

But first he had to clear up some issues at the White House. He met with Ickes and told him he was not interested in managing the Clinton reelection campaign. He did not mention the pregnancy; it was still too early. But he did say, "You need somebody who can deal better than I can with the permanent government establishment." And then he added an exquisite Begala-ism: "You need someone with wing tips, not cowboy boots."

Soon thereafter Begala sidled into Carville's office, lay down on his couch, and confessed that he had not been kidding during their meal months before about moving to Texas. And like everyone else associated with life in the White House who heard the plan, Carville said it all made eminent sense.

.   .   .

The change made even more sense because Austin was home
to Public Strategies, the powerhouse public relations firm Jeff
Eller had joined. Begala courted them, and they eagerly
courted back. Both he and they stood to make massive sums
of money by arranging a "message" for corporations the way
he had arranged a "message" for politicians like Clinton.
Such a clear voice, conveyed to lawmakers and the public by
an organized network of loyal corporate employees, had
become the fastest-growing method of marketing and lobbying. And because it worked, it was a very big seller. Part of
this was what corporations prefer to call "grassroots lobbying." But it is really more like Astroturf, obviously artificial.
In any case, Begala decided to go in for its serious cultivation.
So much for populist rhetoric. Corporations are much more
proficient than the government at controlling their illusions.

He also agreed to write a political column and to teach a
class at the University of Texas on, of all things, politics and
the press. It was hard to think of any group of students Begala was less qualified to teach than budding reporters. He
had referred to the press as "the enemy" and the revered
David Broder of *The Washington Post* as a "gasbag." Still, he
obviously had made the right choice in leaving.

When Clinton flipped on his budget strategy in the spring
of 1995 and abandoned most of his own party by advocating
an end to the deficit by a date certain, he did not even talk to
Begala about it. And that was just as well. It did not resonate
for the consultant. He thought the new line made the President sound too Republican, and, ironically, he sided with
Panetta, who counseled that Clinton show more patience.
Washington is indeed an odd place.

For most of the summer, Begala stayed at home with his son,
Johnny, though he did make the same hunting trip to the
ranch that Eller had made before he joined the firm. The real
attraction for Begala was not the guns, though, but the run-

ning path along the river right outside the firm's office in Austin. His mind was made up.

After telling Carville, Begala arranged to meet with Clinton. In the Oval Office, he told the President he was leaving and did not give him a chance to talk him out of it. Then came the story line: "I'm absolutely certain you're going to win re-election," Begala told him. "I think I could do more for you being out there." They both had to laugh.

In August, Carville held a going-away party for Begala that symbolized the journey they both had taken. Carville no longer lived scrunched on a couch in a Capitol Hill basement but in a sprawling mansion in rural Virginia. Half of it was a renovated 200-year-old farmhouse, and the other half was a thoroughly modern addition, complete with indoor swimming pool and a windowed, two-story living room looking out at nothing but trees and meadows and sparsely traveled roads. He certainly had done well for himself.

But his new life was a very long way from Washington, and that said something too. Carville had literally put a mountain between himself and the city that made him famous, and Begala was about to better that distance. And nobody at the party blamed either of them for the preference. They agreed with it. Envy, not sadness, was the chief reaction to Begala's departure. His colleagues understood what he had gone through. Many of them had experienced the same, and those who still worked at the White House wished they could arrange their own escapes as neatly as Begala had.

Begala had come far indeed. His wife had cried at the inauguration because they had been kept at a distance. Now they could not get away fast enough. "Was it worth it? Yes," Begala said. "Was I suited for it? No." If he had really been smart, he acknowledged, he would have set out for Austin after the election nearly three years before. But who could have known what hazards he would face?

The Illusion of Control

NO ORGANIZATION CAN MANAGE ALL THE JOBS THE AMERICAN people think the president can. Even with the aid of an able staff, a single official cannot at the same time dictate the laws of the land like a king, negotiate compromises like a prime minister, and also act as a spiritual leader. But that is what the public expects.

As a result, the arc of the modern presidency follows the life of the cherry blossom. A new president rides into office on an enormous wave of promise that blooms, at first, into a pink mist of optimism. But, as with the tree, the blossoms quickly fade. Enthusiasm and hope give way to disappointment and anxiety. We see the presidency for what it is, not what we wish it to be. We learn the president is not king. He is one politician in the middle of an increasingly complex world, who must struggle to make even tiny improvements. He is not our spiritual leader; we have many other people to fit that bill. And he is not the head of government. Congress is too fragmented a place for him to exert consistent influence. A president inexorably falls prey to the cherry blossom syndrome, and with him so does his staff.

That is one explanation of why the White House is a madhouse. But there are other reasons too, and all of them hit the working stiffs in the West Wing hard. These loyal aides are the ones who experience the adventure of the presidency most personally and suffer most when, as is so often the case, the journey turns precarious.

How could it be otherwise? Too much goes on too fast for the president and his staff to deal with. Deeply considered decisions are rare luxuries at 1600 Pennsylvania Avenue. Just as the tide of one scandal, say Whitewater, subsides, another vexing trouble spot, like the war in Bosnia, explodes. Controversies, problems, and outright mistakes never stop. Not for an instant. Not for anyone. Certainly not for the people who work at the White House.

True, the Clinton White House was more fraught than others. Unlike the model of a good organization, the Clinton presidency never had, at the same time, a strong chief executive, a highly competent head of operations, and a clear set of objectives to shoot for. It probably never could run smoothly.

Yet the system is overwrought by its very nature, regardless of who is in charge. The constant state of reaction the White House staff must labor under is a prescription for disaster. The inevitable turf battles and petty jealousies among staffers only make matters worse. It is difficult to see how any group of aides could not wind up frustrated.

The root of this unfortunate conclusion is an excess of wishful thinking on the part of the American electorate. No secular institution is as burdened with expectation as the presidency. The president is the first public official children get to know, and they view him with almost pure admiration. Surely he is the most powerful man on earth. And, yes, one day you can grow up to be president too. Just listen to the words of a twelve-year-old boy interviewed in 1970:

> The President of the United States is a man or a woman or whatever who is, like, picked by the people to head the country. And they try and make the person almost perfect. I mean, if he does anything wrong, they down him . . . because if a person is going to be the head of a country like the United States for four years, he just has to be just about perfect.

This opinion is reinforced as the child grows older. The bedrock elements of American identity—honor, patriotism, and strength—are inextricably linked to the presidency. Thomas Langston, a political scientist at Tulane University, has identified an entire set of "fables" about our presidents, which by now are embedded in our culture. These include: "The President is a crusader for freedom," "The President symbolizes America's commitment to democracy," and "When extraordinary action is necessary, the President must take the lead." The president is nothing less than an American icon.

In reality, a contemporary presidency cannot live up to its billing. The presidential scholar Hugh Heclo lays the blame for this on "rampant pluralism." "A more politically volatile public, a less-manageable Congress, a disappearing party hierarchy [and] proliferating groups of single-minded activists," he says, lead to "unnegotiable demands, political stagnation and stalemate." In other words, a president and his staff cannot get things done simply by saying they want them done. Not even close. The world they face is too fractured and intractable for that.

So what happens when the myth of the powerful president meets the reality of the madhouse? Disillusionment. Burns

Roper, the pollster, once observed, "When a President takes office he has nowhere to go but down"—and he usually does:

A winning candidate has been successful in building voter support and starts his term with something approaching a consensus. As he takes office, he is the focus of the nation's hopes. Since he hasn't done anything yet, there is nothing to criticize, and those hopes can become pretty expansive. In a sense, presidential elections are quadrennial myth-builders which every four years make voters believe some man is better than they later conclude he is. The President takes office with most of the nation on his side, but this artificial "unity" soon begins to evaporate.

Whether we like it or not, the presidency is a train wreck waiting to happen. Americans' excessive expectations inevitably collide with the president's limited ability to deliver. Absent a national emergency that brings people together, the chance of a president being seen as a leader, rather than a victim, in a world increasingly devoid of a single set of identifiable values, is slim. Academics have discussed this since the publication in 1960 of the classic *Presidential Power* by Richard Neustadt. The study of presidential power, he pointed out, is really an examination of weakness and how to overcome it. "If the President envisages substantial innovations," Neustadt wrote, "then almost everything in modern history cries caution to such hopes unless accompanied by crises with potential for consensus."

But the public has never caught on. According to Langston of Tulane, the relationship between the people and their president is dysfunctional, and the presidency itself is "an implausible office" if not an impossible one. In the end, he says, disaffected voters almost certainly will turn the president they once revered into "a tragic or sinister figure."

. . .

So why did Bill Clinton exacerbate the problem by naming such outlandishly young aides? His initial staff was scored for being a kiddie corps, overrun with long-haired, sandal-clad near-teens with rude and overbearing attitudes. And, in truth, there was plenty of juvenile foolishness to go round. On Texas Independence Day, March 2, of Clinton's first year in office, Paul Begala, age thirty-two, did not stand on ceremony when he came to work in the West Wing. A graduate of the University of Texas, he wore his loud orange U.T. polyester tie that played "The Eyes of Texas" when a button was pressed. He also sported his black cowboy boots with a red, white, and blue map of Texas on the front. Vice President Gore, a Tennessean, joked that Begala was supporting the wrong U.T. and rolled his eyes every time Begala played his tie.

"That's nothing," Begala said. "I'm wearing my orange-and-white U.T. underwear."

"Show us now," Gore urged. "This is the Clinton administration; anything goes."

So, in the middle of the Oval Office and at the recommendation of the Vice President, Begala pulled the top of his undershorts over his jeans and exposed them to the highest officials in the land.

Many of Clinton's other senior aides were young too. Dee Dee Myers was only thirty-one. Bruce Reed was thirty-three, Gene Sperling, thirty-four, and Jeff Eller, thirty-seven. Were not these people simply too inexperienced to handle their assignments at the top of the federal government? Were they not too green to see the wider importance of their tasks and to take them more seriously? Should not the responsibility of governing have been given to older hands?

The answer, experts surprisingly agree, is no. Although statistics are difficult to compile given the different ways White House staffs have been structured over the years, the upper reaches of the Clinton White House have probably been not much younger than those of any White House of recent vintage. In fact, White Houses in the post–World War II era have tended to be populated by young people.

Ted Sorensen, one of President Kennedy's top aides, was thirty-one when he held sway in the West Wing. Richard Nixon took pride in having youngish top staffers, in their thirties and forties. He hoped their presence would be taken as a sign that he really was a lot less square than people thought. Dick Cheney was Gerald Ford's chief of staff when he was still in his midthirties. Jimmy Carter's top aides were renowned and reviled for their youthfulness; many, like Clinton's, were in their thirties. Jody Powell was thirty-three, and Stuart Eizenstat and Hamilton Jordan were thirty-four when they got to the White House. Even Ronald Reagan's and George Bush's staffs were not as seasoned as some might have thought.

The country's foremost expert on White House staffing, Bradley H. Patterson, Jr., himself a veteran White House aide and author of the well-regarded *Ring of Power,* concludes: "Possibly with the exception of the Eisenhower staff, the staffs of Presidents have tended to be very young, full of get-up-and-go, and full of impatience."

Basically, the White House is a place for young people. Few others are able to survive its rigors. In addition, the staff is almost invariably young because it is drawn from among the new president's former campaign staff. And that, of course, is filled with youngsters. "They are people who don't need much money and who are willing to work twenty hours a day for the love of the adrenalin rush and the glamour," says Stephen Hess of the Brookings Institution. "You tend to give assignments at hand to the people *at hand.*" Hess speaks with some authority. Until White Houses got even younger, he held the record for being the youngest senior aide to the president, at the age of twenty-six, during the Eisenhower administration.

· · ·

But in the most significant ways, chronology is beside the point. Presidential scholars contend the relative youthfulness of current-day White House staffs is only part of the problem. Indeed, Clinton's most senior aides, much like the topmost aides of his predecessors, have not been as young as the rest of the staff. The people with whom the President met the most—in fact, daily—during his first year in office were in their forties and fifties. Mack McLarty, the chief of staff, was forty-six; National Security Adviser Tony Lake was fifty-three; National Economic Adviser Robert Rubin was fifty-four; Domestic Policy Adviser Carol Rasco was forty-four; and Budget Office director Leon Panetta was fifty-four. Clinton's top lobbyist, Howard Paster, at forty-eight years old, was the most elderly person ever to hold that job, save for one in the Reagan administration.

The bigger issue has more to do with the staff's inclination and education. Since the Kennedy administration, the White House has been run by politicos, holdovers from successful political campaigns, rather than by people with an interest, let alone much experience, in government. And the two functions are very different. Electioneering mostly involves the manipulation of images or perceptions; it is largely a public relations effort, shallow and short-term. Governing also entails political posturing, but it is, fundamentally, the process of making real changes in programs that affect, on a very direct level, the daily lives of individual citizens. Not only is making those kinds of changes a far more complex task, especially given the entrenched interests of Washington, but it also is a matter of far more seriousness and gravity. A White House is not just about rhetoric, but it is also about taking action and following through.

In other words, the difference between campaigning for the White House and working in the White House is like the difference between drawing an idyllic farmhouse scene and actually finding, and buying, an available plot of ground for the farmhouse, then designing, planning, and constructing not just the house itself but the gardens that surround it, and tending it all for four long years.

Bruce Reed had his own description of the difference. Moving from the fast-paced world of a campaign to the laborious realm of governing, he said, was like running into water: the deceleration was disorienting and massive. Some former campaign aides grow into this larger challenge. But many find they are over their heads. Some campaign folks are outright contemptuous of government servants. "The people who went into politics first, often come into the White House deliberately not wanting to go into government," said Ronald Moe, an expert on government at the Library of Congress. "They consider it eyeglazing." And, indeed, it is. But that is part of the job.

The best a president and his aides can hope for is to achieve the illusion of control. Ronald Reagan was perhaps the most proficient at this—until the Iran-contra scandal blew his cover. Then it became clear that even the only president to serve two full terms since the 1950s was unable to solve the mystery of how to marshal the White House staff.

The war-torn Clinton White House tried mightily to find its own way to appear in control. In his third year in office, Clinton started using more vetoes and executive orders to give the impression that he was in charge. But neither was a foolproof way to get things done. In fact, with Republicans in the majority in both chambers of Congress, the notion that the President was master of anything became even more ludicrous than usual.

In the end, Clinton and his staff did what every White House has had to do—ride the wave. Fighting the current—trying to make the presidency more potent than it really is—proved futile. The illusion of something more stable and strong is simply unsustainable. So Clinton accepted the voters' admonition in 1994 and positioned himself not as America's chief policy maker but as a go-between—someone who would try as best he could to moderate the Republican Congress in a way he thought the never-radical public preferred.

One way to reduce the wear and tear on the White House staff—and to burnish the reputation of the presidency—would be to allow the leading presidential candidates to begin naming their top officials, preparing for governance, with a more formal shadow government before election day. This would require a change in law as well as considerable sympathy by voters for the problems a president faces. Such appointments should not be viewed as arrogance or overconfidence on the part of the contestants but rather as an attempt to make the office of the presidency less calamitous than it has traditionally turned out to be.

But truly to make the White House less of a madhouse, voters have to take another leap of faith. They must accept that a president is not really in charge, that the blossom of any new presidency must wither. Until then, the ill-named commander in chief will continue to be a source of frustration. What is more, anyone who works in the White House will surely live in turmoil.

By the start of Clinton's fourth year in office, only two of the six staffers featured in this book still worked in the White House. Gene Sperling kept himself busy until all hours defending yet another rendition of the President's budget priorities. He struggled especially hard to keep in law at least some portion of the increase in the earned income tax credit he won the first year. Bruce Reed also remained in the Old Executive Office Building, but with a new job. He was given the thankless task of devising a reason for a second Clinton term. Both men asserted they were happy. But they were not as contented as the four others who had managed to break out of the madhouse.

ACKNOWLEDGMENTS AND SOURCES

THIS BOOK WOULD NOT HAVE BEEN POSSIBLE WITHOUT THE guidance and support of Peter Osnos and Jonathan Karp of Times Books/Random House. They are the best editors a writer could have had. I also am indebted to my wonderful colleagues at *Time* magazine and *The Wall Street Journal* for their encouragement along the way. But my deepest thanks must go to my patient and generous subjects: Paul Begala, Jeff Eller, Dee Dee Myers, Howard Paster, Bruce Reed, and Gene Sperling. They tolerated me and my questions longer than I deserved.

The bulk of this book comes from my own interviews. But other reporters and publications were invaluable sources of anecdotes and quotations as well. My chief guide to the chronology of events that underlies the narrative was the justly respected *Congressional Quarterly*. In addition, *The Wall Street Journal, The Washington Post, The New York Times,* the *Los Angeles Times,* and *Time* magazine were regular sources of information. Books about the Clinton White

House by Ronald Kessler, Elizabeth Drew, and Bob Woodward also were invaluable.

Parts of the profile of Howard Paster were taken from an article by Lloyd Grove in *The Washington Post*. David Rogers and Paul Barrett of *The Wall Street Journal* dug up some of the facts on Zoe Baird's decline, as did several reporters from *The Washington Post*. Part of the Lani Guinier story came from reporting in the *Los Angeles Times* by Jack Nelson and Robert J. Donovan. And Jill Lawrence's work for the Associated Press contributed some facts that described the final days in the White House of Howard Paster.

Sidney Blumenthal of *The New Yorker* and James Perry of *The Wall Street Journal* wrote pieces that contributed to the way I portrayed Jeff Eller and his media affairs operation. Michael Duffy of *Time* magazine, Brit Hume of ABC News, and Gerald Seib of *The Wall Street Journal* provided some details about the health-care speech and the health-care War Room.

My rendition of Bruce Reed's first day on the job was aided by the reporting of Miles Benson in the Harrisburg (Pa.) *Patriot-News*. Parts of the profiles of Gene Sperling and Bruce Reed were taken from the work of Jason Vest, David Hilzenrath, and Stephen Barr of *The Washington Post*.

The profile of Dee Dee Myers was aided by the reporting of Kim Masters of *The Washington Post,* Thomas B. Rosenstiel of the *Los Angeles Times,* Angie Cannon of the Knight-Ridder News Service, and my colleagues at *People* magazine, including Sarah Skolnik.

Paul Begala's biographical sketch was assisted by the work of Lloyd Grove of *The Washington Post* and Joyce Saenz Harris and Sam Attlesey of *The Dallas Morning News*.

For the academic overview of the presidency contained in the introduction and the conclusion, I credit Bill Moyers, Michael Nelson, Bradley Patterson, James Perry of *The Wall Street Journal,* Fred Greenstein of Princeton University (whose work includes the quotations I used from the young boy and Burns Roper), James Thurber of American University, James Pfiffner and Hugh Heclo of George Mason University, Stephen Hess and Thomas Mann of the Brookings Institution, and Thomas Langston of Tulane University, Charles Jones of the University of Wisconsin, Samuel Kernell of the University of California, George Edwards of Texas A&M University, and Richard Neustadt of Harvard University.

Special thanks also to Henry Ferris, now of Morrow, for his early efforts on the book's behalf, to Robert Barnett of Williams & Connolly for his excellent counsel, and to my colleagues Michael Duffy, Dan Goodgame, Jef McAllister, and Norman Pearlstine. I also benefited in ways that can never be repaid from my family: Esther and Earl Birnbaum, Rhoda Galembo, and Deborah, Michael, and Julia Birnbaum.

Index

ABOUT THE AUTHOR

JEFFREY H. BIRNBAUM covers national politics for *Time* magazine. A graduate of the University of Pennsylvania, he has served as a reporter for *The Miami Herald* and *The Wall Street Journal*. He lives in Maryland with his wife and two children.